FORWARD

The Delaware river is many things to many people and she has gone through many changes through the years. Her waters carry the life's blood of the Delaware Valley and have done so even before the white man set foot on her shores.

The Delaware has made such an amazing comeback that it is now being proposed that the river from Washington's Crossing north be made part of the Scenic and Wild Rivers Program. Portions of the river above the Delaware Water Gap are already part of this program. If this should come about it would be one more in a series of steps to protect the river for future generations.

Anyone who has fished the river in the past few years is well aware of the renaissance the striped bass population has gone through. These fish have given a whole new meaning to the word sportfishing in the river and in Chapter Nine we give you an in-depth look at this exciting fishery.

Likewise, the smallmouth stocks in the river have experienced five consecutive record years, and their numbers show every sign of increasing in the next few years. The Delaware is considered by many to have the east coast's best smallmouth population.

Another fishery that is closely examined is the world class shad fishery. The Delaware is thought to be the king of shad rivers, and it's fish have been used to stock other rivers in attempts to get migratory fisheries established in them. It's major tributaries, the Schuylkill and Lehigh, have had shad ladders constructed on them which allow these fish to migrate up their waters. Shad are also an intricate part in the food chain on the river and are in a large part responsible for the increasing numbers and good health of the other fisheries.

The three major fisheries that we have just mentioned are complemented by the excellent catfish, crappie, largemouth, walleye, herring and panfish populations that abound in the river.

All might seem well with the river, but there are some negatives, the most important being the curtailment of the stocking of walleye and muskie by the state of Pennsylvania. For whatever reason the program is being halted, muskie fishing in some sections will be all but non-existent and the walleye fishing that only a few years ago was flourishing is now on the decline.

Even with the decline of two of the river's fisheries, the Big "D" still has more to offer the angler than any other body of water in the Delaware Valley, or even the east coast for that matter. Once you experience the river's scenic beauty and sample some of the fishing it has to offer, I'm sure that you will find a place in your heart, just as I have, for the Delaware river and it's fisheries.

TABLE OF CONTENTS

CHAPTER 1: KEY FACTORS

WATER TEMPERATURE

Of all the elements that the fisherman has to deal with, water temperature is the single most important. Since fish are cold blooded creatures it's the temperature of the water in which they are found that makes them do the things they do. It tells their body how often they will feed, governs how fast they digest their food and burn up calories, tells them when it's time to spawn, dictates their movements on a seasonal basis, and directly or indirectly affects every part of their life.

The tide water portion of the Delaware is much different than the non-tidal portion in that it is usually deeper, slower moving, more stable and less susceptible to quick change. This means that patterns will hold longer in the deeper waters of the tide water than they will in the shallower non-tidal river. This is why the tide water portion of the river takes longer to warm up in the spring and longer to cool down in the fall.

On the reverse side of the coin we have the non-tidal river. This portion of the river is a hard rock base, fast moving river which abounds in rapids, ripples and other oxygen producing structures. Water temperatures here are much more susceptible to quick changes than in the tidal river. This is a double edged sword, working for the fisherman and against him.

Summer water temps often climb into the 80's on a daily basis.

For all intents and purposes, the warmer the water temperature in a river gets, the more active the fish will be. The easiest way of seeing this is to compare a fish to a car engine. A car engine takes in fuel just as a fish takes in forage. The car engine unites the fuel with oxygen and produces power to run the car. The fish digests the forage and unites it with oxygen to form calories, which in turn power the fish. The faster the car engine goes, the more fuel it must use. Likewise, the warmer the water gets, the faster the fish burn up the calories and the more they must eat.

As the preceding example illustrates, the fact is that fish will be more active in a river system the warmer the water gets. Likewise, the cooler the water gets, the slower the fishes body metabolism is and the slower and less often they will feed.

Water temperature not only regulates how heavy the fish will feed, as well as the speed control at which an angler uses his lures, but it can change the fishes forage base and their way of feeding as well. A prime example of this is the forage on which smallies feed during the warmest portion of the season. The Delaware has huge bug hatches during this period of the year and the smallmouth will feed on them because they are more plentiful than other types of forage at this time. Insect hatches will make up to 70% to 80% of their diet.

Another example is the shad and herring populations in the river. Once these fish have spawned, their offspring will be a large part of the predatory fishes forage base. During the fall it's the water temperature that triggers the fall feed, as well as when these fish will begin moving downstream to the ocean. During this period the small shad and herring will be the largest part of the game fishes diet.

There are two major cycles that the river goes through each year, and the effects they have in combination with that years weather patterns is very different. The first cycle takes place in the spring as the river transforms from a cold water river to a warm water river. A few days of warm air temps pushed by the wind can warm up shallow waters and those found below rapids and ripples very quickly. Flats, eddies, shallow areas around islands and other structures in the non-tidal river can warm up fast and the angler will find some good fishing there.

In the tidal river, this wind driven warm air will unite with water that is pushed into the shallows by the incoming tide. This water is then carried out of the shallows with the outgoing tides and travels along the drop-offs. This can results in good fishing in both the shallows on the incoming tide and along the drop-offs with the outgoing tide.

We have given you the positive side of this cycle, however, there is a negative side as well. When a few days of cold windy air presents itself during the early season, the reverse effect takes place. Water found in the areas we mentioned will chill down and the fish found there will become sluggish. Even if the fish move back into deeper water they will be moving back into cooler water. This results in slower fishing.

The second cycle, that which takes palace in the fall, is a better one for the fisherman. This is when the river will go from a warm water season into the cold water one. A few days of warm air temperatures combined with a good breeze will keep the water warm in the shallow areas, and this will result in some good fishing both in the tidal and non-tidal sections.

If the reverse should happen and a few days of cool temperatures pushed by the wind should occur, the fish will be forced back into deeper water. Since deeper water will retain warmer temperatures longer, these fish will be pushed back into warmer water, thus they will remain active. Fishing the deeper water in this instance will be all the angler has to do to take fish. This pattern will hold true until the water in the deeper areas chills down. In the tidal river, this will usually produce better action with the incoming tide which will usually carry warmer water back onto structures.

During the warm water season, water temperatures can be affected by the volume of water in the river on any given year. During high water years, water temps tend to be cooler as opposed to a low water year when they can get very warm. There can also be a difference of 5 to 8 degrees in shallow areas between night and day, and early morning and late afternoon. Overcast days will also keep the water temperatures cooler since the suns rays can't reach the water to warm it up.

Two definite patterns develop during the warm water season in relation to water temperature. In a cool year which produces water temperatures remaining in the high 70's and reaching the 80's for short periods, fish such as smallmouth will move into the shallow areas in the early evening and early morning and then move just off these areas during the day time. During warm water years when water temps stay in the 80's most of the time, the fish will still feed in the shallows, however, they will move into oxygen rich areas such as ripples or rapids during the daytime. Here, they feed constantly throughout the day to maintain their high body metabolism.

Here are some simple rules with regard to water temperature. Fish found in warm, oxygenated water will be more active, attacking their prey harder, and will be more persistent in their pursuit of a meal. The reverse is true in cooler water or water that has a lower oxygen content.

In water temperatures below 50 degrees, live bait will be more productive; in water above 60 degrees, lures will be more productive. When the water temps are between 50 and 60 degrees, the angler should try both live bait and lures, using whichever is more productive on any given day.

OXYGEN LEVELS

In the Tide Water Regions

It's a well established fact that the Delaware river has one of the richest oxygen levels of any river along the east coast. This was not always so and as recently as the late 50's and early 60's, the tide water Delaware was plagued by poor oxygen counts which were the result of water pollution. It's good to report that these problems have been put to rest for the most part and the pollution block that had hampered migratory fish such as shad, stripers and herring for so many years no longer is a threat. The proof of this is in the record catches of shad and herring in recent years and corresponding explosion in the striper population. I don't mean to say that there is no longer a pollution problem in the tide water portion of the river, however, when compared with the water quality of 20 years ago the river is infinitely cleaner and this is reflected in the current fish population.

Wind   The biggest oxygen generator the river has is the wind. It's this one element that supplies the oxygen that keeps the water healthy. Unlike the upper non-tidal part where the river is fast flowing with plenty of rapids, ripples and water falls to supply oxygen to the water, the tide water portion of the river has to rely on the wind and the movement of the tides for it's oxygen supply.

Rips   Wind direction and velocity affects the river from several perspectives, and there are several different instances that will have a direct effect on the river and the fishing found there. One specific scenario, which can really rile things up when it occurs, is when the wind and the tides are coming from different directions. This will cause a shear that will create real rough water on the main river. An outgoing tide and a stiff upriver wind will combine to give you heavy seas. The reverse, incoming tide and down river wind, can have the same effect.

Blow Outs   Another scenario is when the wind is blowing in the same direction as the tides. This can result in what is commonly known as a blow out. A stiff downriver wind blowing with an outgoing tide can force the water out of the river and this will cause lower than normal tides. It will also hold the incoming tide back, causing the tides to seem to change later than they are supposed to.

Blow Ins   The reverse can happen when an incoming tide is accompanied with an upriver wind. This will cause higher than normal tides and cause the outgoing tide to move slower than normal. Either condition will also cause a very flat surface river.

Cross winds   Winds blowing across the river will cause the water to be better oxygenated on the side that the wind is blowing up against. Likewise, the side from which the wind is blowing will be better sheltered and this will offer the fisherman a place to get out of the wind during the cold water season. How these winds will affect the water temperatures will depend on how warm or cold the air is when the wind is blowing.

In the non-tidal regions

The one thing that separates a river from other bodies of water is the rich oxygen levels that are found in a river. Since a river is constantly moving, it's waters are constantly being united with oxygen. Ripples, rapids and other river structures act as circulators, constantly mixing air with water. These high oxygen levels greatly influence the fish that call a river their home.

Because a river receives high amounts of oxygen through it's moving waters, weather conditions have a quicker and more direct effect on a river, more so than a lake or other body of water that doesn't possess a current. This can work for the fisherman or against him. If weather patterns are favorable then they can affect a river's water in a beneficial way. Of course, the reverse can be true.

Rapids are a main supplier of the river's rich oxygen supply.

Another thing that the rich oxygen levels of a river does is to allow the fish to tolerate the high water temps that a river can reach during the summer months. As stated in the water temperature section, the combination of rich oxygen levels and warm water temperatures will cause fish to burn up calories faster, forcing them to feed more often to maintain their higher body metabolism.

Playing the Oxygen Levels   One of the keys to being a successful river fisherman is knowing how to play these rich oxygen levels. In the spring you should concentrate your efforts in areas of a river where the oxygen causes the water to warm up quickest after a few warm days. Small eddies, ripples and other shallow areas are top choices in the spring. Should the weather turn cold, concentrate your efforts on the deeper sections. The fish, however, will not be as active since the spring is when the river is turning over from a cold water river to a warm water one, and the fish will be pushed back into cooler water.

Mid-day Fishing   The best fishing of the warm water season during the mid day hours is in the ripples and rapids, as well as the portions of river structures where the oxygen counts are the highest.

The river's rich oxygen levels also create a good environment for large bug hatches. This gives all types of fish an excellent forage base, thus enhancing the food cycle.

Fall Fishing   As the water begins cooling down during the fall, going from a warm water season to a cold water one, concentrate on the areas of the river that offer a more stable environment such as pools and deep eddies. When the fish are forced from shallow areas back into deeper ones by a few cool days, they are moving back into warm water and will continue to be active. All you have to do is fish the deeper areas to keep catching fish.

WATER COLOR

This is another factor that can change very quickly in a river. You should think of this factor on a weather related basis, as the amount of rain fall and how quickly it falls, along with the current water levels that are present in a river at any time, are the factors that govern the river's water color.

Off Color Water   During the summer months, a quick rain can cause small streams in a certain section of the river to rise and get muddy. This water will flow into the river and create a muddy water break line, which carries all types of forage into the river with it. Fish will stack up along this color change where clear water meets dirty water and pick up the forage as it passes by.

During times when the entire river is on the dirty side, the first places that will clear up are the many small streams that flow into it. Now you will have a clean stream of water flowing into a dirty river, the reverse of the situation we just mentioned. These places are a good bet, as the fish will move into this clearer water for the better oxygen levels and the forage supply they hold.

Heavy rains can often make the river unfishable for periods of time. Once the river starts clearing up, it will go through stages ranging from unfishable brown to gin clear. As the water starts to turn green in color and visibility starts to improve, the fish will begin to feed more heavily. It's at this time when many of the bigger fish are taken. In gin clear water, big fish tend to spook easily. In this type of off color water, however, they will move around more freely.

Gin clear water and low water go hand in hand during the summer..

Gin Clear   Most rivers will have long periods when their water is extremely clear. In most rivers, gin clear water goes hand and hand with low water conditions. As previously stated, this is when the fish will be the most spooky. When these conditions are present the fisherman must use extra caution when wading and using a boat. He must also learn to take advantage of the opportunities that a river offers to allow him to cope with these conditions. (See Light Penetration section of this chapter.)

Whenever possible, camouflage the bottom of your boat to cut down on any glare that might reflect into the water when the water is extremely clear. If you are a wader, keep from wearing bright colors as they are more visible to the fish during such times. Dark colors and camouflage patterns will work best. No matter how you fish, keep from making fast or sharp movements, as they are more visible when the water is clear.

Another case is the muddy water break lines that occur around the small streams that flow into the river. This can affect the river on a smaller scale and isolated rains can cause these small streams to get dirty. This will force a stream of dirty water into the main river and the break line that results is ideal for a variety of fish from stripers to channel cats. The reverse can also happen when the river is dirty from too much rain. The small streams that flow into the river will clean up first and they will pump clear water into the main river; this will also create a muddy water break line. Fish from the dirty river will also gather in the clean water of these streams and this makes them a good place to look when these conditions are present.

Clean Water Pockets   All the conditions that we have just covered pertain to the tidal river with one notable addition. The largest portion of the river is made up of a body of water that moves back and forth with the tides. The effects of rain on the river and the streams that flow into it will take longer to affect this body of water. In many cases the dirty water flowing into the tidal section of the river from the upper river and from streams that flow directly into the tidal river will isolate this body of water. This will result in a clean block of water that will move in and out with the tides. As a result, you will find that after heavy rains the water will be dirty with the outgoing tide and then clear up once the tide starts coming in. This is an excellent condition to play during the spring when you are fishing for stripers.

Water Releases   Another factor that comes into play is the reservoirs that have been built in the head water regions and those that have been built on the tributary streams which are used to maintain certain water flow rates. On normal years these reservoirs are replenished by precipitation and run off during the winter and spring seasons so that during the summer months, when the water levels draw down due to lack of rain and evaporation, water can be released to help preserve water levels.

During the summer months when water is released from these impondments, the water levels can often come up in short periods of time and this cooler water that is released can drop the water temperature. Both of these factors can change the fishing conditions.

The Effects Of Rainfall   Another factor that comes into play has to do with the amount of rain that falls in any given area in a short period of time. This is very common during the summer months when storms can pour heavy amounts of rain over a small section of the river, causing small streams and creeks to spill large amounts of water into a river. This will, in turn, raise the water levels in certain areas for short periods of time and also create dirty water conditions in these areas. This water will move downstream in a block and will raise the water level in different sections for short periods of time as it passes through. This condition can change water temperatures, color and levels on the short term.

There are several factors that control how much any amount of rain will affect a river: how saturated the ground is, whether or not the ground is frozen, whether or not the leaves are on the trees, how high the water levels are when the rain occurs, and how fast the rain comes down in relation to the amount that falls. All these factors will have an effect on how the rain influences a river.

In the case of frozen ground, rain will run off faster, taking top soil with it, and this will produce adverse effects on a river's condition, more so than if the ground was unfrozen and could absorb some of the rain. During the late fall, winter and early spring, the lack of leaves on the trees and vegetation will cause the rain to fall directly to the ground. This in itself will create a faster run off and will have more of a negative effect on the rivers conditions. If you couple this with some frozen ground, the adverse effects are even greater.

The water level a river possesses when the rain comes down will also be a determining factor on how it affects a river. If the water levels are already high it will take larger amounts of rain to affect the river's condition. Because of the larger volume of water in the river, small rain storms, unless they are very severe, will not seriously affect a river's condition. If the water level in a river is on the low side, even small amounts of rain can have an adverse effect. It will suffice to say that fast heavy rains will adversely affect the river's condition faster than a slow gentle rain, which has time to be absorbed.

Fish Under High Water Conditions   A simple rule to follow when it comes to high water levels is to always fish in areas and on structures that offer the fish a place to get out of the river's swifter currents. Fish will stack up along shore lines and stay out of the main stream of the river. This can often make for some easy fishing during times of high water.

Fish will migrate to slower moving, quieter areas during times of high water.

You must remember that high water levels go hand in hand with swifter currents and off color water. For the angler, speed and depth control under these circumstances will be crucial to his success. High water conditions will give the boat angler better access to sections of the river he can't reach when the water is low. It deadens the effects of sound and sight to a certain degree, which will allow the angler to get closer to the fish without being detected.

How high water levels affect fishing can be influenced by when they occur. As an example, if you have had low water conditions throughout the summer and into the fall, a heavy rain can raise water levels, changing water temps too quickly, turning off the fish. Simply put, drastic differences between the temperature of the rain and the temperature of the water can have adverse effects on the fishing.

Fish Under Low Water Conditions   As previously stated, low water conditions go hand and hand with gin clear water and slower currents. When the currents of a river are not as strong, the fish will spread out more and will relate to a wider variety of structures. Since the pressure of the river's current is lessened, they will roam more and chase lures and bait much further. Low water conditions allow water temps to go higher during the summer since the sun has less water to warm up.

When low water conditions are present during the warm water season they will push the fish into areas of decreased light and high oxygen levels. Surface fishing is greatly enhanced under low water conditions because the lures are more visible and closer to the fish.

LIGHT PENETRATION

Another key factor that affects the river is the amount of light that penetrates into the water, and the river offers the angler many different ways of coping with this. Ripples which defuse the light, deep water, shadows from mountains, fog, etc. can have a direct effect on the fishing, both in how you fish and the amount you catch.

Many anglers believe light penetration is the element that triggers some fish movements in a river in the morning and evening. If you fish a river often enough you will realize that most structures on a river are evolving structures. Once you realize this it is easier to see the association between light penetration and how it affects where fish are found on river structures.

Shadows   One of the first ways of dealing with light penetration, and one of the best I might add, is by playing the shadows. Shadows cast onto a river by the mountains through which it flows will cause the fishing to last longer in the morning and start earlier in the afternoon, thus giving the angler more time when the fish are active.

Another way shadows can help you is if you fish on the shady side of bridge pilings, rocks and other obstructions in the river. Bass and other fish will hold in these shadows during the day time and they are a prime target for the angler.

Over Cast Days   One of the best ways of coping with the effects of light penetration is to fish overcast days whenever possible. I have spent many gloomy days on the river knocking the socks off the fish when other fishermen have stayed home because of the dreary weather. Once the fish begin to feed on a cloudy day, they will often feed throughout the day and do so close to the surface, making them easy to get. The fish aren't as spooky and you don't have to worry about casting shadows on the water. Keep in mind that over cast days will serve you best during the warm water season of the summer when the effects of the sun are not so desirable.

Overcast days produce some of the biggest fish.

Fog   Besides over cast days, another condition that will increase your chances of taking good numbers of fish is the fog that is common on the river during certain weather changes. Fog is more common during the changing seasons of spring and fall when the difference between the water temperatures and air temperatures are more common and more distinctive.

8

Fog helps negate the effects of light penetration.

There are two scenarios that are conducive to fog. The first, which usually comes into play during the spring, is when the water temperature is cooler than the air. The second is when the water temperature is warmer than the air and is the reason fog occurs during the fall. Fog occurring during the early fall is usually more productive than that which occurs in the spring.

Fog can be hazardous to the river fisherman because of the sight problems it can cause for the boater and wader, so use caution when fishing under foggy conditions. As with overcast weather conditions, the fog will cause the fish to feed closer to the surface and be less spooky. As the sun breaks through the fog, the fish will begin to move into their deeper haunts or under cover, so you will have to change the way you fish.

If water temperatures are warm enough to support lure fishing, surface and shallow working lures will be your top choices. Since much of the fog that occurs on a river does so when conditions are prime for live-bait fishing, live-lining will work well in a foggy situation. Once the fog starts to lift you will have to adjust the way you fish your live bait based on the type of water you are fishing.

Night Fishing   Another way of coping with the effects of light penetration is to fish after dark. This is especially true when fishing for such noted nocturnal creatures as walleye and stripers. Beside allowing the fish to move around more because of the decreased light penetration, there is also less traffic to spook the fish as well. You will find that the warmer the water gets in the summer, the more fish like stripers, catfish, walleyes and even largemouth will be active after dark.

TIDES AND MOON PHASES

There is a saying that "neither time nor tide waits for no man". The person who said this was obviously waiting for his spouse to finish getting dressed for a dinner engagement, however, it does have it's applications for the angler, in particular those who ply the waters of the Delaware for its tidal inhabitants.

Tides play an important part in fish movements on a daily and seasonal basis. The effect that the tides have on fish movements are influenced by external factors such as water temperature and moon phases. Moon phases, on the other hand, have more influence in the tidal river than they have on the fish in the non-tidal river because of their effects on the tides.

In order to understand the effects of the tides on fish in the river we should first understand what makes the tides work. In technical terms, when the moon is in

MOON PHASES

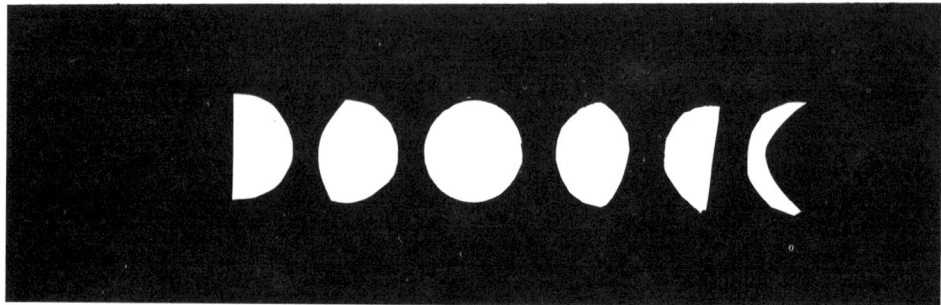

apogee it is at the farthest distance from the earth. Perigee, on the other hand, is when the moon is closest to the earth. For our purposes, during the full moon and the new moon is when the moon's influence on the tides is at its greatest. The last quarter and first quarter is when the moon's influence is at its lowest. The best fishing usually occurs between two to six days after the full and new moons.

During certain times of the year, certain tides will be more productive and this has to do with the water temperature. During the early and late season when the water temperatures are on the cool side (50 and below), the outgoing tide will be the preferred tide. This is because the lower water temps will cause the fish's metabolism to be sluggish and they will not feed as often, nor will they travel as far for a meal. In this case they will stay in deeper water and wait for food to come to them with the outgoing tide.

During the warm water season the reverse is true. The warmer water causes the fish's metabolism to rise, burns up calories faster and makes him more aggressive. In this case he will feed on both the incoming and outgoing tide, with the incoming tide being more productive. This is because he will move into shallow water to feed and when the tides are low there will be very little water in places like flats, bars, reefs, etc. The incoming tide will pour water into these places and the baitfish will come with it. This is especially true when the river is full of spawning herring which will move into the shallow water to spawn. Striper movements in particular are closely tied to the migration of the herring up river to spawn and the herring will move with the tides during this time of the year.

Another time when you will find the incoming tide productive is during the summer months when the many fish take on nocturnal qualities. This can cause you to lose plenty of sleep because some of the best fishing will be when the incoming tide occurs after dark. You will want to start fishing just after the tide turns and starts coming in just off the channel edges and gradually work your way into shallow water. Many of the silt bars that are located at the mouths of tributary streams where the water from the streams will collide with the moving water of the river are prime structures during this time of the year.

Tidal rise and fall in some areas of the river are as much as seven feet under average water conditions. The upper most limit that comes under the influence of the tides it the Trenton area. This is where the effects of the tides are most pronounced and the tidal currents are their swiftest.

CHAPTER 2: EQUIPMENT

Because the Delaware river has many different fish populations, along with a diversity of structures and a variety of conditions under which the angler must fish, fishermen will find that a wide range of equipment will come in handy. It's true that fishing tackle is for the most part a matter of personal preference and finances, however, there are some basic needs that have to be met by the river fisherman in order to fish the river with a reasonable chance of taking fish. Whether you choose to fish from a boat, by wading or from the shoreline, personal safety and comfort will have to be taken into consideration when choosing your equipment.

WADING

Waders The equipment that the wader uses will vary greatly with the time of the year. During the cold water season (early spring and late fall), a good pair of insulated waders are a must. Most veteran anglers prefer them over the use of hip boots, as they provide better protection against the cold air and water. Moving around in a river, especially on a windy day when water can splash above your waist or a slip on the seat of your pants can get you wet in places where you don't want to get wet, provides another reason for the use of waders over that of hip boots.

In recent years, the use of neoprene waders have increased, and many anglers prefer this type of wader over the traditional type. They are more costly, but offer

Wading is one of the best ways of fishing the river. Note wader bags and life jacket.

better insulation against the cold.

No matter what type of wader you choose, it must be remembered that when you fish a river you will be dealing with the force of a river's current. Cold water is a killer, and a slip into the river can cause your waders to fill up fast. A good way of preventing this is to wear a tight belt around the top of your waders. This will help keep them sealed up and prevent water from getting into them if the unthinkable should happen.

Footwear Another invaluable piece of equipment that goes along with wading a river is some type of footwear that will give you the traction that you need to walk on the slippery rocks that adorn it's shoreline and bottom. For this need the angler has several choices.

11

Felt soled waders or over shoes are one choice. The heavy deposits of algae that form on rocks, however, can often cause felt soles to slip. They can also present a problem when the shoreline is frozen, so most anglers prefer some type of spiked boot or overshoe.

During the summer months, the use of an old pair of golf spikes is a common practice among anglers. These can be purchased in a second hand store for a few dollars and will give you the traction you need at a modest price. If you choose to use an old pair of golf spikes for wading a river, be sure to look for a pair that are stitched as well as glued together. If the pair you choose is only glued together, it is a good bet that they will come apart after being used several times. It must be remembered that golf spikes are not made to walk on such rugged terrain and some of the less expensive pairs are not as well constructed. Another option you have is to take a your golf spikes to a cobbler and have him stitch the soles to the shoe for added strength. You can also take a pair of sneakers, desert boots or other type of soft shoe to a cobbler and have him put a pair of spiked neoprene soles on them. Not all cobblers do this type of work, so you will have to shop around.

The most common type of spiked footwear used for wading a river are Walt's Walkers. These are rubber over shoes with removable golf spikes on their bottoms. The advantage of this type of spiked footwear is that they can be worn over boots during the cold water season and over shoes and sneakers during the warm water season, giving the angler year round use. For a modest investment and with the proper care, they will give the average angler several years of service. You can remove and replace worn out spikes very inexpensively when necessary.

Another type of footwear common to river fishermen are corkers. These are sandal type overshoes that can be placed on any type of footwear. They lace onto your boot or shoe and do provide good traction. The one drawback is that they will sometimes become loose or untied, causing them to slide around on your feet.

One thing that many anglers have begun doing in recent years to fish shallow water flats during the warm water season is to doctor up a pair of sneakers by adding a pair of felt soles. If you like to tinker and work on your equipment yourself, you can purchase a pair of replacement felt soles of the type used to replace worn out soles on boots. Your next step is to take a wire wheel and grind the ridges off the sneakers until the bottoms are smooth. Next, take contact cement and

Angler wades on flat during the summer. Spikes or felt soles are recommended for wading the slippery river rocks.

coat both the bottom of the sneaker and the felt sole and let them sit until they get tacky. Once they reach this state you combine the two and place something heavy on them and let them sit overnight. The next day you can trim any excess felt off and

12

you are in business. If you use them on a regular basis it is best to hand stitch the soles onto the sneakers to help keep the edges from coming undone. The glue will hold the soles in place as long as you dry them out after each use. If you use them on a daily basis and they don't have time to dry out completely, they will start coming loose around the edges. Stitching them will prevent this from happening.

Angler using a wading stick.

Wading staffs are in common use among river fishermen and are an excellent addition to your wading equipment. There are several produced commercially, however, an old broom or mop handle can be easily adapted for use as a wading staff. All that need be done is to drill a hole at the top of the staff and tie a length of cord to it. At the other end of the cord, a clip can be added so that you can attach it to your clothing, allowing the staff to hang free when not in use.

There are several safety devices that will be of benefit to the river wader. Several companies produce a life vest that will inflate at the pull of a ring or cord and can get you out of a sticky situation if it should arise. One company makes a pair of suspenders that can be used with waders (or even your britches) that will inflate and provide flotation in an emergency. It is always wise to wade with a partner and to use the proper safety gear in a river, especially if you are a non-swimmer or it's the cold water season.

Wading Bags & Vests   There are several schools of thought when it comes to what type of equipment is best to carry lures, hooks and other necessities when wading a river. Many anglers choose to use a fishing vest or jacket and this method of carrying tackle has been a standard among river fishermen for many years. Fishing vests, like most other types of fishing tackle, are more a matter of personal preference and price tag than anything else. Most fishing vests that are on the market will do the job, however, many seasoned river fishermen choose another option.

The use of a wading bag is considered more practical while wading by a good many anglers for several reasons. When doctored up properly it can hold all the tackle a vest can hold and more. A belt type bag is the best type of bag to use for wading. A standard mili-

Wading belt bag & spare rod holder used by many river fishermen.

13

tary ammo or gas mask bag can be purchased in most Army/Navy stores and sporting good shops. Several plastic boxes can be placed in it to store your tackle needs. It is always best to place a grommet in the bottom of the bag so that if you should wade past it the water will have a place to run out of when the bag comes out of the water.

If you use swivels or snap swivels for your fishing you can take a large snap swivel and sew or pin it onto your bag. You can then take the smaller snap swivels that you use for your fishing and attach them to the larger one. This will allow you to take one at a time instead of keeping them in a small box, which you may have to open in the middle of the river and may get knocked into the water.

When it comes to storing hooks, strip lead, split shot and other necessities, you can use an empty 35 millimeter film container to do it. All you have to do is to drill a hole in the bottom of the film container. Your next step is to take a small length of cord or shoe lace and double it over, tying the ends together in a knot. You can then pull this loop through the hole so that the knot is left inside to keep it from sliding out. The container can then be pinned onto the bag or looped through the belt and used to store the above mentioned needs. A retractable pin-on can be used to hold these containers, as well as a pair of forceps, which comes in handy to remove hooks from the fish. This will keep the smaller items you need in one place and make them easy to get at when you need them.

Two Rods Are Better Than One   Many anglers who wade the river for smallmouth, stripers and other fish find it advantageous to use more than one fishing rod. A scabbard can be sewn onto your wading bag that will hold one and even two extra rods in place, out of the way along side of the bag while you are using the other. There are several advantages to using this system. In a river you will come up against many different situations. A good example of this is during the early morning of the summer when you are fishing a flat area. Your main tool will become some type of surface lure, however, you may find a small eddy that is better fished with some other type of lure. Carrying a second rod will allow you to keep a different type of lure on each rod, letting you fish the same water with two different lures without having to take time and go into your box and change lures. The use of two rods while wading will allow you to fish close in with one type of lure while having a lure that will afford you greater distance on the other. Many times you will spot a fish feeding that is out of range of the lure you are using and by the time you change lures he has moved away. When you have two rods rigged up, all you have to do is switch rods and you will get a shot at that fish that you might have otherwise missed.

BOATS

The Delaware river is a diverse body of water, ranging from the deep tidal sections found from Trenton to the bay to the shallow water and fast moving rapids of the upper river. It's because of this diversity in water conditions that just about every type of boat can find a home some place along the Delaware. However, no one boat will suit all your angling needs, thus certain types of boats will perform better in different areas and are better suited for certain types of angling.

In the tidal river below Trenton, just about every type of boat can be used. With a channel capable of handling ocean going vessels as far upstream as Trenton, draft is not a problem for even the biggest of boats. Since the river is very wide in the tidal sections, is vulnerable to the effects of the wind in most places, and is used for commerce by larger sea going vessels and tugs, you should choose a boat that is as

Author's V-bottom boat used on the tidal river.

sea worthy as possible. Two and three foot swells are common on this part of the river, and wakes from larger vessels can be a danger to smaller boats. Because of their design, flat bottom boats are not suitable for this part of the river. Rough water will cause this type of boat to bounce and give the boater a very poor ride. It's for this reason that vee hulls and heavier fiberglass boats make better choices for fishing in the tide water river.

Once north of Trenton you enter the non-tidal river and you will find a very different river. No defined channels exist above Trenton and swift rocky, shallow water replaces the slow moving deeper sections of the tide water. Deep water sections are restricted by rapids, and depths in excess of twenty feet are the exception, not the rule. The shallow water of the summer months can compound these conditions.

It's in the type of water we just described that the flat bottom jon boat, modified vee, pram, rubber boat and canoe are at home. All the aforementioned vessels are shallow draft boats and, with the proper modifications to their motors, will serve you well. Aluminum is the preferred material for boats that will be needed to fish a productive river of the type we have described. The weight of fiberglass adds weight and draft to a vessel. Fiberglass is also much more easily damaged. Other hull materials such as Ram X and Kelvelar are not as widely used because of price considerations, weight and other factors.

Wide-body, flat-bottomed boats with a shallow draft offer better stability in the shallow waters of the non-tidal river.

For the best results when choosing an aluminum boat for use in the river, the bottom thickness of the boat should be at least .070 and the seams should be welded or riveted and welded for extra strength. Your beam should be at least 60 inches or better for good stability.

Flat Bottoms and Prams One of the best all around boats to use in shallow rock base rivers is a wide body jon boat in the 12' to 16' range, with 14' considered to be the best all around length. This type of boat offers

15

excellent stability, easy handling, shallow draft and plenty of on board space. They can be easily modified with pedestal seats, live wells, rod holders, lure racks, floor and navigational lighting and many other connivances that can make them as comfortable and convenient to fish out of as a factory made bass boat. Their price tag is also much easier on the wallet, and their maneuverability on and off the trailer makes them a top choice among river fishermen.

Several boat manufacturers are even producing boats of this type specifically designed for use in a shallow rocky river. Their modified hulls draw very little water, their wide body design gives them excellent stability and their lightness allows them to be pushed with less horse power. The last feature makes them easier on the wallet in the fuel department.

Motorized canoes are a good vessel for the non-tidal river.

Canoes   The canoe is at home on a river and has been since the beginning of time. It makes an excellent light craft for one or two persons to fish out of. Although not as comfortable and stable as other vessels, it does offer the angler benefits that other boats can't. With the addition of a small motor, it will get you into sections of the river that most other boats can't travel. It is easily car topped and can be launched from anywhere along the river, without the need for a ramp. It is the vehicle of choice on most float trips, though a small jon boat is preferred over it by many anglers for this purpose.

Both double end and square back are in wide spread use on the river, however, the square back is more popular among fishermen. The reason for this is that it makes a better craft with which to use a small gas outboard. Since a fisherman's needs are different than that of a canoer, who's main purpose is to paddle a river, the square back is a better boat for him. The addition of a motor on the square back will give the mobility that he would not possess in a manually powered craft. It will allow him to go against the current more easily.

This will come in handy when you have drifted through a productive area and want to make another pass. It is also a benefit in that you will be able to move much faster through an area you don't want to fish, thus giving you more fishing time. Most small gas outboards under 5 hp are very fuel efficient and easy to transport.

The canoe will allow you to effectively fish flats and other shallow areas by using it to get to them and then beaching the canoe and wading the desired areas. Because of the streamlined shape and light weight of the canoe, another option you have is to use a catch line to tie it off to your belt and wade a productive section with the canoe trailing you downstream. This is a tactic commonly used during the summer season for fishing ripples, rapids and sections that have an abundance of small eddies.

Rubber Boats   The use of a rubber raft, although not as commonly used as the other crafts that we mentioned, does have plenty of applications on a river. It can be doctored up to give you many of the comforts that you enjoy on larger, hard hull

vessels. A good many anglers shy away from them because of a lack of confidence in their durability, however, in this day and age most of the rubber boats that are produced by reputable companies are very durable. They also have many advantages over other types of vessels.

Rubber boats make excellent crafts especially on float trips.

Since you are riding on a cushion of air they are very light, and this will work for and against the angler in a river. Their lightness makes them easy to maneuver, but a windy day can make them difficult to handle.

Their one main advantage over other types of crafts is their ability to be very compact when deflated. If you have a space problem either in your vehicle or home, they offer you easy storage.

Because of their buoyancy, they make excellent vehicles for a down river trip in that they can hold large amounts of gear and still move easily through shallow water. Most of the better ones make provisions for the use of a small motor. The one draw back that they have is that they are usually a wet boat, and this can cause you problems during the early and late part of the season when getting wet can be just plain cold.

Float tubes are a popular way of combining wading and floating the river.

Float Tubes   Although not considered a vessel in most states, the float tube is an effective way of fishing a river for a very moderate cost. There are numerous float tubes on the market today and your choice in tubes can be as elaborate or as spartan as you yourself make it. The use of a float tube is sort of a cross between the use of a boat and wading. It offers the angler the best of both styles of fishing, along with several other advantages. It allows the wader to stand in shallow water and gives him the advantage of being able to fish deeper sections of the river while floating in the tube.

Besides the fishing advantages, a tube is compact and easy to store and transport. Among it's disadvantages is the fact that it is limited in mobility from the stand point that it is not powered and cannot be used to go against the current. This makes planning your fishing trip more important. The best way of using one is to fish with another fisherman who has a float tube and use two vehicles. One vehicle can be used to transport you to a starting point and the other can be left at the point you expect to end your fishing trip. You can then fish a predetermined area combining wading with floating. This makes an excellent way to fish a river during the summer months.

During the warm water season, a float tube can be used with a pair of shorts and sneakers or spiked shoes. It makes a good way to cool off and get some good action in at the same time. Throughout the cooler portion of the year a float tube can still be employed, but a pair of insulated waders will become a necessity. Despite their relatively higher cost, many anglers who use this mode of fishing prefer the use of neoprene waders for the flexibility and warmth that they afford.

MOTORS

Since the non-tidal Delaware is a fast moving rocky type river, the need for high speeds to traverse large distances is replaced by the need for the ability to maneuver in shallow waters and swift currents. Here, large engines are replaced by smaller, lighter weight and shallower draft motors.

Shallow water tilt system on Mercury motor.

In order to maneuver in shallow, swift, rock filled waters, you will have to protect your lower unit and prop. This can be done in several ways. A shallow water tilt system is a necessity, and most of the major outboard manufacturers equip their motors of 20 horse power or less with factory made systems. On larger engines it will be necessary to improvise a bracket to tilt your motor, and the way you go about this will vary with the different makes of outboards.

For OMC engines and other makes that do not employ a claw type locking system, you can use a piece of flat bar steel to fasten your bracket. It should be bent in the shape of a "U" and holes should be drilled into the sides of the bracket so that it will fit over the tilt pin. The bracket should be able to swing free so that it can be moved into an out-of-the-way position when not in use. Tailor make the bracket so that the motor will ride at a 45 degree angle when it is in the shallow water mode.

For Mercury engines and other motors that employ a claw type locking system that hooks on to the tilt pin when the engine is in the idle mode, round bar steel will have to be used in the construction of the bracket. The shape of the bracket is the same, however, the bracket side bars will have to be designed so that they fit into the tilt pin holes and can be locked in through the use of a cotter pin. This will keep the bracket from popping out when the engine puts pressure on it.

No matter what make of motor you use or what type of shallow water bracket system you employ with your motor, always make sure that your motor is not locked in position while running on the river. As long as your motor is hanging free when running, it will kick up when it hits something, thus greatly reducing the damage to the lower unit. Even though most manufacturers of power trim systems use a break away feature that is supposed to achieve the same end, all need a certain amount of force to pop them free. By the time this happens, however, the damage is done, and for this reason power trim units are not of benefit to river fishermen.

Jet drives are another option that the angler has available to him. Here, too, a jet drive will cause a 20 to 30 percent loss in power. The expense of this type of unit is another factor that keeps many anglers from using it. Small rocks and pebbles can present a problem with this type of unit when they get sucked into the intakes.

There are several ways of protecting your lower unit from the rocky terrain with a steel guard. Some manufacturers produce a circular guard that fits around the prop and attaches to the lower unit. These guards do protect your prop, but many fishermen do not like them because of the 15 to 20 percent power loss they create. They are also not available for larger engines.

An inexpensive way of protecting your lower unit is to use a piece of angle iron. It can be fitted around the front of the lower unit and down along the skag to a length of two inches below the skag. A steel strap can be used to hold it in place near the top of the guard. Be sure when positioning this strap that it does not cover the water intakes for your cooling system. The angle iron can be compressed over the skag with a vise or C clamp so that it fits tightly in place. You can then drill a hole through the skag, and a bolt can be used to lock the lower portion of the guard in place. This guard will protect the lower unit and

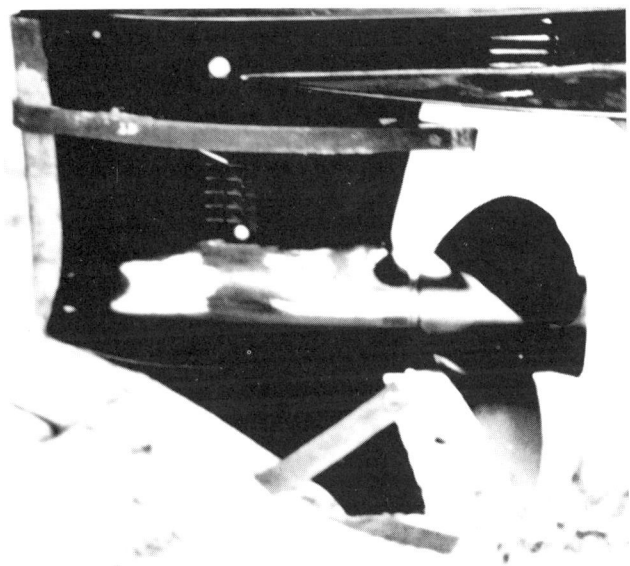

Steel bracket used to safeguard lower unit from rocks.

prop to a certain extent. The only time damage to your prop will occur from hitting a rock is when your motor is turning and the points of the prop come in contact with the rock. Using your engine at slow speeds in conjunction with the shallow water tilt system that we previously described will save your prop and lower unit from most damage. One problem you may run across is some cavitation that will occur when running at high speeds. You can alleviate this problem through the use of a Dolefin or other type of hydrofoil device.

Whenever running your motor in waters of which you are uncertain, always proceed slow enough so that you can see the water ahead of you and make sure it is free of obstructions. This not only makes good sense when it comes to personal safety, but it can save you the price of a costly repair job.

Trolling motors are another piece of equipment that can come in handy, however, forward mounted foot controlled motors will present problems. They are easily damaged when they strike an under water object while moving downstream because the weight of the boat is amplified by the current. This will often result in bent shafts and cracked housings.

The more applicable choice in electric motors is a stern mounted trolling motor that will hang free when it is being used. This will allow it to bounce off most objects and the rocky bottom without causing damage. Electric trolling motors can be used to power canoes when floating down river. In most cases they will not have enough power to move a canoe or other vessel upstream against the current.

Most electric motors will lock into place while they are in use. This may be fine for running in a lake or other deep body of water, however, as we mentioned, it is unwise to run any motor in a locked position when running a river. Many veteran anglers will file or cut the teeth off a section of their trolling motor mount to allow it to hang free. Another trick that is commonly used is to bolt a piece of metal or wood in place to keep the motor from locking in place.

One place that you will find trolling motors handy is in the quiet waters of the tide water river. Fishing coves and backwater areas in this portion of the river is much the same as fishing a lake or pond. Trolling motors make excellent tools for working drop-offs and other structures that are found in these areas.

MISCELLANEOUS BOAT EQUIPMENT

Anchors   Of all the items that you will have to stock on your boat, the anchor is one of the most important. It must always be remembered that anchoring a boat in the river with it's current is very different from anchoring a boat in a lake or reservoir where there is no current. All too often anglers venture out into a river with an inadequate anchoring system, and this not only cuts down on their fishing efficiency but can present some safety problems as well.

The only type of anchor that will effectively grab onto the rocky bottom of a river is some type of grappling hook anchor. There are several that are marketed commercially, however, it is less costly and more efficient to have a welder make one for you. After many years of using different anchor designs, the one which has proven itself as being the most effective is a four pronged grappling anchor. It can be made by taking a length of two inch bar steel about two feet long and welding an eye to one end. The prongs that are used to grab the bottom are made from three foot lengths of half inch reinforcement iron which is shaped and welded to the base of the anchor in opposite directions; a slide bar is welded to the main bar of the anchor so that if the anchor gets stuck you can get ahead of it and the chain will slide to the '

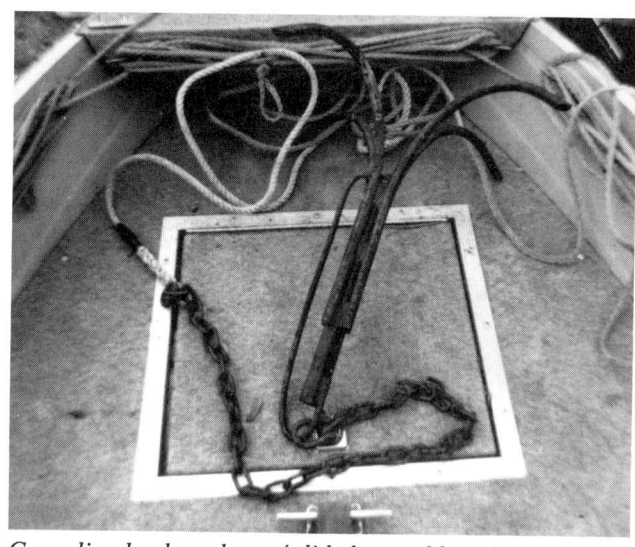

Grappling hook anchor w/ slide bar and length of chain.

back of the anchor and you can pull it out backwards.

If the anchor is made properly, the half inch reinforcement iron of which the prongs are made will enable the angler to make the anchor line fast to his boat and pull it out under power if it should become stuck in deep water. The prongs will bend, however, once the anchor is free they can be bent back in place. A length of pipe that will fit over the prongs of the anchor can be kept on the boat and used to bend the prongs back in shape.

A two to three foot length of heavy chain should be used ahead of the anchor to insure that the points of the anchor will remain pointed downward where they will do the most good.

Anchoring in a River's Current.   When it comes to the amount of line that you must pay out when anchoring, a simple rule to follow is to allow six feet of line for every foot of depth and never anchor over the stern of a boat in a river's current. When casting your anchor into the water, always make sure that all persons in the boat are seated so that if the anchor should grab suddenly they will not be thrown off balance. Allow the anchor to catch and then slowly feed out line until the proper anchoring position is achieved. Never just throw the anchor over the side and then go about your business without first making sure that the boat is secured.

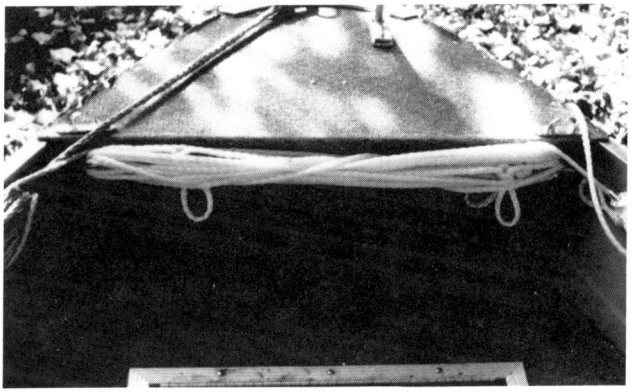
Note anchor chalks on both sides of boat.

When it comes to anchor lines, there are several things that you can do to make your anchoring system more efficient. Keep several lengths of anchor line on your boat and tie loops on them every twenty five feet. This will allow you to place your anchor in one spot and use the current to fish different areas by releasing some line every time you wish to move. It will allow you to fish along a structure by using the current to move your boat down the structure without having to retrieve your anchor each time.

Another tip is to always start your boat prior to picking up your anchor and moving. This will ensure that your boat will be able to make a clean getaway without floating into dangerous water while you are trying to start your engine.

Nets   When it comes to the nets that the angler will find useful for river fishing, his choice will be governed by the fish for which he is fishing and how he is doing the fishing. Anglers fishing from shore will find a long handled net better suited than it's short handled counterpart. Those wading, on the other hand, will find that the opposite is true. Boat fishermen will find that a net with an extendable handle will be better suited for their purposes. There are several of this style net on the market today. When not in use, the handle collapses for easy storage. When the net is needed, a simple push of a button will extend the handle. One tip for the use of nets is to tie a length of cord on the bottom of the net and use it to hold the net to the handle while you are maneuvering the net to take a fish. Once the net is under the fish, all the angler has to do is release the cord and the net will balloon out, engulfing the fish.

Life Preservers   Besides being the law (one life jacket for each person in the vessel), it only makes good sense to put your own personal safety first. In addition to the normal flotation vest that most fishermen use, a throw type life saver (seat cushion or ring) makes an excellent accessory. It can come in handy if you should ever have to render assistance to a downed boater or drowning person. It is always wise to wear your life jacket while the boat is moving and in waters that are unfamiliar to you. Likewise, non-swimmers and youngsters should always wear life jackets while on the water. Numerous persons drown each year not because they don't know how to swim but because they hit their head or received another type of injury that incapacitated them as they fell from a boat without a life jacket. Had they been wearing one they would have remained upright in the water and in most cases would have not inhaled the water and drowned.

Emergency Kit   If you fish from a boat often enough, sooner or later you will have a mechanical problem. The best way to cope with the minor problems that might arise is to carry an emergency kit. This kit should be stocked with spare spark plugs, electricians tape, duct tape, spare light bulbs that will fit your navigation and trailer lights, fuses (if your boats uses them), a length of electrical wire, and wrenches and screw drivers that will fit the nuts and bolts on your boat and motor. All the aforementioned items should be kept in a water tight container and permanently stored in your boat.

In addition to the spare parts and tools that we just mentioned, there are certain items that you are better off carrying in your boat no matter how small it is and whether the law requires them or not. A hand held air horn is an excellent signaling device for warning other approaching boats or for just getting someone's attention. You will find an air horn especially useful when foggy weather is present.

A pair of water proof flares is another safety item that can come in handy in an emergency. A well stocked first aid kit is another plus, even if you only use it for minor mishaps. Besides the standard items such as band aids, gauze, tape, etc., your kit should include insect bite medication, aspirin or an aspirin substitute, antacid, antiseptic creams for poison ivy and other irritating plants, baking soda and sun screen. A can of insect repellent is another item that it never hurts to have on hand.

Electronics   Because of the shallow nature of the upper Delaware, there are only a few places where a sonar unit will come in handy for reading the bottom. Long quiet deep water pools and sections of a river that are dammed up are two of the places where they will have some applications. One problem that you will face when using a graph in a river has to do with the current. The current will cause leaves and other objects to pass under your boat, and the transducer of your graph will quite often mistake them for fish. This is very common during the fall season and during periods of high water when plenty of debris has found it's way into the river.

On the other hand, you will find a sonar unit very useful on the tide water Delaware. The water in this portion of the river is much deeper and the structures, in many cases, are different. Locating drop-offs, wrecks and other under water objects can best be done with a dependable sonar unit. Sonar will also come in handy when you are trolling along channel ledges in the main river and for locating under water bars and rock piles.

One piece of electronics that will be of great value to you on the river will be a surface temperature gauge. Since water temperature is a primary factor in river fishing, it will come in handy in determining the use of lures and live bait, as well as the methods that you use to present them.

Most commercially produced temperature gauges can be permanently mounted on the transom of your boat to give you constant surface temperature readings. Having a hand held gauge that can be lowered into the depths can also be of benefit in that it will allow you to see the difference between the surface temperature and the water down under.

The **Delaware River Fisherman's Association** is a group of concerned sportsmen, businesses and fishing clubs dedicated to the preservation an d improvement of the river, it's fisheries, water quality and access, and to promote good sportsmanship among those who use the river. If you are interested in joining the D.R.F.A. or want some information on the Association please write **D.R.F.A., P.O. Box 9, Titusville, NJ 08560**. All interested sportsmen and those concerned about the future of the Delaware are invited to join. Meetings are held the last Thursday of the month at 7 PM at the Sportsmen Center, Route 130, Bordentown, New Jersey.

CHAPTER 3: STRUCTURES

EVOLVING STRUCTURES

Most structures that are found on the Delaware can be classified as evolving structures. In the case of the non-tidal river we mean that the position of the fish changes with the time of the day, thus affecting how you fish for them. In the tidal river, these structures will change with each turn of the tide. For the most part this will be prevalent during the warm water season when the fish are more active and move around more. During the cold water season the fish will, on the whole, seek

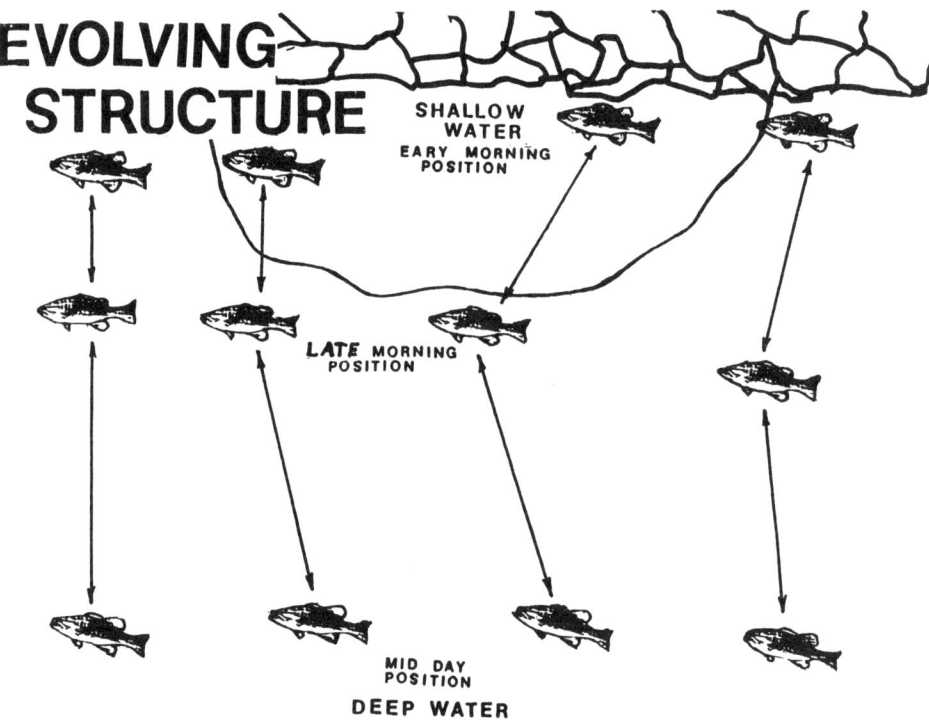

EVOLVING STRUCTURE

SHALLOW WATER

EARY MORNING POSITION

LATE MORNING POSITION

MID DAY POSITION

DEEP WATER

out deeper water and remain there as long as the water temperature remains cold, not moving very far for a meal during this time.

During the warm water season, fish move into shallow water to feed and then retreat back into deep water or under some type of cover. This occurs during two prime periods, early morning and late afternoon. Sometimes fish will move into the shallow water during the late afternoon and remain there until the following morning, moving out of the shallow water when the effects of the sun's light get too bright. This has led many serious anglers to adhere to the theory that the movements of some fish are directly related to the rising and setting of the sun. More specifically, fish movements are triggered by certain levels of light penetration.

On evolving structures such as flats or bars, most gamefish such as bass move onto them to feed in the early morning and begin moving off as the sun's light becomes brighter. You should begin fishing the structure close in with surface lures. As the light of day gets brighter and the fish begin moving away from shallow water, your next step will be to fish swimming plugs and other shallow running lures. As the fish move further from shallow water and into deeper water you will have to use lures that go down deeper. Once the fish have moved into the deeper regions or under some type of cover you will have to dig them out with jigs and jig/rubber bait combinations, along with other lures that will get you to where the fish are.

As you can see, evolving structures get their name because you will have to change the way you fish on them as fish move from shallow water back into their deep water haunts. You'll find that some fish will develop different patterns on most types of structures, based on weather and water conditions, and these will be the key to the fishing no matter what time of year it is.

Very few structures found in a river will not be evolving structures. The ones that are not are what are called constant structures; by this we mean that the way you fish them will not vary according to the time of the day. Among the structures that are considered constant structures are bridge pilings, warm water discharges, deep drop-offs and over hanging trees. In the case of these structures, the only time you change the way you fish them is when the water levels of a river affect them and change their physical make up.

Play the percentages   Most successful fishermen are percentage fishermen. By this we mean that they fish certain structures by the time of day they are fishing. Likewise, they will fish certain structures according to the weather and water conditions that are present on any given day.

Knowledgible fishermen choose their lures according to the conditions that are present and the type of water they are trying to cover. An open mind is one of the top requirements of a good river fisherman, or any type of fisherman for that matter. Never allow yourself to get into a rut by having a pet lure. Your lures are tools and should be treated as such, each having their time and place.

Likewise, you should govern your choices in rod and reels according to the type of lure you are using and the type of water you are fishing. There is no one type of rod or reel that will do it all. The more you fish, the more you will realize this fact and after a while you will begin to see what we mean.

The Three States Of A Fish   One mistake that many fishermen make is to fish one spot too long. Knowing when to leave a productive spot and when to stay will only come through experience. Likewise, fishing the same place day after day is another mistake that a good many anglers make.

There are three basic states of a fish. The first state, most commonly referred to as the "active state", is the one that most of us dream about. It's during this time that the fish will hit anything that moves and it's also during this time that the largest numbers of fish are taken. For most fish, this active state will occur more often during certain times of the year and certain times of the day. This is when your chance of taking them will be greatest. It will also be governed by external factors such as weather and water conditions.

Unfortunately, the active state is not as common as the second state, best known as the "neutral state". Fish will spend 60% of their time in this condition. When they are found in this state they are not as aggressive as when they are active, however, if something should come close enough to them they will take it. Since this state is the one in which the fish will most likely be found, it is the most important to the fisherman. Anyone can catch fish when they are actively feeding; the neutral state, however, takes a little more effort as well as skill.

25

Proper lure presentation becomes a vital ingredient when fish are found in the neutral or middle state, and speed and depth control are crucial to an anglers presentation. Knowing how to read the water of a river is another factor that figures into the successful river fisherman's formula, and his ability to present his offerings in a current will be crucial to his success.

The third or "passive" state of a fish is one that we all would rather forget about. Although fish that inhabit a river are very seldom found in this state, due to the rich amounts of oxygen found there, it does happen from time to time. Fish that are in a passive state are usually fed up and/or turned off by weather or water conditions. No matter what you do or how good a fisherman you are, the chances of making them hit are very slim. You may take a few on days such as we are talking about, but by and large the fishing will be tough, and passive fish simply will not be interested in your offerings.

When we talk about fishing percentages with regard to the different states of a fish, it's easy to see that the active fish are where the percentages are the highest. Thus you should play the percentages for the best catches. If you fish a structure and take some fish and then the fishing slows down, don't be afraid to move. Fishing dead water as it's called is only wasting your time and costing you fish. Moving to a similar spot as that where you caught the fish will often produce more fish. Once you feel that you have fished a spot thoroughly (knowing when that is done will come with experience), move and keep moving until you find more fish that are active.

FISH THE SHADOWS

The non-tidal Delaware is a clean, rock base river that flows through hills and

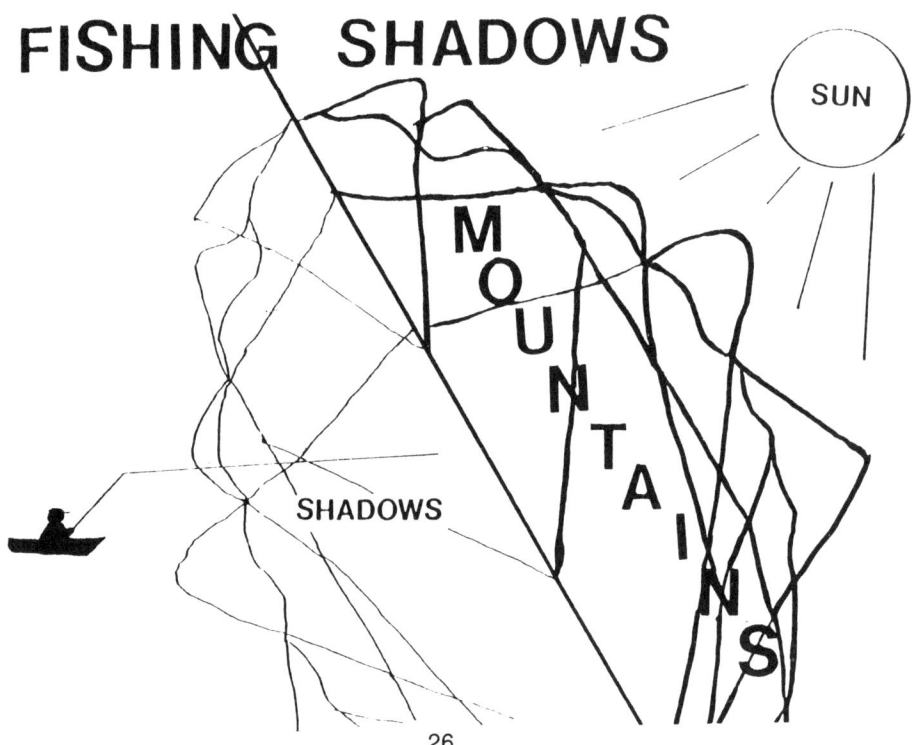

mountains. These hills and mountains cast shadows on the river and it's structures during certain times of the day, thus directly affecting fish movements on the structures affected by the shadows.

Structures having shadows on them during the morning hours will have fish movements that last later into the morning. Those having shadows on them earlier in the afternoon will have fish movements that begin earlier in the afternoon. Keep this in mind when choosing a place to fish to put the odds on your side.

A good tip to fishing structures that have shadows on them is the color of the fish that you catch. Fish, especially bass, will change color. When found in shallow water they will be pale and when found in deeper water or under cover they will be dark in color. When you are fishing a shallow structure and take a dark color fish, chances are he has moved into shallow water from deep water or from under cover. He is usually a front runner and more will follow. The reverse is true if you catch a pale color fish in deeper water.

KEEP A FISHING LOG

There is an old saying that "no job is finished until the paper work is done". If

you are a serious fisherman then this pertains to you, especially if you fish the same places on a regular basis. I know most of us have a dislike for paper work, however, a little paper work can make a big difference in the number of fish you catch. If you stop to think about it, how many times have you found yourself saying "I think it was around this time last year that I was taking fish on spinnerbaits in the ripples, or was it a few weeks later." A fishing log will take the guess work out of your fishing.

Keeping a fishing log will help you pin-point fish movements when certain conditions occur.

What a fishing log will teach you is that fish are creatures of habit, having definite preferences when it comes to times of day, times of year, forage, etc. and they will develop definite patterns in relation to weather and water conditions. A log will clearly define these things for you and will help you pick up on them and cope with them when they occur in the future.

My personal logs extend back 33 years. What keeps many fishermen from keeping a log is that you won't see any results quickly. It will take a couple of years of keeping one before you will be able to see any patterns developing on the waters you fish or get any significant information from a log.

Some of the things that you should keep in your log are water conditions, weather conditions, numbers of fish you catch, what you catch them on, places you fish and the amount of time you spend fishing there, moon phases, wind speed and directions, and any other information you feel makes a difference in how successful your are or are not.

BASIC EDDIES

One thing all river structures have in common is that they will be some form of eddy structure or will have eddies located somewhere on or around them. This makes understanding the basic eddy very important. Likewise, certain parts of an eddy will be productive at different times of the day and under different water conditions, thus certain lures will work better along different parts of an eddy.

The basic eddy is composed of four parts: the object that causes the eddy, the current line or lines that pass around the object and form the third part, the dead water pocket, and the shallow downstream area located below the eddy. Fish can be found in all these portions of an eddy at one time or another, depending on random elements such as water levels, direction of the sun, amount of light penetrating the eddy, time of day, and other factors.

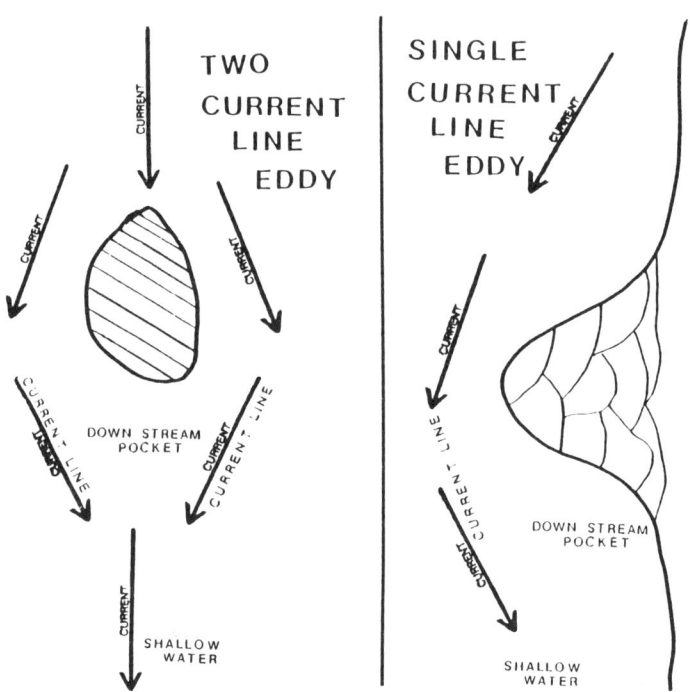

There are two basic types of eddies, single current line and double current line eddies. Eddies are either structures by themselves or parts of larger structures. (A look at the diagram above will illustrate the difference between the two.)

FLATS

If I had to pick the most exciting place to fish, especially for bass, there would be no contest; the abundant shallow flats that are found on the river would win hands down. There is nothing more spectacular than a smallie taken in shallow water as he goes airborne in an effort to throw the hook. One might think that this is only true when surface fishing, but when smallies are taken in only a few inches of water, whether it be on a lure, or livebait, they will explode out of the water as there is simply no place for them to go.

Fish found on flats are usually there to feed. Even though there is a certain amount of fish on a flat under most conditions, the biggest numbers will be found during feeding times. Thus, certain times of the day will be more productive. One thing that you should remember when fishing shallow water is that fish spook more easily, especially when the water is low and gin clear. Sound and vibrations travel fast and far in shallow water. As a result, the angler must be very careful when fishing them, whether in a boat, from shore or by wading.

28

FLATS

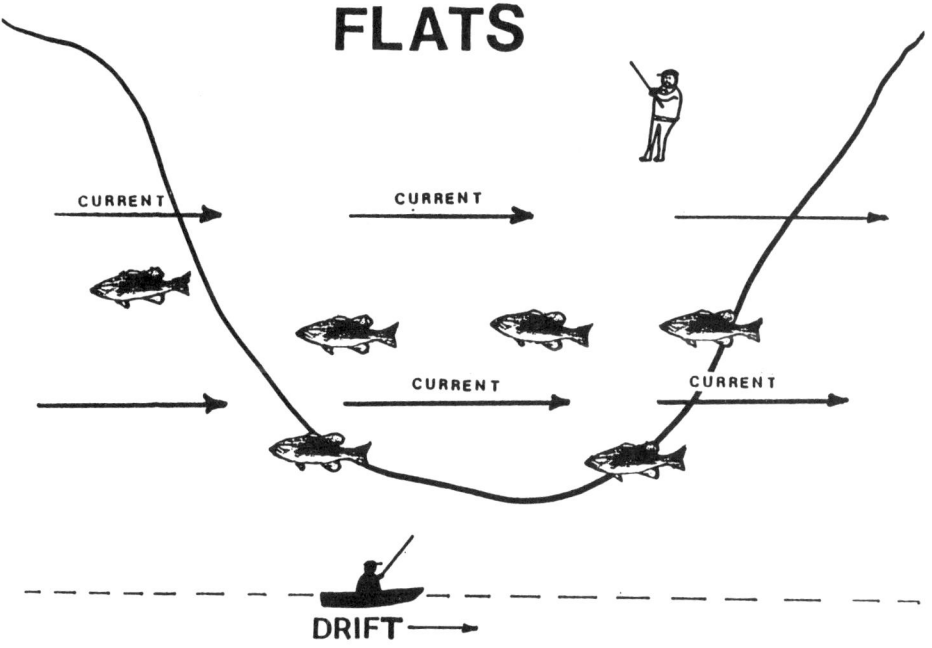

DRIFT →

Water temperature plays an important part in fishing the flats. It will, to a large extent, govern your choice in a productive flat during certain times of the year.

During the summer when the water temperatures are at their highest, shallow flats that have a slight to moderate current passing over them will be your most productive flats. Oxygen levels on them will be higher and bug hatches more plentiful, thus giving the fish two of their most important needs, food and oxygen.

There are four prime times when fish will be found there in good numbers. The first is during the early season as the water begins to warm up. Since flats are shallow and are very susceptible to a few days of warm weather and breezes, they are some of the first places to warm up in the spring and one of the first places the fish will become active. Live bait, spinnerbaits and swimming plugs fished during the late afternoons when the water is warmest will be your top choices during this period. The second period is during the spawning season when bass and other fish move onto them to spawn. Jig/rubberbait combinations and crankbaits will be your best bet at this time.

The third and most productive portion of the year is during the summer months when bass and panfish feed in the early morning and late afternoons. During the summer months, flats are typical evolving structures with the fish moving on them to feed during the early morning and late afternoon. Many anglers, myself included, ascribe to the light theory. This is the belief that the fish are triggered by certain levels of light. As day breaks, fish on the flats will start feeding in the shallow areas, hitting anything that presents a target on the surface. As the light of day gets brighter they begin moving into deeper water or into some type of cover. You should fish in close, moving gradually into deeper water or towards the closest cover, as the sun gets on the water.

During periods when the water is gin clear, the fish's movements will be of

29

shorter duration and will usually occur during the beginning and end of the day. When the light penetration is diminished by either a shadow or by off color water, fish movements will last longer. Movements will also last longer on cloudy or overcast days. The diminished light levels will often keep the fish feeding throughout the day.

The fourth period of the season when fishing will be better than average on a flat is during the fall feed. Schools of the returning shad or herring will often feed on insects for several days at a time, giving you good action with spinnerbaits, swimming plugs and live-lined minnows.

Angler takes a smallie off a flat in the early morning.

When wading a flat you should always fish it going upstream whenever possible and fish it with the sun in your face. Always try to keep your shadow from being cast onto the flat. Move slowly and keep from making any loud noises or fast movements that might spook the fish.

When fishing from a boat, drift along the flat with the sun in your face and as far from the area you are fishing as possible. Cast your lures towards the shoreline and work them back. If you should spot fish feeding on a school of baitfish, position yourself away from them and cast at them. Drift as slowly as possible, employing a drag anchor as needed to slow down your drift.

POINTS OF LAND

Points of land are an excellent type of single current line eddy structure, and their productivity or lack of it has a lot to do with the water levels present on the structure when you are fishing. Another important factor is the depth of the water in the area in which they are found. There are several fish producing parts of a point of land. The first is the upstream pocket and it is usually an early morning or late afternoon spot. During the warm water season, small surface lures, swimming plugs and crankbaits will produce best. Live-lining and jigging minnows and other livebait will be your top producers during the cool water season. The fish will stack up there because the current will sweep forage into this pocket as it moves along the shoreline.

When low water conditions are present, fish will usually be found along the current line that sweeps around the point while they are feeding and along the inside of the current line where it comes into contact with the dead water pocket when they are resting. On points of land that are located in deep water, the fish will move into any shallow water that is found close to the point. Many times points of land located in shallow areas will be more productive when the water levels of the river are on the higher side. When fishing a point of land from the shore or by wading, there are three places to position yourself. The first is along side the upstream pocket and casting to it. The second is to walk out onto the point of land and cast at the upstream pocket, the downstream pocket and the current line. Surface plugs and swimming

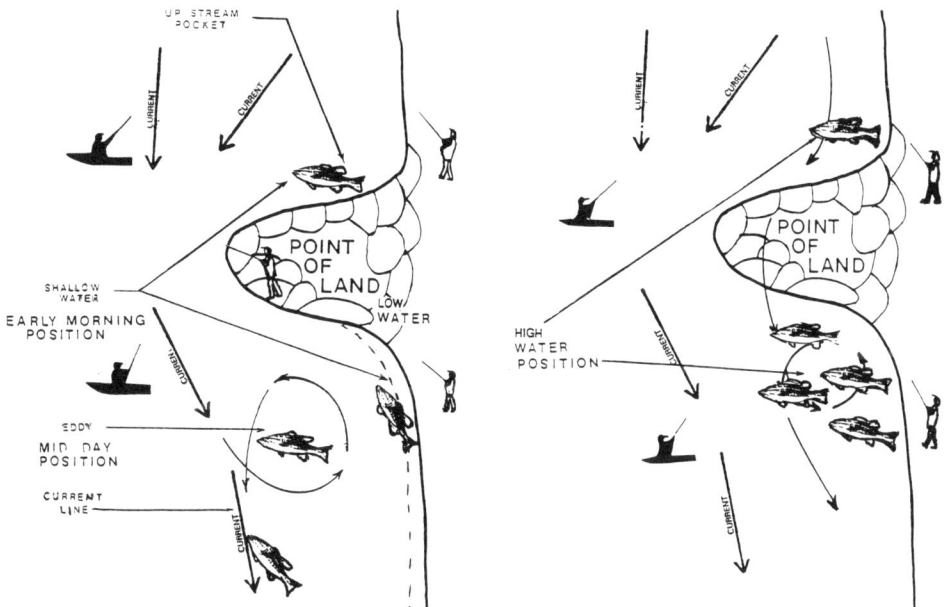

plugs should be used in the downstream and upstream pockets, and crankbaits, sinking swimming plugs, spinnerbaits and lead body baits in the current line.

The third place you should position yourself to fish a point of land is along side of the downstream pocket; cast at the current line with swimming plugs, crankbaits, jig/rubberbaits and spinnerbaits.

Point of land at the mouth of a tributary stream.

When fishing livebait from all three positions, the method you will use will be determined by the swiftness of the current you have to deal with. In slower currents you can liveline or cast and retrieve livebait. If the water is on the faster side then your best bet will be to fish jig/livebait combos.

When fishing from a boat, always position yourself across from the point and cast at the three positions we named. You can also drift slowly along the point, working surface lures and swimming plugs during the early and late hours of the day and crankbaits, jig/rubberbaits and sinking swimming plugs during the mid day hours. Just as when fishing from the shore or by wading, the way you use your livebait will be determined by the swiftness of the current that is moving along the point of land.

When high water is present on any point of land, the fish will be forced up close to the shoreline in the dead water pocket. They will gather here in good numbers to escape the swifter currents of the main river.

BRIDGE PILINGS

The Delaware has plenty of bridges that cross it. The pilings on which the bridges sit offer some of the best eddy structures found on the river. The amount of eddies, their size and the swiftness of the currents that flow around them will vary with each bridge. However, they all have essentiality the same type of classic eddy structure found below their pilings.

Low Water   During periods of low water, eddies found below the pilings will have very distinct current lines, dead water pockets and shallow downstream areas.

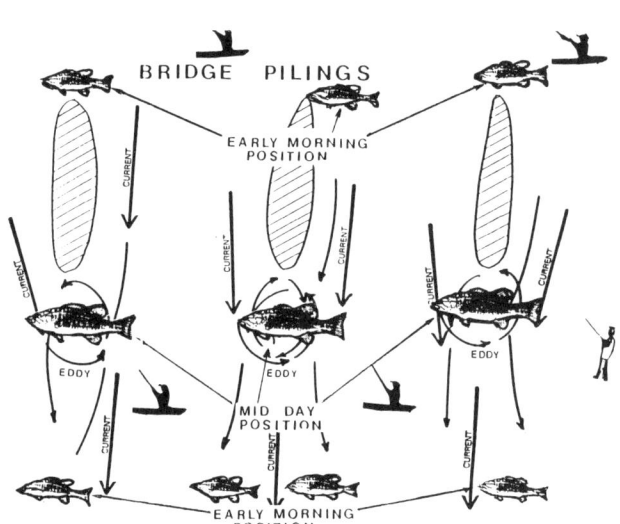

One of the most common mistakes that many anglers make is spending too much time fishing one piling. It's best to move from piling to piling, staying only as long as it takes to check out the eddies below each one. Fish each piling only as long as the fish are hitting and as soon as they slow down, move on to the next one.

Many bridge pilings will have upstream pockets at the head of the piling. This is another place that should not be overlooked, as fish will gather here to feed on insects and the baitfish that feed on them. This is much the same situation as the upstream flat of an island where forage is pushed on to it by the moving current.

High Water   During times of high water, choose the piling with the slowest water behind it. This will be, in most cases, one of the pilings that is closest to the shoreline. Fish will move into these slower eddies to escape the main rivers swift current. You should also check out any secondary structures that might have slower currents close to the pilings or a secondary structure that will slow up the water below a specific piling.

Anglers anchor alongside a bridge piling to fish the eddy located below it.

32

FINGER STRUCTURES

Finger structures are natural rock ledges that jut out into the river and form a type of natural dam. They are different from points of land in that they are solid rock structures, as opposed to a collection of rocks, debris and other objects which make up a point of land.

To the fisherman that enjoys wading, these structures are a prime target since they allow him to get out into the river and at it's main current. Most of them are easily waded and this is one type of structure where doing a little homework during periods of low water will pay off in big dividends during times when the water is higher.

Typical finger structure found on the river.

There are two different types of finger structures, single and multiple. Some of these may go all the way across the river while others may only jut partially out into the river.

Single Finger Structures   A single finger structure will have one set of eddies located below the rock ledge. In most cases, finger structures have an upstream pocket, a sluice or several breaks in the rock pile that will have water moving through them, and one or more eddies located below the ledge. All these areas will hold fish at one time or another.

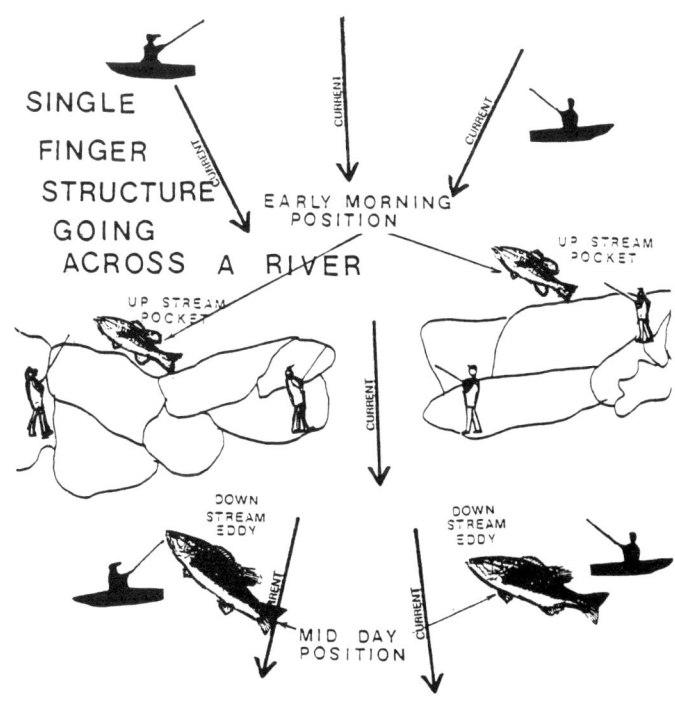

During the summer when low water conditions are present, bass and other fish that haunt a finger structure will be close to the surface during the early morning and late afternoon. The shallow water portions of the upstream pocket and surface of the quiet water portion of the eddy found below will be prime surface fishing waters.

33

The upstream water of a finger structure is very similar to that which is found above a wing dam in that it will have a gradual slope and is best worked with surface lures and swimming plugs.

The eddy found below a finger structure is a typical eddy structure, and the fish will often move from the bottom of the eddy to the top during low light periods to feed on insect life and other forage that is washed through the breaks in the finger.

Active fish found around finger structures will usually haunt the current lines that pass around a finger structure that does not go all the way across the river and the current lines that are caused by breaks in the finger. If a finger structure has more than one current line, always choose the deepest ones. Jig combinations, small spinnerbaits and deep running crankbaits will be the top producers here.

During the warm water season, fish holding to a finger structure will move into the eddy portion during the mid day hours for the better oxygen contents and the diminished light penetration they possess. When fish retreat here, digging them out with jig/rubberbait combinations and deep running crankbaits will be the way to go.

Under high water conditions, many of the eddies located below a finger will be too fast to fish effectively. If the finger structure has slower eddies along it's side, the fish will stack up there to get out of the faster currents. During the warm water season, jig/rubberbait combinations, swimming plugs and crankbaits are excellent choices. If this happens during the cold water season, livebait either live-lined or jigged will be the answer. Whether you choose to jig or live-line your bait will be determined by the depth of the eddy and the swiftness of it's current.

Multiple Finger Structures The major difference between a single finger structure and a multiple finger structure is the amount of eddies, current lines and rock ledges that are found there. The mid section of the Delaware is rich in shale and

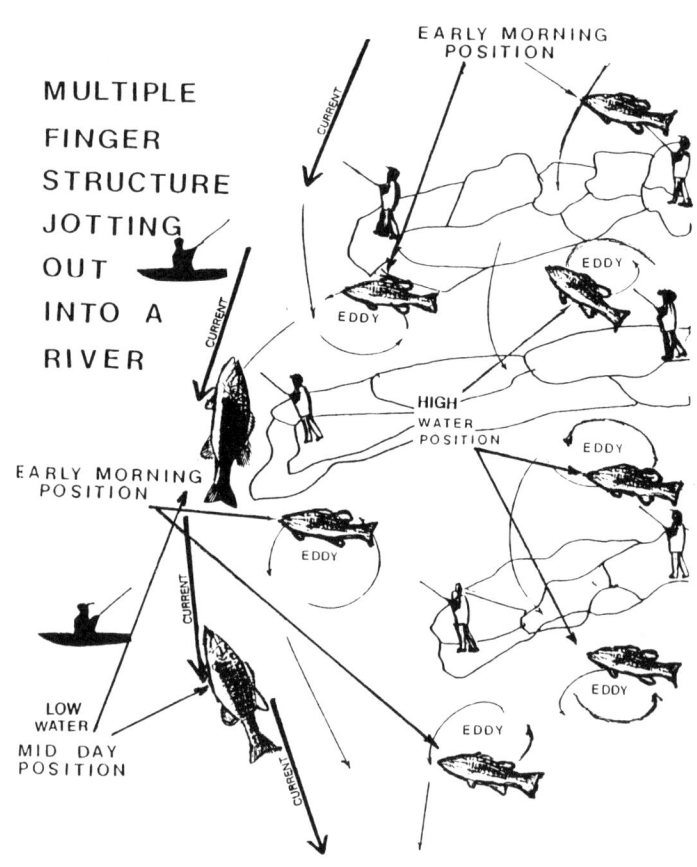

MULTIPLE FINGER STRUCTURE JOTTING OUT INTO A RIVER

other types of flat rocks that are the prime ingredients in finger structures. This results in several rock ledges making their way out into or across the river one after the other, creating multiple fingers. Each one of these ledges will have it's own set of eddies and current lines to fish, and this type of finger structure is excellent for the wader.

This type of finger structure provides some top-notch fishing during the low water periods of the summer. Surface fishing is excellent during this time and small popping plugs, buzzbaits, spinnerbaits and swimming plugs will be your top producers. If you are a fly fisherman, this type of structure will give you some great results on popping bugs, streamer flies and dry flies during the early mornings and late afternoons when good hatches occur. Mid day hours will find the fish in the numerous small eddies that dot these areas, and good results can be had on jig/rubberbait combinations. For the fly fisherman, streamer flies, nymphs and other sinking flies will be the best choices. As with single finger structures, periods of high water move the fish into the shallower, slower eddies that are found close to shore. Quite often, these areas are high and dry during low water and the rising waters will fill them in, creating productive areas. With multiple finger structures, shallow eddies are more numerous, providing more choices to fish when high water is present.

Your best way of fishing these structures during the late season is to concentrate on the deeper eddies that have slower currents. These eddies will hold water temperatures longer and be more stable later in the year.

STREAM CONFLUENCES

All rivers are fed by smaller feeder streams. These stream confluences are

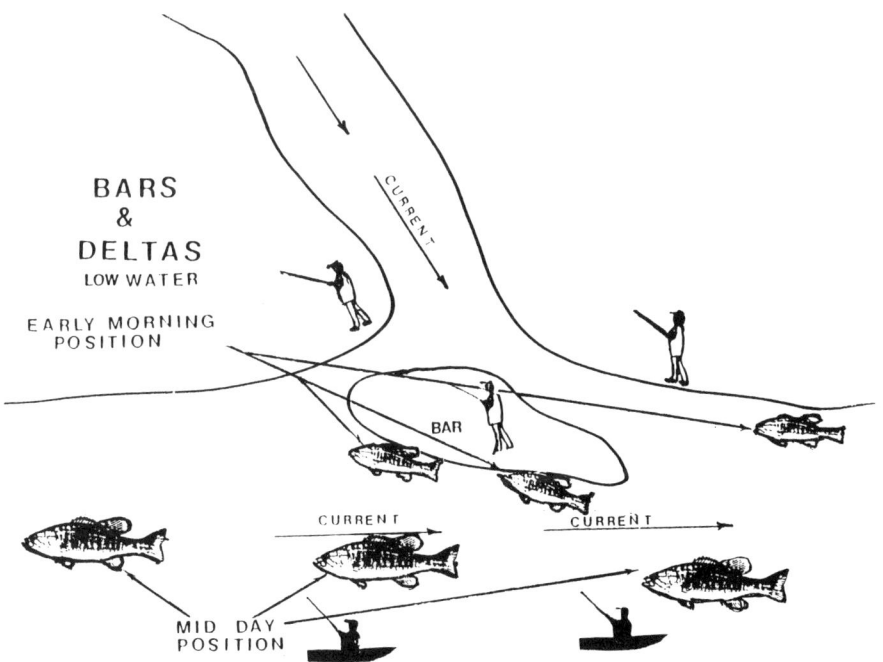

productive the year round under a variety of conditions. Many of them will have small dams and these dams will be as far as the fish will be able to travel up the tributary stream.

Most tributary streams will have a silt bar or delta at their confluence with the main river. This bar will be a prime feeding area during certain times. Since the water that comes from the stream will be warmer than that in the river during the first part of the

Mouth of the Lockatong Creek. Note dam, deltas and current flow.

spring, this area will be a good early season spot, and livebait will produce well here.

Low Water Conditions   As with most river structures, the fishing in and around the mouth of a tributary stream is affected by water levels and the weather conditions which affect them. During low water periods in the summer, the bar and any shallow flats found downstream from it will give you some early morning and late afternoon action. Water from the smaller streams is usually cooler than the main river and thus it will be oxygen rich, making the fish found here more active. Surface lures, spinnerbaits and swimming plugs are good bets here.

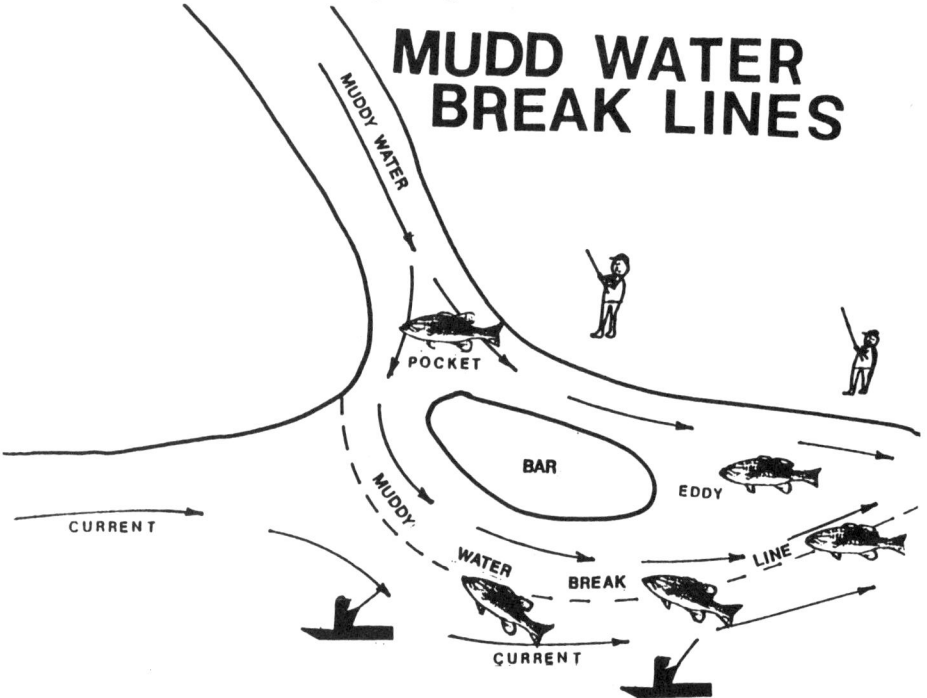

Muddy Water Break Lines   One condition that can really give you some good numbers of fish in a muddy water break line. This can occur two different ways. The first way and the one that is most prominent is when the small streams get muddy after a heavy rain. This dirty water will pour into the clean main stream of the river and a color breakline will form where the water from the stream comes in contact with the main current of the river. Along with the dirty water comes all types of forage, and smallmouth and other fish will stack up along the color breakline, feeding on the forage as it enters the river. Jig/rubberbait combinations, crankbaits and spinnerbaits will work best well here. During the cool water season live lining will be the top producer.

High Water Conditions   During high water periods that are accompanied by dirty water conditions, the tributary stream confluences can really be your salvation. With the main river being dirty, the small streams will clear up first, and good numbers of fish can be found where the clean water merges with the dirty water. The same lures and baits will work in this type of muddy water breakline.

Tributary streams can affect the rivers water in another way. These streams can sometimes be affected by weather patterns far away from a river. Heavy rains upstream in tributary streams can cause them to pour dirty water into the river, which results in the river being dirty from that point down. A good look at the current weather map or a call to some tackle shops can often tell you if the water will be cleaner upstream. In many cases you will be able to fish the river by fishing above where the dirty water comes in.

DROP-OFFS

Drop-offs are prime structures on any type of water, however, there is a distinct difference between drop-offs that are found in a lake and those that are found in a river. As with any river structure, they are affected by the current, and this key element is usually the ticket to fishing them.

The majority of the drop-offs found on the river are situated on river bends. Over the years, currents erode loose soil and rocks until a solid rock shoreline is left;

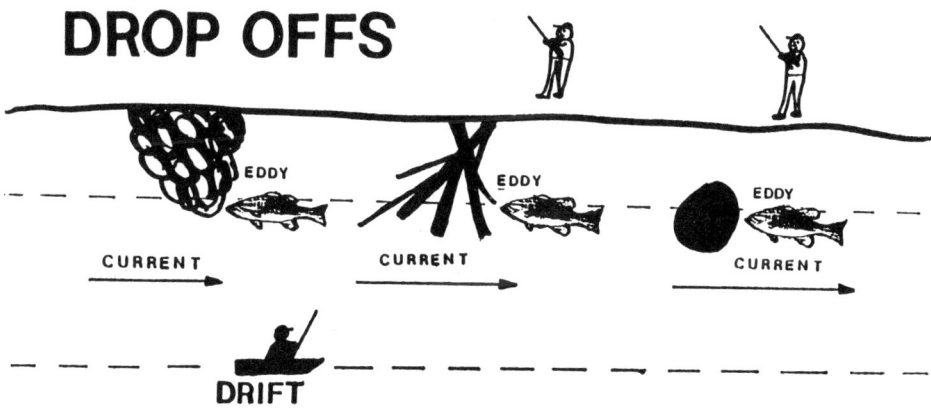

through time, even this solid rock will be cut into. The resulting drop-off usually holds some of the deepest water of a river.

In most cases, high water conditions will not be as productive as low water conditions on drop-off structures found on a river bend. This is not because of the depth of the water but because of the swift currents which accompany high water. The key to fishing a drop-off will be to find some type of object or secondary structure along them. A good sized rock, log, fallen tree or other object located along the drop-off which blocks the current and causes an eddy to form behind it will be the place where the fish are found. They hold behind these objects and grab forage as the current carries it downstream along the drop-off, darting back to their haunts.

How you fish a drop-off will be determined by how deep the drop-off is and the swiftness of the current. If the drop-off has considerable depth and moderate currents, trolling deep running plugs and spinnerbaits will make a good choice, and speed and depth control will be the key to your success.

Another way of fishing a drop-off is to slow drift it, casting to the drop-off and working lures such as jig/rubberbait combinations, jig/livebait combos and crankbaits. Here, too, speed and depth control is essential, especially during the cold water season when the fish will not move as far for a meal.

DAMS

Wing Dams   There are three wing dams located on the Delaware river. The first is located at Scudders Falls and was originally used to power a mill that is no longer standing. The second is at Lambertville and here, again, the dam was used to power the mill that is still standing but has been converted into condos. The last one is located at Bulls Island and is still used to back water up into the Delaware and Raritan Canal. This dam was recently refurbished in 1993 because the old dam did not back up enough water to supply the canal and the Point Pleasant pumping station. Wing dams are not constructed like the dams used to back up water into a reservoir. Instead of a fast sloping dam face, they have a gradual slope on the upriver side. This upstream slope of dam

Bulls Island wing dam at low water.

can provide some good surface fishing in the early mornings of the summer. Fish lay along this ledge in the current, picking up small baitfish and insects as they are pushed up on the ledge just before they go over the dam. Another prime place to fish is the eddies that are formed along the sluices of these dams.

Low Water Conditions   When low water conditions are present there are good sized eddies found along both sides of the sluice way of a dam, and they have swift water and smaller secondary eddies located below them. The gouged out depressions just below the base of the dam will cause hydros to form as water flows over the dam. These areas will all hold fish at one time or another. The eddies are typical eddy type structures and some will have good depth to them. The depth and currents will determine the weights of the lures or sinkers you use to fish them. As with all structures on the river, the currents and the depth of the eddies will be governed by the amount of water that is present.

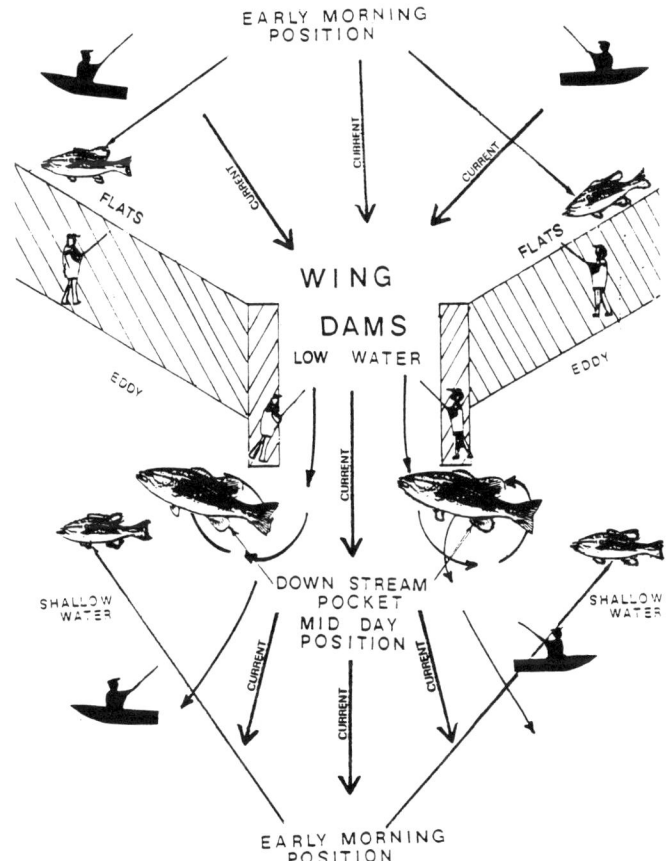

When the water is low and clear in the summer you will find that surface lures used along the front of the dam will give you some good results in the early morning and late afternoon. Jig/rubberbait combinations, sinking swimming plugs and crankbaits will be your ticket in the eddies located along side of the sluice. Spinnerbaits, swimming plugs and crankbaits will be your means to take the fish that will be found in the shallow swift water downstream from the dam, as well as the gouged out pocket below the dam.

High Water Conditions   Rising water levels will drastically change wing dams and the position of the fish. The water going through the sluice and the water going over most of the dam will be unfishable because of the swift currents. As a result, the swift currents will force the fish up close to the shoreline or further downstream from the dam than they would be found when low water conditions are present. Look for any slow water areas such as eddies, pockets or coves that may have formed as a result of the higher water. These are the places where the fish will gather to get out of the fast currents.

If high water conditions occur during the warm water season, jig/rubberbait combinations, sinking swimming plugs and crankbaits will be your best bet in the areas we have described. During the cold water season, jigging minnows and other livebait will give you the best results in shallow and medium range depths. In deeper water, Lindy rig/livebait combinations will work best.

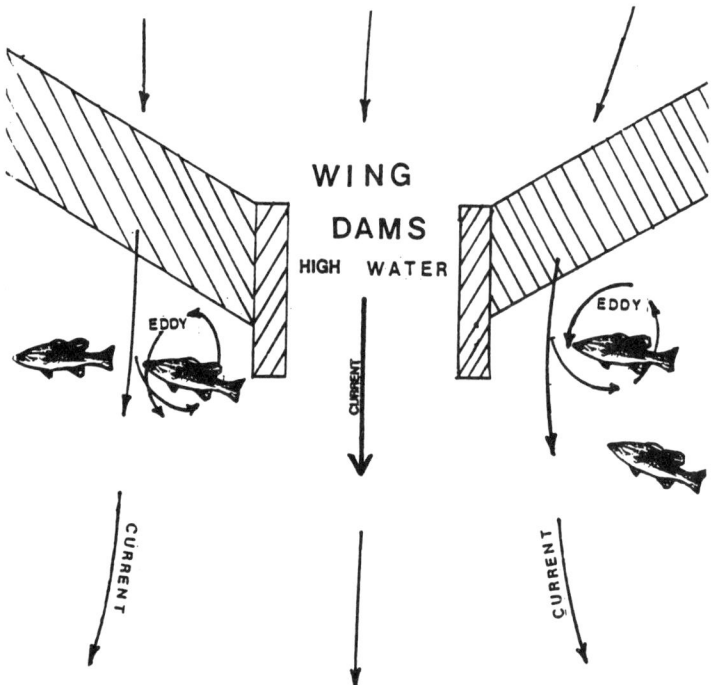

WING

DAMS

HIGH WATER

Secondary Dams Besides the wing dams that are found on the river, there are numerous smaller dams located on the streams that flow into the Delaware, the most notable of which is the dam at the mouth of the Lehigh. Spillways located at the base of these dams can produce some excellent fishing during certain times of the year and when certain conditions are present.

These spillways make great places to fish during high water periods. As the river rises due to heavy rain fall, the waters of a river will back up into the tributary streams as far as the dam. Fish will seek refuge from the rivers faster currents here, feeding on what is washed over the dam by the swollen stream.

Another factor that dam spillways have in their favor is that the stream which feeds them will usually clear up faster than the main river after flooding has taken place. The waters below the dams will hold a pocket of water clearer than that which is found in the main river and these waters will provide some excellent fishing along the edge of the color lines which will form between the clean water of the stream and the dirty water of the river.

During the autumn, the rivers migratory fish populations of yearling shad and herring, returning down river, will move in and out of these places, giving the fish excellent forage on which to feed. This makes them one of the top spots to fish when the fall feed is taking place.

ISLANDS

There are two basic types of islands found on the river. The first is an island located on a straight stretch of river. This type of island will usually have a downstream bar located directly below the island. It's uncommon to have a deep water pocket directly below this type of island unless the waters around the island are influenced by other islands or structures.

The second type is an island located on a river bend. This type of island will still have a downstream bar but in most cases a deep water pocket is usually found directly below the island. The reason for this is the way the water swirls around the

Island with bar on a straight stretch of river.

island, gouging out a hole instead of creating a bar. Both types of islands will be productive, but water levels will have different effects on each of them. Productivity of any individual island can vary with the amount and type of secondary structures that are found around the island.

Islands Located on a Straight Stretch of Water The bar that is located downstream from an island found on a straight stretch of river is a typical evolving structure. During the warm water season, this bar will have some excellent surface fishing close to it. The fish will move further away from the bar into deeper water or into rapids as the sun gets on the water. You will then have to go with spinnerbaits, swimming plugs and crankbaits and eventually to jig combinations to dig the fish out from the deeper water or rapids.

Another key to fishing islands is to fish any secondary structures found on the shaded side of the island. These structures tend to hold fish later in the morning because of the shaded waters the island provides. In the afternoon, switch to the side of the island the shade moves onto first as the sun begins to set; this is where the fish will begin feeding first.

Islands Located On A River Bend Bars that are found below islands

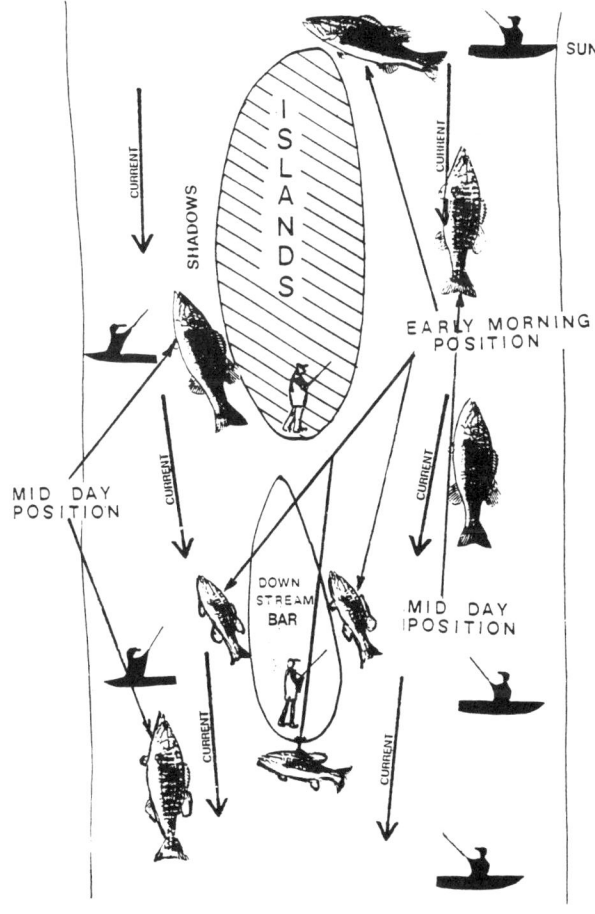

41

which are located on river bends have similar action during the warm water season, however, the deep water pocket located below the island will give the angler better results during the cold water season. It's during this time that fish will move into these deep water pockets and stay there throughout the cold water season. Jig/live bait and Lindy rig/live bait combinations and deep running crankbaits will be the tools you need to fish this situation.

Island located on a river bend. Note upstream bar and downstream pocket.

One thing that both types of islands have in common is that they will have a shallow water flat located on their upstream side. This flat is a prime target of the surface fisherman during the early mornings of the summer. Bass and other fish move onto these flats, feeding during the early morning and late afternoon, and some spectacular action can be had on buzzbaits and surface plugs. The fly fisherman can find excellent action here on deer hair bugs and poppers. During the early fall, these flats are prime places to liveline minnows and hellgrammites. Baitfish and other forage are pushed by the rivers main current onto these flats and this is the reason the fish frequent them.

The flats found around islands serve as spawning places for most river fish as well as most of the baitfish

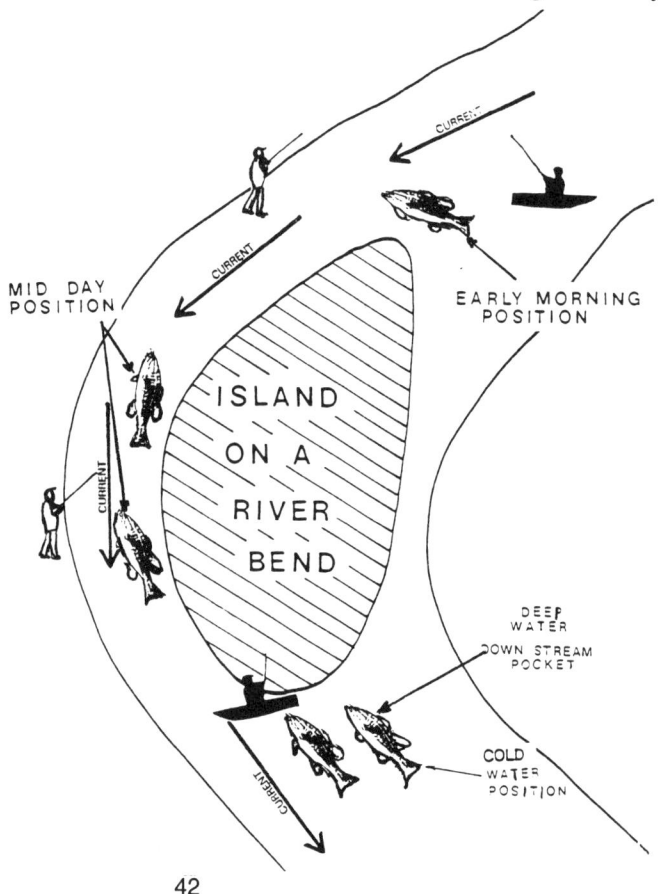

populations in the spring. As a result, the fry of these fish are found in good numbers around islands, and this is another reason the fishing is so good here.

WARM WATER DISCHARGES

More so than any other structure, a warm water discharge is a seasonal one. During the cold water season starting in late fall, throughout the winter and into early spring, warm water discharges can be a real bonanza. During the summer months, warm water discharges tend to be void of fish because of their warm water temperatures.

Warm water discharges are good spots during the cold water season but are poor choices during the summer.

Until the last twenty years, power generating stations routinely used the river's water to cool their generating units and pumped this water back into the river. In recent years, however, most of these plants have built cooling towers which recycle the water back into the plant, and what water is discharged is kept to a minimum. In order for a warm water discharge to be productive, the discharge must take place on a consistent basis.

Just about every species of fish finds their way into the warm water discharges during the cold water season. These fish will often hit when the rest of the river is

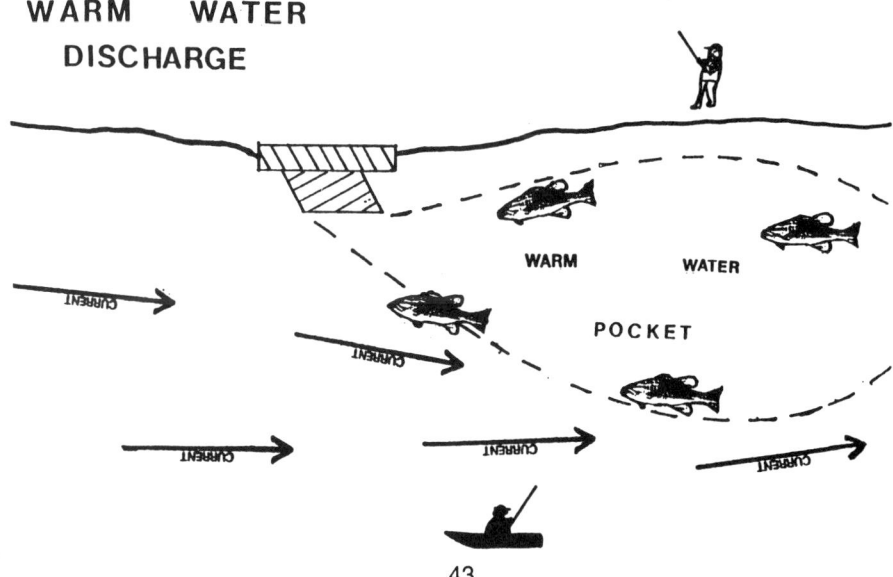

WARM WATER DISCHARGE

WARM WATER POCKET

silent; Lindy rigs dressed with live bait, deep running crankbaits and jig combinations will be a good bet.

The best way to fish a warm water discharge is to position yourself along side of the warm water stream and cast your baits into the eddies that will form downstream from where the warm water collides with the currents of the river. Fish will hold here, feeding along the current lines. It must be remembered that warm water rises, and the farther away you get from the source, the cooler the bottom water will be. The current lines and warm water pocket will remain more stable, traveling the same path unless the water levels rise. In that case they will be pushed closer to shore, and the higher the water gets the more the warm water will be dispersed.

Besides power plant discharges, there are other sources of artificial warm water discharges. By law, industrial discharges are regulated and monitored to keep them within the standards of the Clean Water Act. These discharges are not as large, nor do they have as much influence on the river. They do produce fish on a smaller scale than their larger counter parts.

Water treatment facilities are another source of a warm water discharge. Here, again, they are not as potent as power plant discharges, however, even a five degree change in temperature can spell the difference between catching fish and not doing so when the water is cold. Since discharges from industrial plants and water treatment plants are much smaller, the areas you will have to fish will be greatly reduced. As a result, the angler has to be more precise in his presentation, refining his speed and depth control in order to keep his baits in the smaller strike zone.

OVER HANGING TREES

Not considered a major fishing structure by most fishermen, they are worth mentioning because they can produce some real good catches of smallies and panfish when the conditions are right. Some sections of the Delaware have tree lined shorelines that are covered with fallen and over hanging trees.

During the month of June when the inch worms fall from these trees in good numbers, bass that are not spawning and even those that are will feed heavily on them. This is the time when the prudent angler can score heavily on inch worm imitations, jig combinations and surface lures. The fly fisherman can do a number on these fish with his fly rod, popping bugs and some wet flies.

TIDAL RIVER STRUCTURES
Tidal Coves

The tide water Delaware contains numerous tidal coves, the majority of which were once used for shipping. Over the years, many coves have been abandoned and allowed to deteriorate, creating some excellent structures for bass, crappie and other fish. Old bulkheads, dock pilings, sunken barges and wrecks litter these coves. Most have excellent drop-offs with depths ranging from five to thirty feet. Secondary structures that lie off these drop-offs are excellent fish producing structures.

Some coves have shallow areas which flood with the incoming tide and are often filled with vegetation during the summer. These shallow areas provide good early season fishing because they warm up faster than deeper parts of the cove. The

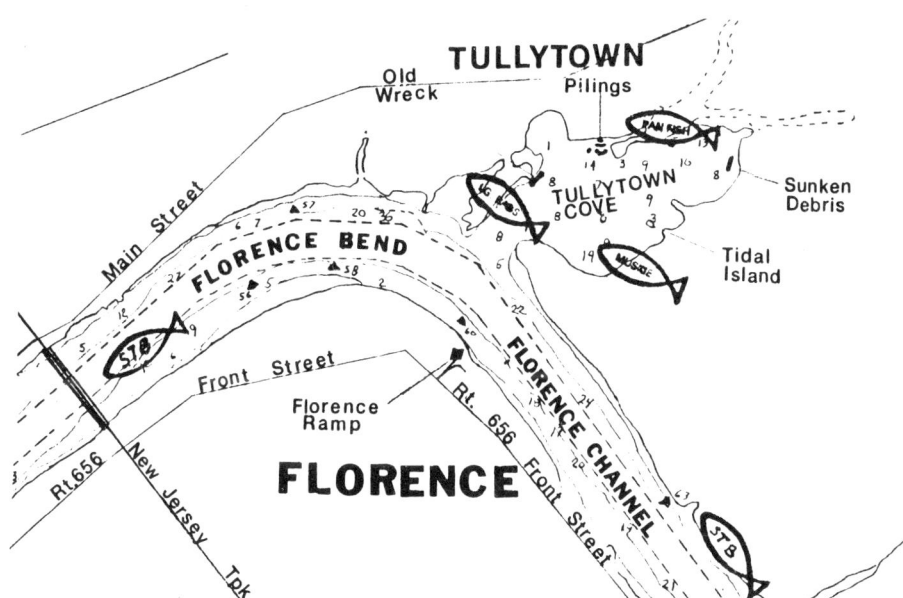

areas of vegetation also produce during the warm water season for bass and other fish that feed there, giving anglers some good surface fishing during the evening hours.

Coves serve as wintering over places for crappie, bass and other fish, thus making them productive during the cold water season; numerous species of fish also use the coves as spawning grounds. As you can see, coves are productive for most of the year for a variety of fish.

Tidal Tributary Streams

Numerous smaller rivers, streams and creeks flow into the tidal Delaware, and their back water areas and marshes offer excellent fishing. The larger streams such as the Rancocas, Neshaminy, Cooper and Schuylkill contribute significant amounts of water to the tidal river and serve as spawning grounds for herring, stripers and other fish. Many of them are also navigable for some distance and numerous marinas are found on their waters.

Most largemouth, crappie and panfish found in these tributary streams are resident fish. Some fish such as muskies and northern pike have also been stocked in an effort to get these fish established in both the tributary streams and the river. Herring spawn in these streams and shad have also been detected spawning here in recent years.

As with any structure found in the tidal river, the best fishing is on the moving tides. One word of caution- many sections of these streams are only navigable at high tide, which limits the time you can fish in these areas.

Besides the fishing that is found in the back water areas, they also make an excellent place to trap baitfish. Killies are the primary baitfish found in these areas the year round, and a good supply can be had by placing a funnel trap in the deeper holes on these streams. Baitfish move in and out of these streams with the tides and hold over in these deeper holes when the tide is out, working their way into the trap.

Tidal Points of Land

Most points of land found in the tidal river are located at the mouths of coves and tributary streams. Fish will move onto them with the incoming tide and back off them with the outgoing tide. Stumps, logs, rocks and other rip rap located along the points are the keys to fishing them. Your best bet is to locate these objects at low water and then fish them on the incoming tide. Bass, crappie and other fish use these objects as stopping points on their migration route into the shallow waters of these structures. Some points of land have vegetation in their shallow water areas during the summer and it will serve as scattering points for the fish that move up on them.

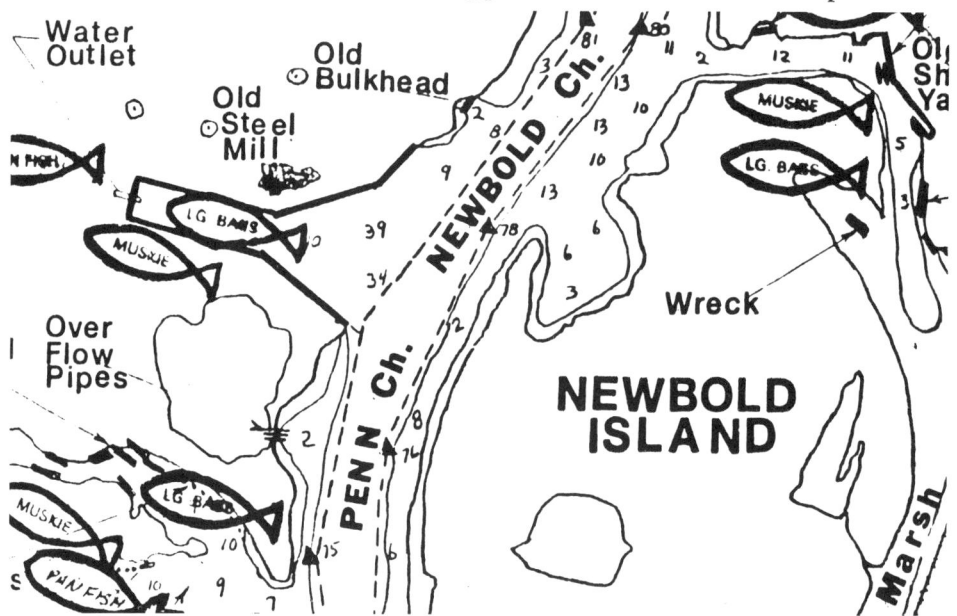

Points of land found at the mouth of a small stream will frequently be accompanied by an eddy which changes with the tides. This eddy is a prime spot and the key to fishing it is to fish the downstream side with the outgoing tide and the upstream side with the incoming tide. Points of land also serve as spawning areas for herring and, as a result, stripers will feed on them, making them excellent places for the striper fisherman to fish.

Flats

Flats are some of the most productive structures found on the tidal river, especially for stripers, perch and channel catfish. They serve as spawning grounds for these fish in the spring and the same fish will migrate from deeper water onto the flats to feed during the warm water season.

There are two prime times to fish the flats. The first is when the incoming tide turns and starts filling the water around the steepest drop-off on the flat. The fish will gather here as they begin to move with the tides, and crankbaits and jig/rubberbait combinations will give the best results.

The next part of the incoming tide that will be productive is when the tide starts flooding some of the objects along the flat or when it starts flooding into any

Tidal flat at Trenton.

vegetation that may be found on the flat. In both cases the fish moving into these places will be chasing the baitfish that also move onto these flats to feed.

Stripers are the primary predators that feed on these flats. One of the keys to fishing these flats is to find flats with good amounts of herring on them. Herring are the prime forage for the stripers and if you find the herring it's a good bet the stripers will be there also.

Some of the larger flats such as the National Park flats, Petty Island flats and Tinicum Island flats are best fished by trolling or drifting. Swimming plugs and good sized jig/twister combos are best for trolling, while bottom fishing blood worms, eels and herring will work best when drifting.

Islands

There are several islands, large and small, found on the tidal river. Most islands will have upstream and downstream flats and these are the most productive waters found around an island. The best way to fish the flats around an island is to fish the downstream flat with the incoming tide and the upstream flat with the outgoing tide. Each respective tide will push baitfish up onto the flats and this is when the fish will be the most active.

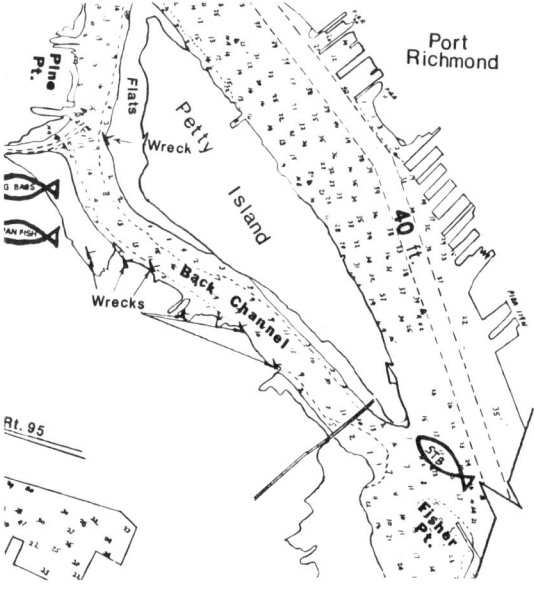

Many islands have pilings, wrecks and other objects that will hold fish, especially bass and crappie, and here again, the moving tide will give you the best results. During the warm water season both the incoming and outgoing tide will produce fish, with the incoming tide being more productive. During the cold water season the outgoing tide will be the better choice since the fish will not be feeding as often and won't travel as far for a meal; they will wait along the down side of the island for the forage to come to them.

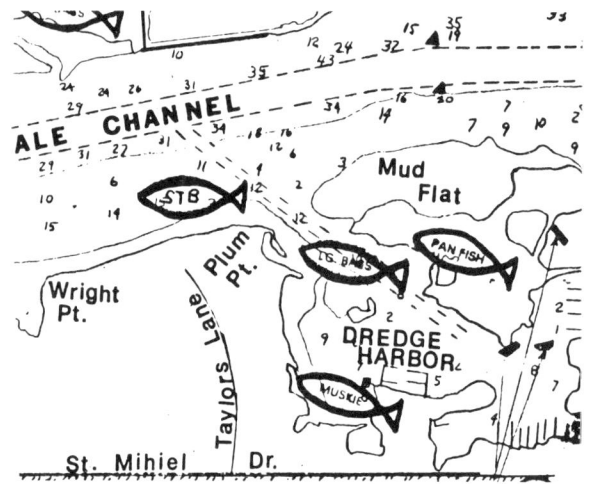

Drop-Offs & Channels

Because the river is used for shipping, drop-offs are a part of the main river, coves and in backwater areas. Like other river structures they are governed by tidal movements.

The main river channel is the deep water sanctuary for catfish, perch and stripers. These fish school along the channel at low tide and then move into shallow areas to feed with the incoming tide. Heavy boat traffic during the warm water season makes fishing the main channel very difficult. Drifting and deep water trolling is the only way to fish the channel when possible.

Drop-offs located in tidal coves are a different matter. These drop-offs will be most productive when they have some type of object laying along them. During the warm water season, fish such as bass and crappie use these objects as stopping points

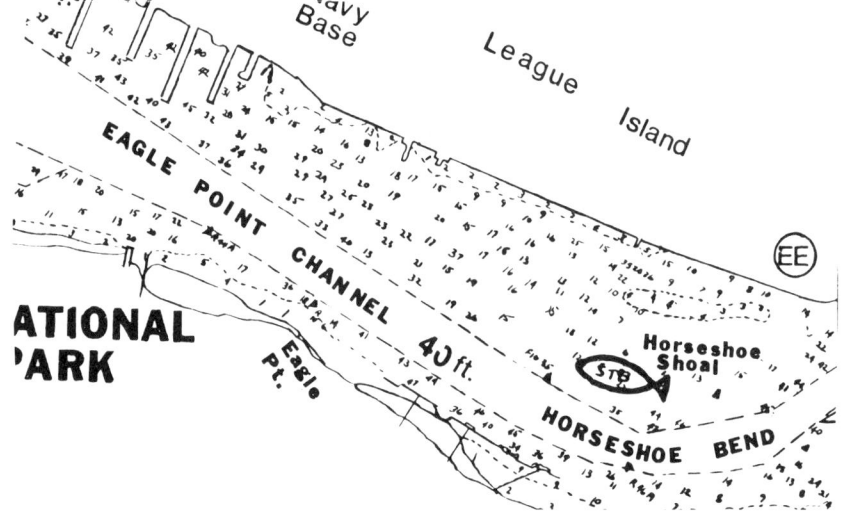

as they travel to and from shallow water to feed. Both the incoming and outgoing tide will be productive during the warm water season. During the cold water season, schools of fish will be found here wintering over and when the water temperature dips below 50 degrees, the better fishing is on live bait with the outgoing tide.

One condition that gives you and edge when fishing drop-offs is when the wind is blowing up against them. Spring and fall fishing benefits most when warm weather occurs to warm up the water along the drop-off. Anchoring upwind and allowing the wind to blow your boat over the drop-off is a prime way of fishing during this time. Once your boat is in the right position you can vertical fish, dead stick or combine vertical fishing with dead sticking to take the fish that are suspended along the drop-off.

Bridge Pilings

The major difference between bridge pilings found in the non-tidal river and the tidal river is that the eddies around the bridge pilings in the tidal river will change with the tide and the eddies below bridge piling on the non-tidal river will not. Stripers, catfish and perch are commonly found below bridge pilings in the tide water river. Most pilings are located in deep water, making them hard to fish. Since anchoring is a problem in these areas, many anglers will tie off to the piling itself in order to fish them.

The key to fishing these pilings is to fish on the downstream side with the outgoing tide and the upstream side with the incoming tide. This is because the location of the eddy that is found around the pilings will change with the tides. Bottom fishing with baits and jigging with heavy jig/rubberbait combinations will give you the best results because these methods allow you to control your baits best.

Wrecks

Numerous barges and other smaller vessels have grounded out or sunk in the Delaware over the years, and unless they impair navigation they have been allowed to remain where they sank. Most of them are located off the main river and are great structures for bass, crappie and panfish. Many are visible during low water periods and are completely covered during high tide.

Countless old wrecks are found on the tidal river. They are hot spots for bass and crappie the year round.

These wrecks hold bass, crappie and panfish the year round and like other structures found in tide water, they are best fished on the moving tide. Some of the better producing wrecks are found along drop-offs and places where they come close to the channel.

Flippin' jigs, rubberbaits, plastic worms and sinking plugs are prime tools for taking the bass that inhabit wrecks during the warm water season. When the water is on the cold side, jig/minnow combinations jigged right in and along the wrecks is your best method.

Old Pilings & Docks

Countless old pilings are found in the tidal river. Most are found in the same places as wrecks, and the one major difference is that some of them are still in use.

Just as with wrecks, the more productive pilings are the ones found along drop-offs and are best fished with the moving tides. They are a favorite of crappie, bass and panfish fishermen.

Pilings found along the main river will often harbor stripers, perch, catfish and, in some cases, crappie. Because of the stronger tides along these pilings, the fishing will not last as long as it will around pilings found in back water areas and coves

Old pilings are favorite spots of crappie and bass anglers.

which take longer to flood. The changes in water depths are also not as prominent, since most of the pilings that are found along the main river are found in deeper water.

Pilings are a top spot for bass and crappie fishermen on the tidal river.

Power Plants & other Warm Water Discharges

There are only a few warm water discharges found in the tidal river and they provide some good early and late season action. In addition to water which is discharged from power plants, warm water discharges can result from factories and water treatment plants. They make excellent choices to fish during the cold water season but are of no use once the water warms up.

These power plant discharges provide anglers with the first shot at the stripers, herring and shad as they move up river in the spring. Bass, crappie, catfish, panfish, etc. also gather in these discharges and can be taken through the winter months on live bait. This is also the first place that bass and other game fish will hit artificials in the spring.

Warm water discharges found in the tidal river will be greatly influenced by the tides. In most cases, the best tide to fish will be the incoming tide since it will back up the warm water that is coming from the discharge, resulting in the warmest water temperatures. It must be remembered that warm water rises, and the farther you get

from the source, the more it will rise to the surface and dissipate. When a warm water discharge is released into a cove such as it is at Trenton's Duck Island power plant, the effects of the warmer water will be more pronounced. When the warmer water is released directly into the river it will disperse much more quickly.

Power plant discharge at Trenton on the tidal river.

Current lines and eddies of the warm water discharge will be the most productive areas. These current lines and eddies will change with the tides. On the outgoing tide, the current lines will be longer and the eddies smaller. The reverse will be true on the incoming tide.

Good-sized crappie taken from piling in the late season.

Angler launching a boat on a tidal river ramp.

CHAPTER 4: LAUNCH RAMPS AND ACCESS

THE TIDE WATER RIVER

With the ever increasing striper population in the Delaware and the attention this fishery gets from fishermen, the CHESTER launch ramp, which is located off Flower Street in Chester, PA at the foot of the Commodore Barry Bridge, has become one of the most heavily used ramps on the lower river. It is operated by the Pennsylvania Fish Commission. One word of caution- because of it's location it has been the site of numerous car break-ins, so exercise caution when leaving your vehicle at this ramp.

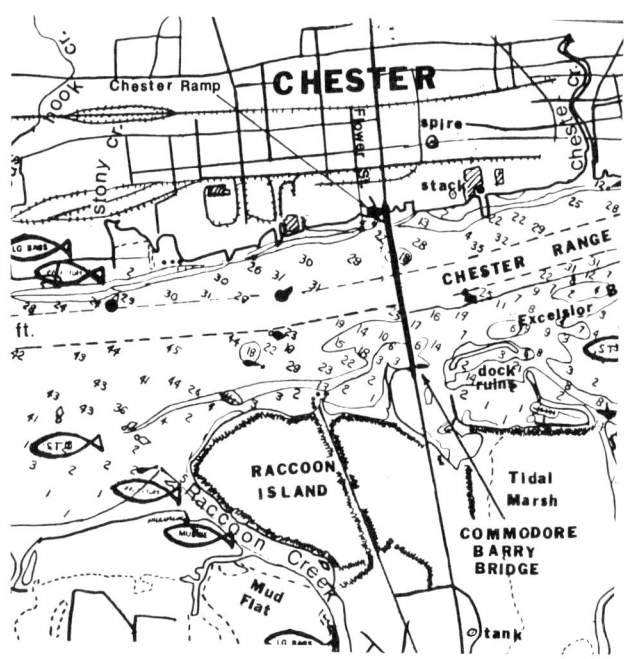

The FRANKFORT ARSENAL ramp, which is located on the site of the old arsenal, is one of the best ramps on the river. It offers three ramps from which to launch and plenty of parking. It can be accessed from Route 95, and is maintained by the Pennsylvania Fish Commission.

The LINDEN AVENUE ramp is another excellent ramp which is located off the street whose name it bears. A paved ramp is complimented by ample parking. The ramp and it's surroundings are well kept and the access puts you in touch with some of the best bass, crappie and striper fishing found in the upper tidal sections of the river.

Access to the NESHAMINY STATE PARK ramp can be had from 4th Street off of State Road. One word of caution: the ramp is located on State Park property and the rules governing the ramp and adjacent parking area are the same as those in all Pennsylvania state parks and are strictly enforced. The ramp and it's parking facilities are ample and well maintained.

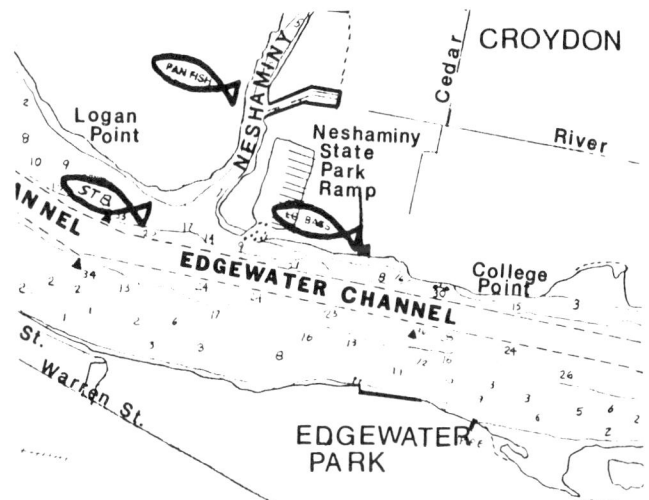

BURLINGTON MUNICIPAL ramp, located off Pearl Street in Burlington, New Jersey, is owned by the town of Burlington and is well kept with a paved ramp and ample parking. There is a fee for it's use.

Another recently renovated ramp is the FLORENCE MUNICIPAL ramp in Florence, N.J. This ramp is run by the town which charges a fee for launching from April through the month of October. It is in excellent shape and has a limited amount of parking. Much controversy has surrounded this ramp in the past year because it was built with Green Acres money and the fees charged for it's use are excessive in some cases. The town charges $25 a year for residents, $50 a year for in-state non-residents and $500 per year for non-state residents. These fees are currently in effect although several groups are trying to have them rescinded.

BORDENTOWN MUNICIPAL launch is located at the mouth of Crosswicks creek. The Route 295 bridge is currently under construction here and this can cause some problems. At present there is no paved ramp here but one is scheduled for construction as soon as the bridge and road over the mouth of the creek is completed. At the present time this access will give you problems at low water, and care should be exercised when launching under these conditions.

This past year, the CITY OF TRENTON access became a joint venture between the city of Trenton and the county of Mercer. This joint ownership has proven to be of great benefit to the sportsmen as the ramp has under gone extensive repairs. The parking lot has been paved, the drop at the bottom of the ramp has been filled in, picnic benches have been added and the ramp is patrolled by the city police. It is in the best shape it has ever been in and should serve as a model for other launch ramps along the river. It has no launch fee, ample parking and is heavily used.

THE NON TIDAL RIVER

TRENTON to LAMBERTVILLE

Numerous species of fish abound in this section of the river. The most prevalent are smallmouth, largemouth, walleyes, muskies, and a variety of panfish. During spring months of May and June, the river holds very good amounts of stripers which provide anglers with some superb surface action for these fish when

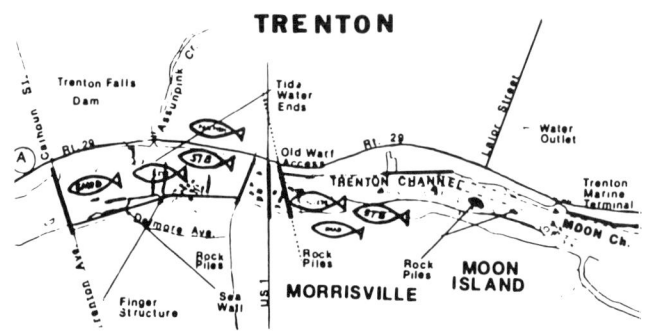

conditions are favorable. Another important factor about this section of the river is that it gives anglers their first significant amounts of shad and herring as these fish make their way upstream to their spawning grounds. Bottom fishermen will find this section well stocked with good sized carp and channel cats for their angling pleasures.

When it comes to good fishing structures this area holds a good selection for the angler to fish. The eddies and flats around Rotary Island are a favorite of smallmouth, striper and walleye fishermen. To the north of Rotary Island there are several deep holes located close to the West Trenton railroad bridge. A little further upstream there are several holes located at the site of the former Yardley/West Trenton bridge which was washed out in the '55 flood. One of the top favorites of the early season shad fishermen is the Scudders Falls wing dam and the deep holes located below the dam and near the Route 95 bridge. These are also a good bet for bass and walleye and some occasional musky, as well as a variety of panfish.

The next productive area in this section is the Washington Crossing/Titusville area. It offers anglers some excellent surface fishing for smallmouth and striped bass in the area of the Washington Crossing State Park and the waters upstream from it. Two productive points of land jut out into the river, one on each side of the river. The Titusville rocks and the Fife & Drum rocks both give fishermen access to the deep water pool that is located in the Titusville area. Perennial production of walleye and musky in this area is excellent and several New Jersey state record muskie have come from this region.

The next section which lies between Titusville and the Lambertville wing dam holds several structures of interest to the fisherman. Several excellent flats are located in the area of Fiddlers Creek that produce some good smallmouth and striper fishing. The deeper water located just off these flats holds some good walleye and channel cat action, and a few good sized muskies are taken here each year. One of the better known fishing spots in this area is Fireman's Eddy. Here the main fisheries are smallies, walleyes, stripers, shad and herring. North of the eddy are the turbulent waters found below the Lambertville wing dam. This is a difficult and dangerous section to fish, but excellent catches of stripers, smallmouth and walleyes are common when conditions are favorable. Typical structures that are found in this area consist of numerous small eddies, pools and ripples.

Anglers will find this section of the river very accessible with the entire shore line on the Jersey side being part of the Delaware/Raritan Canal State Park. Your main access road along the Jersey side is Route 29. WASHINGTON'S CROSSING STATE PARK bounds the river in two spots, and several places allow you access along Pennsylvania's Route 32, which runs parallel to the river from Morrisville to New Hope. Boat access in the area of Scudders Falls/Yardley is the YARDLEY access, which is operated and maintained by the Pa. Fish Commission. It is an excellent ramp, however, it will give you some problems, especially with large boats, during times of low water. There is a primitive boat access located just below the Fife & Drum rocks on the Pennsylvania side a short distance from Washington's Crossing State Park. Another primitive access with no paved boat ramp is located at Fireman's Eddy on the Jersey Side. Both of the previously mentioned ramps are car top launches, however, the launching of trailered boats is possible with a four wheel drive.

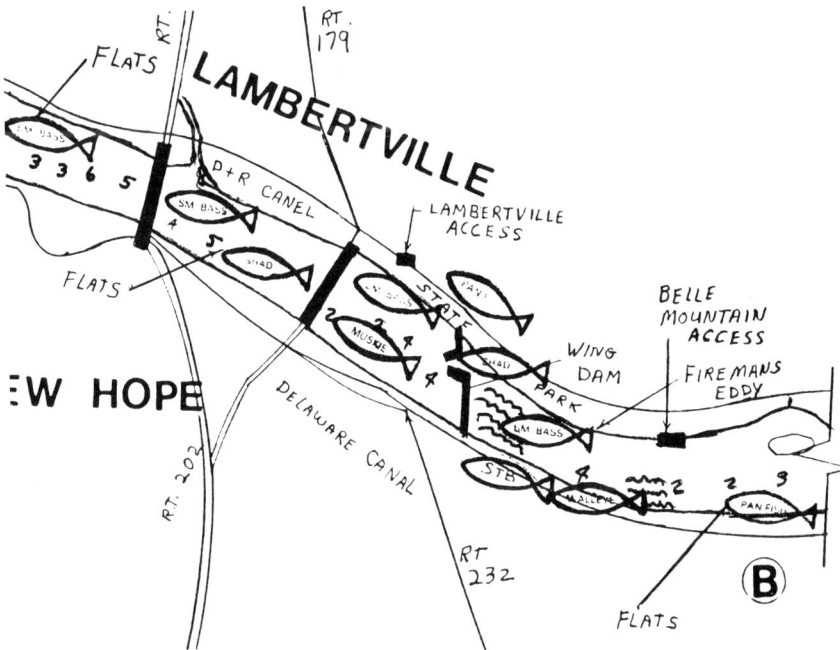

LAMBERTVILLE to FRENCHTOWN

Smallmouth fishing is the top offering for the angler in this area, with just about every type of structure found in the river available to the angler. The waters above the Lambertville wing dam are well known for their early season shad action and this area is very crowded during April and the early part of May. In the last few years, increasing numbers of stripers have been moving into this section just after the shad run winds down, and action is in prime time during the months of May and early June. The area is also well known for the excellent smallmouth, walleye and panfishing found here. Some of the top places to fish include the Route 202 bridge, along with the deep holes and shallow water flats found around it; the flats around the mouth of the Alexhauken creek; the rocky area across from the Kingston trap rock quarry; and the eddies below the Stockton bridge.

Traveling upstream we find the Bull's Island section of the river. This area is one of the more accessible areas for the angler. The recent reconstruction of the wing dam has given better access to the waters around the dam. Below the wing dam, the deep waters located around the pedestrian bridge are another good bet. Both areas produce smallmouth, walleye, stripers and panfish, along with a few musky. During the spring season these areas are a prime spot for shad and herring.

Upstream from the wing dam there are several productive areas. Walleye, smallmouth and channel catfish are available to the angler from the deeper waters of the Bryam pool. Point Pleasant Eddy, which became very controversial over the pumping station that was built in the late '80's, has always been a top spot for the shad fisherman. It is also a prime area for walleye, smallmouth and panfishing. This area has also become a prime area for the striper fisherman as well. A pair of excellent points of land, various flats and the deteriorating bridge pilings from the washed out Point Pleasant bridge are located just upstream from the eddy.

As we travel upstream, we reach the Devil's Tea Table area, which gets it's name from the cliffs and rock structures that cast their shadows on the river from the Jersey side. Some of the most notable finger structures on the river are located in this area. They make excellent structures for the angler to wade for smallmouth, panfish and stripers. Under the right conditions they make top-notch spots for spring shad fishermen. Along with the numerous finger structures found in this area, there are many small and good sized islands in this section. Adjacent to these islands, the angler will find excellent flats, eddies and deep holes that give up some good amounts of smallmouth, walleye and panfishing.

Downstream from the Frenchtown bridge, the waters are shallow in nature and are top spots for smallmouth and panfishing. This is another section that is tailor made for the wader and produces good results for the surface fisherman when conditions are suitable during the summer season.

There are five boat ramps found in this section, the first of which is the LAMBERTVILLE access. It offers anglers access to the waters above the Lambertville wing dam as far upstream as the Stockton bridge when average conditions are present. It is a well maintained access, co-operated by the D & R State park and the Lambertville Boat Club, and has no fee and ample parking. The next access is the BULLS ISLAND access, which is part of the state park of the same name. It gives fishermen access to the waters below the wing dam for about a mile. BRYAM access, which is located above the wing dam, will put you in touch with the waters from the dam to Prahis Island. Both of these ramps are top notch paved ramps with

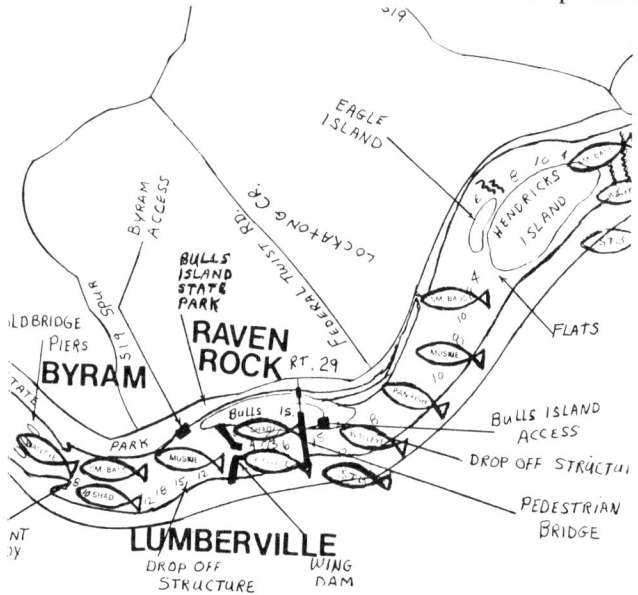

plenty of parking and are open all year. They are heavily used during the spring shad season and summer months. The twin ramps of TINICUM PARK access on the Pennsylvania side and the KINGWOOD access on the New Jersey side are both located about a mile and a half below the Frenchtown bridge. Because of the shallow water found in this area, both of these ramps only give the angler limited access. Both will also give you problems during periods of low water. Shoreline fishermen and waders will find excellent access along the Jersey side which is part of the D & R Canal State Park on the Jersey side. Your main access road along the Pennsylvania side is Route 32, which parallels the river, giving the angler only intermittent access.

FRENCHTOWN to PHILLIPSBURG

Finger structures, different sized eddies and numerous small islands highlight the structures found in this area. For the most part this section is shallow. Smallmouth and panfish are the primary fish, with stripers increasing in number each season. Upstream from the Milford/Upper Black Eddy bridge, the angler can choose from finger structures, eddies, points of land and a power plant to fish. Since the construction of cooling towers, the plant only discharges warm water on a sporadic basis. A pair of good sized pools, the first stretching from the bridge to Milford rocks and the other extending from the rocks to Lynn Island, produce smallies, walleyes, stripers, muskies and panfish, as well as shad during the spring.

Another well known area found in this section is the Reiglesville area. Known as a top shad producing spot, it annually produces some of the better sized smallies every year as well. Finger structures with good sized drops, several flats and a small stream confluence are found along the Pennsylvania side of the river below the Reiglesville bridge. Above the bridge, a sizeable deep pool with rock edges is an

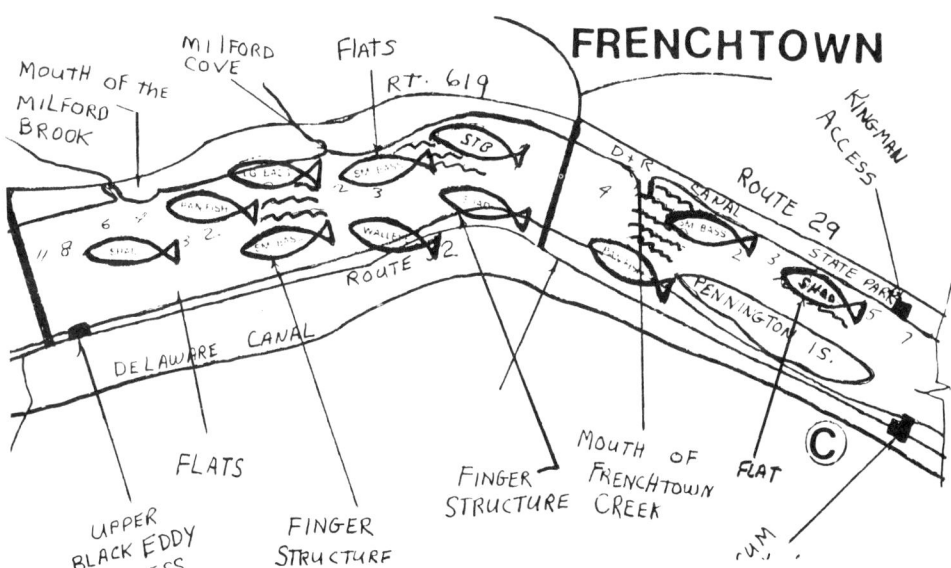

ideal structure for the smallmouth and panfish fisherman. The mouth of the Pohatcong creek and Musconetcong river enter the Delaware in this area and some nice trout are taken from their confluences with the river each year.

The 35 foot plus deep hole located below Raubs Island is the best known structure in this area. In addition to the deep hole, there are several other areas that produce some good fishing. As you come out of the deep hole the river winds it's way through a stretch that is full of huge boulders which form numerous eddies and deep holes. These structures produce smallies, walleyes, stripers and panfish on a variety of baits and lures. Although the anglers can fish this area from the shoreline, a canoe is the preferable way of chasing your quarry.

The section of river which lies downstream from the Phillipsburg/Easton area is a prime place for smallmouth, walleye, stripers, muskies and panfish. It is highlighted by good sized flats, drop offs, islands, the Route 78 bridge and several good sized deep water pools. Anglers will find that just about every lure and bait will take fish from this area when the conditions are favorable.

With the lack of a public boat ramp in the Rieglesville area, this section has become the favorite of shore line fishermen and waders. Your access road is Route 627 on the New Jersey side. This area can be fished by canoe or car top boats launched from several places along the rivers banks.

The UPPER BLACK EDDY access lies below the Milford/Upper Black Eddy bridge on the Pennsy side. This ramp is maintained and operated by the Pennsylvania Fish Commission and has limited parking. This ramp can present a problem for boaters during times of low water, especially with larger boats. Approximately three miles of river are available to the angler from this ramp. Shore line access along both sides is scattered but ample and the section is excellent for wading. Route 627 parallels the river on the Jersey side and Route 611 is your access road on the Pennsylvania side.

The HOLLAND CHURCH access is a primitive car top and shore line access that is part of the Delaware River Access program of the State of New Jersey. It has very little parking, and has been largely neglected over the years. It does provide access to some good smallmouth and panfishing.

PHILLIPSBURG/EASTON TO MARTINS CREEK

This portion of the river is known as a good smallmouth and walleye producing area. It possesses a good selection of structures for the angler to fish, and boat and shore line access is very good here.

The PBurg/Easton area is one of the top spots for the shad fisherman, and

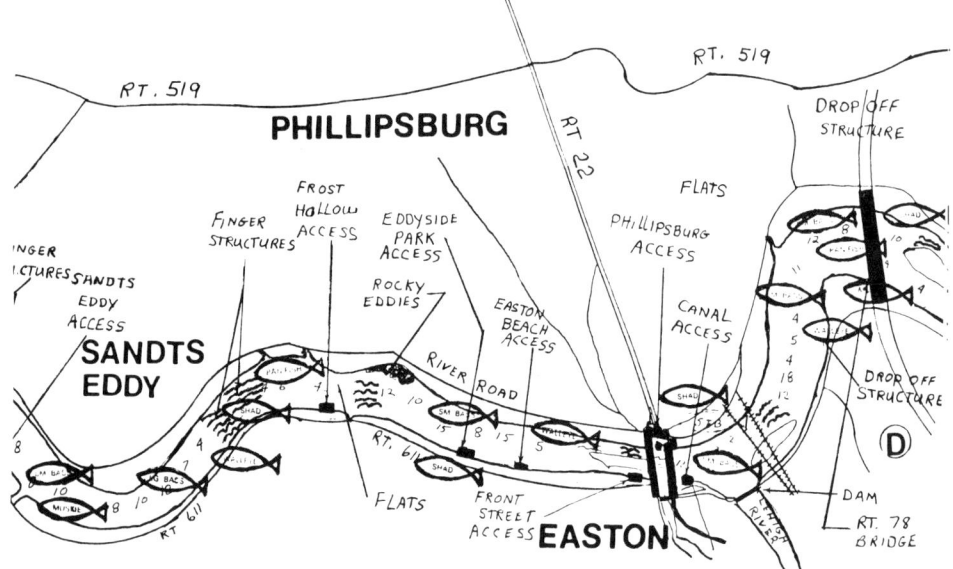

smallmouth and walleye fishing are also excellent. The confluence of the Lehigh River and the Delaware occurs between the bridges that cross the river at this point. The river here is very narrow and deep, making it ideal for shad fishing. This section of the river is host to the "Forks of the Delaware" shad fishing contest which is the largest shad contest held annually on the river. Walleye fishing is very good in the early and late season, and this is also a top spot for stripers in the late spring.

Upstream from the PBurg/Easton area, the river takes several bends, causing the rivers currents to sweep against the shore line, making them top places for the shore line shad fisherman. One of the best known spots in this area is at the base of the Route 611 overlook along the Pennsylvania side. This is a deep section preceded by some small eddies and finger structures that provide some of the best smallmouth fishing on the river along with some good walleye and panfishing.

Standt's Eddy is noted as one of the better smallmouth and shad producing areas on the river. Upstream from this point, Keifer Island and the deep waters around the old railroad trestle are top walleye spots. Plenty of small eddies, pools and finger structures can be found in this area and are excellent places to fish for smallies and panfish.

Your main access roads in this area are Route 611 on the Pennsylvania side and River road, which parallels the river on the Jersey side. Shore line fishing and wading are excellent along these roads. Of the several boat ramps located in this area, the best are the PHILLIPSBURG access on the Jersey side and the FRONT STREET access on the Easton side. Both ramps have limited parking and give you access to the waters between the bridges and downstream.

STANDT'S EDDY access is one of the better known ramps on the river and offers ample parking. It is very heavily used during the shad run and can present problems during times of low water.

MARTIN'S CREEK to THE GAP

Premium smallmouth and walleye in one of the most picturesque settings you'll find on the river and the fact that it is not easily accessible make this one of the better sections on the river for the fisherman who wants to get away from the crowds. It is ideal for a down river canoe trip and has many different structures to fish. Foul Riff is well known as one of the most dangerous sections on the river. It's fast currents and sharp rocks are known to be tough on even experienced canoeers. It is a top section for the fly fisherman during the summer months when smallies and panfish surface feed on the numerous bug hatches. The deep pool located at the base of the Riff, known as The Trench, is traditionally a top walleye producing spot. The Martin's Creek power plant and it's warm water discharge, when in operation, gives anglers some cold water fishing for a variety of fish.

Upstream from Martin's Creek the river twists and turns as it flows past Belvidere. It's in this area that the Pequest river enters the Delaware, and trout are often caught at the streams confluence with the river. The numerous flats and shallow water structures found here make it ideal for surface fishing and wading.

The Portland/Columbia section of the river is and has been one of the best known shad fishing areas and is heavily fished during the spring run. Two railroad bridges, a pedestrian bridge and a vehicle bridge span the river in this area and occasional trout are taken from the mouth of the Paulinskill, which flows into the river here. Plenty of eddies provide anglers with some good smallmouth fishing and walleyes can be taken from the deeper sections found here.

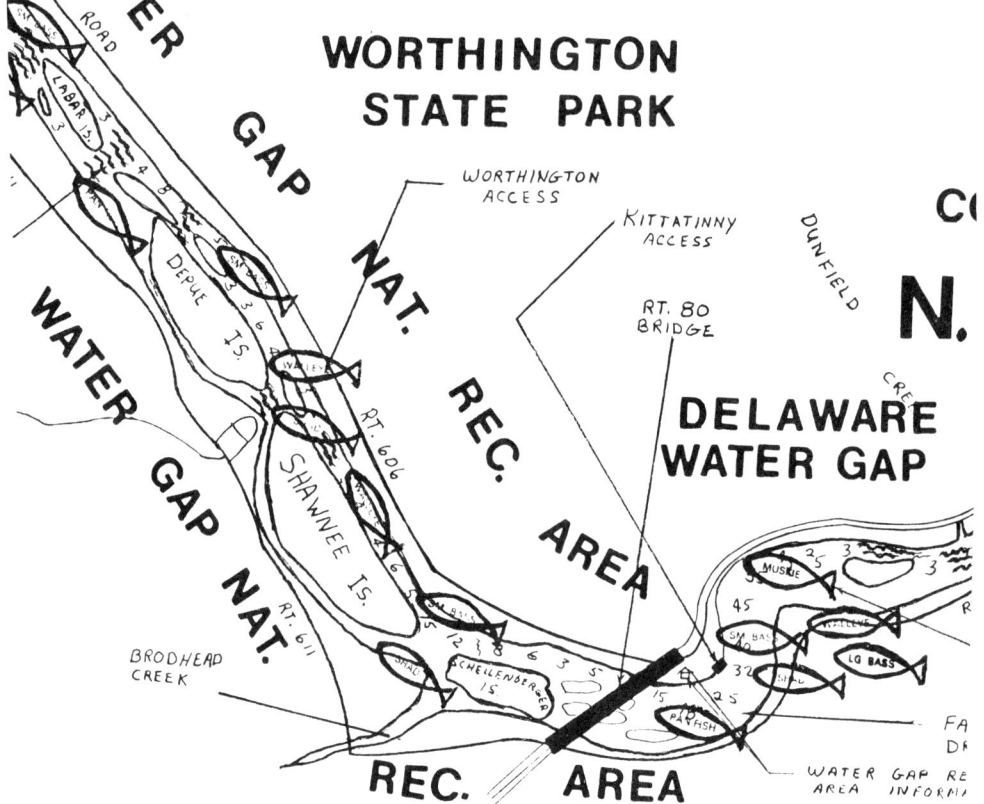

The Delaware Water Gap possesses some of the deepest water found on the river and is world renowned for its picturesque beauty. Contrary to several popular legends which put these waters at a 100 feet deep and more, the waters at the base of the Gap are only fifty feet deep. They traditionally produce some good sized walleye, smallmouth and shad. In the past several years, good sized stripers have been taken from these waters as these fish continue to make their way further and further up river each season.

Shoreline access in this area is sporadic, however, there are several boat ramps that will give access to the river's waters here. MARTIN'S CREEK access, which is operated by the power company, gives the angler limited access to the Foul Riff/ Martin's Creek area. This access in not in the best of shape and can give you problems during times of low water. The MET ED access is maintained and operated the Met Ed power plant in Portland. Because of it's location, the amount of water the angler has to fish is limited, especially during times of low water. KITTATINNY access, which is located behind the Visitor Center off Route 80, is well maintained and has plenty of parking. It gives you access to the deep water of the Gap.

Good shoreline access is available in this area with Foul Riff Road, Route 46 and Route 80 running along the river on the Jersey side close to the water, however, parking can be a problem in some areas. On the Pennsylvania side of the river, Route 611 parallels the river along it's entire length, with many side roads branching off from it where it is not close to the river.

THE DELAWARE WATER GAP NATIONAL RECREATION AREA

This portion of the river comes under the Wild and Scenic Rivers Act and is under Federal jurisdiction. The only section which is not under federal jurisdiction is Worthington State Forest which is run by the state of New Jersey. Although this area gives the angler plenty of access, much of it requires the angler to do some walking. Camping is only permitted in designated areas, however, canoeers and back packers are permitted to camp along the banks of the river. Federal regulations regarding life jackets, speed limits and alcohol consumption are in effect and enforced by federal park rangers.

The river north of the Gap has numerous good sized islands, the best known of which are Shawnee, Depue, Labar and Tocks. All are typical island structures, having good sized flats around them which make them ideal for summer surface fishing for bass and panfish. Several also have deep holes located below them which produce walleye and muskie. The islands also narrow down the water as it passes between them and the shore, making excellent places for shad fishing in the spring.

Some of the best walleye waters are located between Poxono and Depew islands, with the deep hole located below each of these islands being two of the prime spots. Plenty of flats situated around these islands provide top notch smallmouth fishing during the summer months and they are some of the best areas to fish with live bait during the fall season.

Wallpack Bend, which is the most famous bend on the river, is the next area of interest to the angler. The scenic cliffs that cast their shadows on the river as it twists it's way though this area provide the picturesque setting for some premiere smallmouth and walleye fishing. Bushkill creek flows into the river on the Pennsylvania side and the Flat Brook enters on the Jersey side. Both of these streams are stocked with trout and many of these fish work their way into the river in this area, especially during high water years. Numerous eddies, deep pools, points of land, ripples and other structures adorn this area and give the angler plenty of places to fish.

The portion of the river that flows between Wallpack Bend and Dingman's Ferry is one of the more secluded sections of the river. Access is sparse, and this area is one of the best for one and two day float trips. It offers a variety of structures from

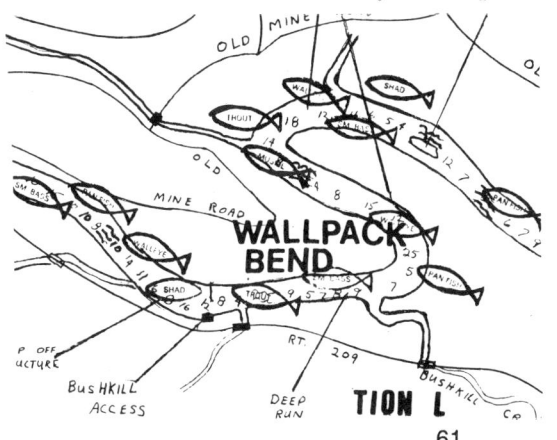

which to choose, with flats, eddies, islands, deep pools and quiet slow moving stretches providing some of the best smallmouth and panfish found on the river. Fishing surface lures, jig and spinnerbaits are your top methods during the summer months, with live-lining and jigging minnows tops during the cold water season.

The legendary reputation of Dingman's Ferry among shad fishermen has made this area one of the most heavily fished places during the spring shad run. The banner shad fishing also overshadows the smallmouth, walleye and panfish action that is present during the rest of the year. The numerous flats found in this area are typical of this portion of the river, and surface fishing during the warm water season is the top way of fishing. The deeper sections hold some quality walleye fishing.

The Milford, Pa. to Matamoras stretch of the river is another quality shad area during the spring and provides top smallie, panfish and walleye action throughout the rest of the year. Namanock, Minisink, and Mashipacong islands are the major islands found in this area. Among the other structures found here are long quiet stretches, deep pools, eddies and flats. This is another stretch of river that is excellent for canoe and down river fishing trips.

The majority of boat ramps found in this area come under the jurisdiction of the National Park Service and are well maintained. New Jersey owns and operates the WORTHINGTON STATE PARK access, which is part of Worthington State Park, which includes a campground that makes an excellent base for the angler who would like to spend a few days fishing. POXONO ISLAND access is a well maintained ramp with plenty of parking, and it gives you access to the waters near Poxono island. Both ramps give the angler a limited amount of water to fish and do have problems during periods of low water. Our next access is BUSHKILL access, which is operated and maintained by the Pa. Fish Commission, and puts anglers in touch with the waters around Wallpack Bend. SMITHFIELD BEACH access is another excellent boat access in this area. It offers ample parking and sanitary facilities, and is popular with shad fishermen in the spring. DINGMAN'S FERRY access is probably the most heavily used ramp during the spring shad season and it is in excellent shape, with plenty of parking and other amenities. The MILFORD BEACH access, which is run by the National Park Service is another excellent ramp. It gives the angler limited access to the river in the Milford, Pennsylvania area.

Shoreline access to the river along the Pennsylvania side is from Route 209 and is sporadic, as the road veers away from the river in several places. On the New Jersey side, Old Mine Road gives you access from the Gap to a few miles below Dingman's Ferry. From that point north, Route 521 parallels the river from Dingman's Ferry and Montague. On the Jersey side the roads wind away from the water. In the areas where the roads come close to the river the angler will still have to walk a considerable distance to get to the river. Using Dingman's Ferry as a starting point the angler can canoe through this section on one and two day trips, and there are several outfitters located in the area that can be of help on such an adventure.

PORT JERVIS to BARRYVILLE

Smallmouth, walleye, panfish and shad are the main fisheries found in this portion of the river. The twisting and turning nature of the river in this area produces some excellent shoreline fishing and wading. There are no large sized islands located in this stretch but there are several smaller ones. The principle streams that enter the river in this area are the Mongaup and Neversink, along with the Shohola creek. The confluences of each are good early and late season fishing spots. Besides the stream confluences and small islands, slow moving stretches, deep holes as deep as 40 feet, ripples, rapids and flats round out the structures found in this area. The deepest water in this area is Pond Eddy, who's waters are forty plus feet deep and

62

produce some good walleye fishing each year.

The only boat access located in this area is the MATAMORAS access, which is operated and maintained by the Pennsylvania Fish Commission. This ramp offers the angler only limited access because of the rapids that are located above and below it. Sporadic shoreline fishing and wading is available to the angler who is willing to do a little walking. The lone access road into this area is Route 97, which parallels the river along the New York side.

BARRYVILLE to NARROWSBURG

Smallmouth, panfish and walleyes supply the bulk of the action found in this section of the river. This area is a major spawning area for shad and provides fly fishermen with excellent action when conditions are right. The twisting and turning nature of the river in this area creates some excellent places for the shoreline fisherman and the wader. The major stream tributary flowing into the river here is the Lackawaxen river, which flows from Lake Wallenpaulpack and is subject to periodic water releases during low water periods. There are also several smaller streams that flow into the river in this section. The deepest water on the non-tidal river is the Narrowsburg eddy which has water between eighty-five and one hundred feet deep. This, however, is the exception to the rule. The rest of the river in this area

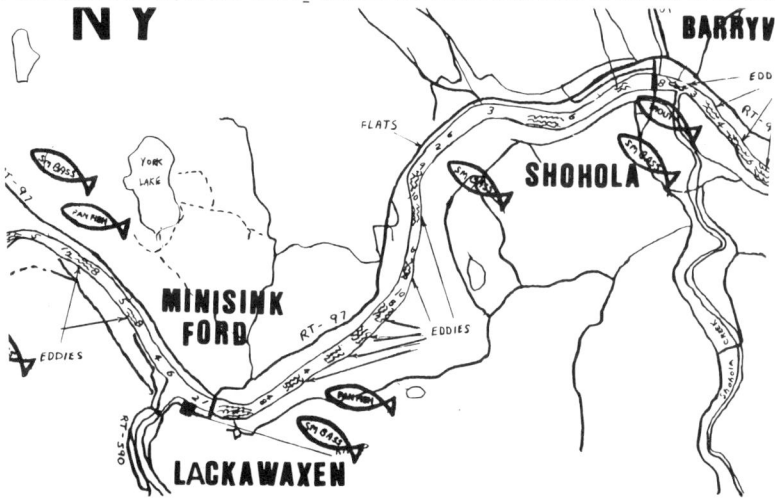

is fairly shallow. As a result of the shallow nature of the river here, rapids, ripples, flats and points of land are the prominent structures.

Three major ramps offer the boater access to the river in this section. The LACKAWAXEN access (Zane Gray Inn Access) is a Pennsylvania Fish Commission access and is in excellent shape. Located below the mouth of the Lackawaxen river, it puts the angler in quick touch with some good fishing. The water you can fish is limited because of the rapids above and below the access. This is especially true during periods of low water.

A pair of accesses are located at the Narrowsburg eddy, one on the PA side of the river (NARROWSBURG access PA) and the other on the New York side (NARROWSBURG access NY). Both are excellent accesses and are located only a short distance from the deep water of the eddy. Ample shore line fishing is available to the angler not only at the eddy but also above and below it. The main access road into this area is Route 97 along the New York side. The Narrowsburg/Damascus Road runs along the river between Narrowsburg and Damascus on the Pennsylvania side of the river.

NARROWSBURG to LONG EDDY

With the closeness of Route 97 to the river along the New York side of the river in this section, stop and go fishing allows the angler to cover plenty of water in a short time. Both shoreline fishing and wading will allow the wader to sample the numerous eddies, flats, ripples and abundant river bends that make up the principle structures found here. Some sections of the river border private property and it's best to make sure it's all right before crossing posted land.

Superb smallmouth fishing is found in this section, and along with better than average trout fishing, panfish and shad make this area an excellent section to fish. The numerous shallows, flats and several small islands make this area ripe for the surface fisherman and it is a favorite area for fly fishing buffs. The ripples and plentiful small eddies make this an ideal area to fish during the mid day hours.

Skinners Falls, which is one of the most dangerous sets of rapids, is located just south of the town of Cochecton. A private campground located up from the Skinners Falls bridge can be used as a base for anglers wishing to spend a few days fishing

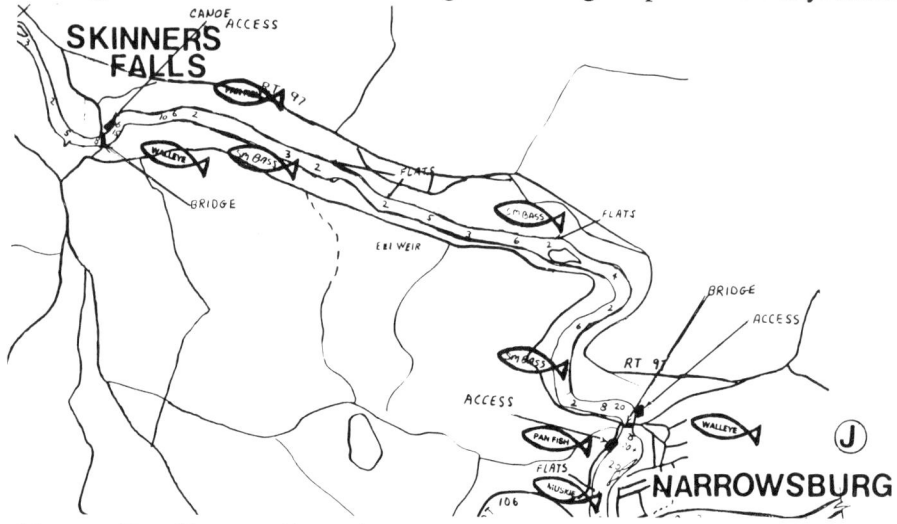

in this area. Excellent smallmouth and sporadic walleye fishing can be found just downstream from the falls. Canoes and car toppers can be launched from a small shoreline access located below the bridge, but canoeers and boaters will have to transgress the falls to get into the more productive portion of the river.

Limited boat access is available at both Damascus and Callicoon. The DAMASCUS access is a Pennsylvania Fish Commission ramp and offers the angler a paved ramp, parking and other facilities. Rapids located above and below it limit the water you have to fish during low water periods. Upstream from the Damascus bridge is the COCHECTON access, which is maintained by the New York Department of Environmental Conservation. It is a car top access and is ideal for starting canoe or raft fishing trips. The shore line fisherman will find some good access both upstream and downstream from both of the aforementioned ramps.

Traveling upstream we find the CALLICOON access, which is operated by the Pennsylvania Fish Commission. It is located a short distance downstream from the Callicoon bridge and here, too, the ramp only offers limited access during summer months because of the rapids that are found upstream and downstream from the ramp. Shoreline fishing and wading is excellent both up and downstream from the access.

LONG EDDY TO HANCOCK

This last section of the river we will cover provides anglers with some good smallmouth, trout, panfish and shad fishing. The river in this area narrows down considerably and is shallow in nature. The deepest water is found near Lordville, and the river is full of small eddies, rapids, ripples, several small islands, flats and many twist and turns. Route 97 parallels the river as far north as Long Eddy and then spins away from the river until it nears the river again downstream from Hancock. Route 191 runs along the river from Equinunk to Balls Eddy on the Pennsylvania side.

There are four boat accesses located in this section. Because of the numerous rapids and the shallow water found in these upper sections of river, most of the ramps are used by canoeers and car toppers to start float trips. The first is LONG EDDY access, which is located off Route 97 at Long Eddy, New York. There is no launch fee for use of this ramp. The next ramp is BUCKINGHAM access, which is on the Pennsylvania side, Route 191, and is operated by the Pennsylvania Fish Commission. It is a poor ramp during the summer months when the water is low. It is mostly used by fishermen during the spring for shad.

The HANCOCK access is a public access located at the south end of the town of Hancock. Here, again, it is most often used during the spring by shad fishermen, and boaters will have problems launching during the summer months.

Our last ramp and the one located the furthermost upstream is the BALLS EDDY ACCESS, which is the only ramp located on the west branch of the Delaware. It is operated by the Pennsylvania Fish Commission and is located off Route 191.

In many cases the shoreline fishing is better than the boat fishing, especially during the summer, around the ramps we have just discussed. There are also many back roads that will put you on the river along both sides in this area. Much of the land, especially on the west branch, is in private hand and in some cases is posted.

FOOT NOTES

Launch ramps owned and operated by the Pennsylvania Fish Commission require your boat be registered if you are a Pennsylvania resident, no matter how small or large, or what type of propulsion is used. If your boat is not registered or you are an out-of-state resident, you need user stickers, for which there is a $5 annual fee. All trash must be taken away by the boater since under the current law, enacted in 1991, no trash receptacles are provided on Fish Commission lands and state parks. Only properly registered and equipped vessels may be launched from Fish Commission ramps. This excludes tubes and other items not considered as vessels.

Boat registrations are reciprocal in the Delaware river and no operators license is required of non-New Jersey residents to operate a boat in the river. Fishing regulations while fishing from a boat are dictated by the side of the river from which you launch and pick up your boat.

Blue Cat taken from the tidal river.

CHAPTER 5: CATFISH

THE FISH: (ICTALURUS)

The Delaware river has excellent populations of several different types of catfish. Besides the major populations of channel catfish, bull heads and white catfish, there are also several sub species that abound in the river.

The top catfish among sportsmen is the channel catfish and it's for good reason that he's number one. Simply put, he more often than not forgets he's a catfish and will readily attack all different types of lures, including surface baits. This results in numbers of these feisty fish being taken by anglers while fishing for other types of fish, especially when fishing after dark. They are also school fish, gathering in good numbers during certain times of the year, creating some fast action from time to time. Some of the best fishing for them is in the early morning just before and after dawn, and the early evening just before and after sunset. This is when they will be most active and moving into shallow water to feed the same as most gamefish.

The Spring & Spawning Season   During the spring, good numbers of cats are found in the deeper coves off the main river, along drop-offs, channel edges and any warn water discharges. They move there during the cold water season for two reasons. First, baitfish move into such places at this time. Second, the catfish will not have to expend as much energy to stay in these areas, as opposed to being in the main river, during the cold water season when they are not as active.

As the water temperature starts to climb in the spring, they move into and around the feeder streams which flow into the river. The deltas and bars found at the confluences of these feeder streams are some of the top spots to look for good sized cats, since old Whiskers will move into these areas prior to and during spawning time. As water temperatures near the 70 degree mark, the mature catfish will start their annual spawning ritual; the greater part of the spawning taking place when water temps are between 71 and 85 degrees. Channel cats are very prolific, producing plenty of offspring when conditions are favorable. The eggs and young are very resilient and are not as affected by changes in water conditions as are other river fish.

Summer Patterns   Once spawning is over, the majority of the catfish move back into the main river and take up residence in deeper waters. Besides the main channel, channel cats haunt such areas as slack water pockets behind bridge pilings, mouths of coves, back water streams and channels, and river bends in the tidal river. In the non-tidal river, cats move into deeper water if it is present, as well as eddies, ripples and other high oxygen areas.

This catfish hit a jig/twister combination.

Throughout the warm water season they follow many of the same patterns as most game fish, moving from deep water haunts into shallow areas to feed. They spend a good part of their time in these areas because they provide cooler water, higher oxygen levels and a haven from the sun. The river's currents will trap forage, such as dead shad, in these areas, giving them a good food supply.

Nocturnal Habits   In the summer months, catfish become very nocturnal, dining by the light of the moon. This makes the phases of the moon very important when fishing for catfish during the summer. Just as with several other species of fish that live in the Delaware, prime fishing will occur a few days after the full moon and the new moon. The full moon is your number one choice and the new moon is your second. This is when the influence of the moon's gravitational pull on the river is at it's peak. It is more prominent in the tide water river where it will cause the tides to run faster, higher and lower than during any other part of the month. Other factors such as wind direction and water levels can come into play as well.

Tides   The moving tide will give you the best action, however, once the cats have moved into a shallow water structure, unlike most game fish, they will feed during the slack period. The last two hours of the incoming tide, through the slack tide and into the first hour or two of the outgoing tide will give you the most action in the shallow water feeding areas.

Good catches can also be had on the low tide by fishing the channel edges and deep water. The fishing will peak during the last two hours of the outgoing tide, slow up during the slack tide and them pick up during the first two hours of the incoming tide. Catfish are known to continuously feed during the warm water season. Water temperatures in the Delaware can reach into the mid 80's, and this is the reason they feed so constantly. The warmer the water temperatures, the better the action.

One thing that you will find true during summer is that the cats are more likely to hit artificial lures. This is especially true in the non-tidal river and many smallmouth and striper fishermen find this out each year while top water fishing, when they receive a smashing hit and a good fight, only to find out that the fish that caused their blood to stir is a good sized channel cat.

The Fall Season   During the early fall season, like most other river fish, catfish will feed on returning herring and shad offspring. Using a cast net or drop net will get you a good supply of small herring or shad. It's during this time of the year that the use of small herring or shad will give you the best results.

Once returning shad and herring are out of the river and water temps start dropping, catfish will start migrating into their cold water haunts, moving back into the coves and back water areas in the tidal river. In the non-tidal river, they migrate into the deeper quieter sections. Another place to look for them is in any warm water discharge that is active. Some warm water discharges hold fish through the winter, especially if they are located in a cove or inlet off the main river where a warm water pocket can develop.

BEST BAITS

Worms   When it comes to the best baits for catfish in the Delaware, the most often used bait is worms. Worms can be had from any bait shop or gathered from a lawn after a rain and their popularity results from availability and the fact that they are so easy to use.

Cut Baits   There is no doubt worms take their share of the cats but most veteran catfishermen will tell you that cut baits, such as shrimp, calves and chicken livers, and herring will take more cats, and bigger ones as well. Cut baits such as shad and herring are the baits of choice among many anglers. Serious catfishing addicts will stock their freezers with these baits in the spring time and use them throughout the year. Some tackle shops along the river will also stock up on them so they have a good supply through the season. When using shad for bait, most anglers will fillet the shad and then freeze it. They can then cut the shad in strips as needed. Herring, on the other hand, is usually frozen whole and then cut into chunks as needed while fishing. Both of these baits are oily and strong smelling. Since catfish use their sense of smell and feel, this makes them easy to detect by the cats.

Both calves and chicken liver are commonly used as catfish bait. Chicken livers are usually used whole, while calves liver is cut into chunks or strips. Both can be purchased in any food or meat store. Some catfish anglers allow the liver to sit out a day or so before using it so it has a very pungent odor. Once the liver is cast into the water, the odor acts as an attractant.

Shrimp have always been a top catfish bait, however, their cost has often kept their wide spread use down. Here, too, many anglers allow their shrimp to ripen (as it is commonly called) for a day or so before using them. Peeled shrimp is also considered a better bait than using it whole.

Minnows, both dead or alive, are another good bait for catfish. One thing that you will find when using minnows, which many anglers like, is that channel cats will hit them more often than other types of catfish. This is a big plus since channel cats are the most sought after catfish.

TACKLE

When it comes to tackle, just about any type of spinning or conventional outfit will be sufficient. Many anglers prefer light action spinning or conventional tackle when fishing from a boat, since you can position your boat over a productive spot and you can chase a larger fish if you hook one.

Anglers who fish for big channel cats from the shoreline will often employ 8 to 10 foot surf fishing outfits. This type of gear gives them the range they need to put their baits into the channel from good distances. It also allows them to use heavier weights to hold the bottom when the tides are moving.

In the line department there are two schools of thought. First, if you fish for fun, then light line is the way to go. In the second case, fishing for the table, heavier line will suit you better. In either case catfish are very tough fish, and even when they are gut hooked they'll survive if you cut the leader. Their strong digestive system will dissolve the hook in a few weeks.

Another factor that comes into play when choosing line is the type of tackle you intend to use. If you are fishing from a boat with light tackle, light line is more appropriate. It will enable you to use light line with less break offs. On the other hand, if you are fishing from the shoreline and are using heavier tackle, it will be too easy to snap your line while setting the hook or playing the fish. In this case heavier line will be more appropriate.

Your choice in hooks will be determined by your choice in line, tackle and baits. For the majority of baits, hooks in sizes 2 through 2/0 will fit most needs. A simple rule to follow is the heavier the tackle the heavier the hook and vice versa. Keeping all your gear in the same class will help you get the most from your equipment. Large catfish are very powerful and if the hook you choose is too light for the tackle you are using the big cats will straighten it, thus causing you to lose the fish. So keep your equipment balanced for the best results.

When it comes to the weights you use to get the bait to the fish, you have several choices depending on the conditions you are fishing. When the cats are found in shallow water, light bottom walking sinkers, egg sinkers and split shot can be used to move baits slowly across or drift them across shallow waters. The key to fishing these areas is to move or allow your baits to be moved slowly along the bottom. You'll have a better chance of getting your baits to the feeding cats by moving it, since they will also be on the move.

The use of heavier weights goes hand and hand with fishing deeper water. The three most commonly used weights are the bank sinker, bottom walking sinker and the pyramid sinker. If you wish your bait to move across the bottom with the tide or current, your best choices are the bank sinker and egg sinker. Their design allows them to roll along the bottom. If you choose to move the bait in a controlled manner, your best option will be a Lindy or bottom walking sinker. Hitting a distant channel and holding your bait there is best accomplished with a pyramid sinker.

The weight of the sinker you choose will be determined by the strength of the tides or current, the depth you are fishing and the size of the bait you are using, as well as the type of tackle with which you are fishing. Sinkers such as a pyramid will not be as effective when used from a boat and is always more effective when used from the shoreline.

TOP STRUCTURES

Many top structures that produce catfish in the Delaware are seasonal ones. By this it is meant you will find fish on them during certain times of the year. Because catfish are nomadic creatures moving around constantly in order to find food, they will naturally be found where the food sources are more plentiful. Most fishermen think of catfish as scavengers, however, they are more of an opportunistic feeder than a scavenger. Sure, if there is an easy meal to be had, they will take it, but for the most part they follow baitfish populations just like most gamefish. Since the baitfish are found in different areas during different times of the year, so too will the catfish be.

It must be remembered that water and weather conditions change the places in which you will find the catfish. As a result, there are no set rules to where you will find them, however, weather conditions, water conditions, time of year and available forage will be the keys to finding and catching old Whiskers.

Channel cat taken on the non-tidal river.

Coves   Tidal coves will be most productive during the cold water season. This is when the cats move into these areas to winter over. During the summer you will find that blue catfish and mud catfish will be more prevalent in the coves. The reason for this is that the different types of catfish like different types of water. Mud cats and blue catfish prefer slow moving water, where as channel cats have a preference for the faster currents of the main river.

Coves found on the tidal river were at one time used as shipping coves and some are still in use. As a result, they have some very sharp drop-offs. Over the years these drop-offs or channels have silted in and many have debris that has drifted in and built up along them. These are the prime spots to look for catfish. In the winter season the cats gather here because they offer shelter and forage throughout the cold water season. In the warm water season, mud cats and blue cats are found here because dead fish and other forage will get hung up in these areas as the tides move in and out of the cove.

Some coves have small streams that flow into them and these are another place to look for the catfish, especially after a good rain. Rains can create muddy water breaklines flowing into the cove, washing in worms, hellgrammites and other forage. This gives the catfish an excellent feeding opportunity and they will gather here as long as the conditions last. Anglers should never overlook these places when the conditions avail themselves.

During the spawning season, look for the catfish to be found in amongst the pilings, old docks and piers that can be found in many of these coves. Most of the coves have old decaying, sunken barges and boats in them, and these are other good places to look during the spawning time.

Bridge Pilings   The bridges crossing the Delaware are good places to look for catfish. The eddies found around bridge pilings are typical two current line eddies. There is one major difference between bridge pilings found in the tidal river and those that are found in the non-tidal river. The difference is that the eddies change with the tides in the tidal river, while they don't in the non-tidal river. On the incoming tide, the eddies will be found on the upstream side of the pilings. The reverse is true when the tide is outgoing. Thus the productivity of the pilings will change with the tides.

One problem you will face while fishing bridge pilings that lie in deeper water is boat control. Many bridge pilings located in the tidal river will be in 30 and 40 feet of water and when the tide really starts to rip, anchoring will be difficult. Add in the sometimes heavy boat traffic and things can get really sticky. Tying off to the pilings is one option, however, this may not always be possible. Your other option is to use

a trolling motor or outboard to hold your boat position. Using bait/jig combinations and bottom walking rigs is the most effective way of fishing the eddies located below the pilings. It's almost impossible to hold your bait in one place under these conditions, so controlling the movement of your baits becomes very important. The size of the eddies that form downstream and upstream from the pilings is determined by the portion of the tide you are fishing. The stronger the tide, the more defined and smaller the eddy will be. The closer the tide is to slack tide, the less defined and larger the eddy is.

When fishing bridge pilings on the non-tidal river you should fish the quiet water pockets that are located below the pilings. These eddies are best fished by anchoring your boat at the base of the piling and casting your weighted baits into these pockets. Your main concern is to keep the bait in the dead water pocket as long as you can. When high water conditions are present, fish the pilings with the most quiet water behind.

Nice stringer of cats taken from the tidal river.

Drop-offs & Channel Edges   Since deep water is the home of the catfish most of the time, the channel edges that follow the shipping channel are prime spots. Anywhere you can find some debris along the channel will be a place that will hold catfish. Your next best bet is where the river takes a bend. These areas are productive because the current sweeps up against them, pushing food into these areas. In many cases you will be able to spot the catfish on your sonar set; getting the bait down to the fish and keeping it there is the key. In most cases, bottom walking rigs will be the best way to fish these areas.

Another type of drop-off that produces are the ones found in coves off the main river. Coves still in use will have sharp drop offs while those that are no longer in use will have silted in areas or may have debris located along them. These drop-offs are easier to fish since much of the current of the tides is negated. Here, jig/bait combinations are the way to go. These drop-offs are more productive in the cold water season, as was previously mentioned.

A third type of drop-off is those found in the feeder streams. Catfish will concentrate in these areas during the warm water season, feeding on the bait populations that move in and out of them and also on the forage such as insect life, crayfish and other food that is washed in by the creek. They are some of the best catfishing on the river and since they are smaller than those in the main river, they are easier to fish. Locating a bend, debris, wreck or old piling is the key to fishing them. If the current is slow, drifting jig/bait combinations or baits weighted with egg sinkers or split shot will give you the best results. If the currents are swift then bottom walking rigs will be the way to go.

Flats and Bars   Since catfish move from deep water to shallow water to feed during the warm water season, this makes flats and bars sort of a dinner table for them. First let's take a look at bars. There are two basic types. The first is a bar that is found on the main river. These bars are humps in the river's bottom and can be made of rock or silt deposits. What separates them from a flat is their size. Flats are longer and bigger in overall size.

The second type is that which is found at the mouth of a creek or stream. This type of is made of silt washed in by the stream and is usually very shallow. One thing that both bars have in common is that they can change from year to year. Storms, swift currents and high water levels can effect them and they can shrink, grow and change size.

The best way to fish them is to drift your baits over them. How much weight you use will be determined by the depth and swiftness of the current flowing over them. If the current is slow and the water shallow, split shot will be all you need. If the current is swift and the water deep, an egg sinker will be needed to drift your bait. If the current is swift but the water is shallow, the use of an egg sinker rig is still recommended. (Some anglers will substitute the use of pencil lead or caterpillar weights as sinkers.)

Pilings & Wrecks   Most pilings found along the river are close to deep water since most were or are used for shipping. Like other structures, those that are found on the main river differ from those found in coves and back water areas.

Pilings located on the main river will usually be good fishing with the incoming tide during the warm water season, as the catfish will move from the deep water into the pilings to feed. Fishing jig/bait combinations and bottom walking rigs close to the pilings will be the way to fish them.

Pilings found in coves and areas of the main river will produce better during the cold water season because these spots serve as wintering over spots for the cats. Another reason that the catfish are found here is the heat generated by the pilings when the sun shines on them. The cats will hover close to the pilings, and jigging your baits right next to them will give you some good results. This is the reason why many crappie fishermen hook into good sized cats while fishing for crappies during the spring and fall season.

Another time that finds cats in these areas, be they on the main river or in a cove, is during the spawning season. It's not uncommon to see small schools of small black catfish swimming in and out of the pilings once the spawning season is over, which is proof that catfish spawn in these areas.

Warm Water Discharges During the summer when the water temperature in the main river is well into the 80's on an average year, warm water discharges will be of no use to you. During the cold water season, however, they can be a real honey hole. The Trenton power plant is one of the last plants actively discharging warm water into the river on a regular basis. Other plants discharge on an off and on basis and none of these are of any use unless they discharge warm water for an extended period of

Nice catfish taken from a warm water discharge in the early season.

time. There are also some municipal and commercial water discharges which will be good from time to time.

Fishing a warm water discharge is as simple as anchoring your boat in the stream of warm water and getting your bait to the fish. There are two times when the warm water discharge will be productive. The first is when the tide is coming in. This will back up the water in a pocket and the fish will concentrate in it. When the tide is going out the warm water discharge will get very narrow and will be more difficult to fish.

CHAPTER 6: LARGEMOUTH BASS & CRAPPIE

LARGEMOUTH BASS

General Factors

Good-sized largemouth taken from a tidal cove.

Because of the physical make up of the tide water Delaware, the largemouth bass shares the crown with the striped bass for the dominant game fish. 99% of the time, striped bass keep to the main river and tributary streams, while the largemouth are found both in the main river and in the coves and back water areas. The slower moving, deeper waters are more to the liking of the largemouth, and the numbers of smallmouth decrease the further down river you go from where the tide water ends at Trenton. The channel in the tidal river ranges from 15 feet at Trenton to 45 feet and deeper in the Wilmington area. Even the coves and back water areas have good deep channels and pockets.

Because the river below Trenton is tidal, structures found there will change every six hours, and the largemouth will relate more to the tides than any other factor. Other factors will, however, affect the tides and thus the largemouth fishing. Time of year, wind direction and velocity, water levels, water clarity, etc. will affect the largemouth and the portion of the tide on which they will feed.

The Cold Water Season   During the cold water season (late fall through early spring, until after spawning season), the bass will be found in large numbers in coves and back water areas off the main river. There are two things that force the bass into these places during the cold water season. First, a bass's body metabolism is very slow since his blood temperature is the same as the water temperature. This means he won't feed as often and will not travel as far for a meal. Second, because of the previously stated reason he will not have much energy to fight the currents in the main river; as a result, they will seek out quieter places to spend the winter months. It's easier for a bass to grab a meal and retreat back into a quiet water area, taking his time to digest his food without having to fight the rivers current.

How early the action begins to pick up is governed by how fast the water warms up. This, in turn, is affected by the weather patterns of any given year. You'll find the best action always comes on some part of a moving tide no matter what time of the year it is and slack water will produce the slowest fishing. This is simple to understand, since a moving tide forces the bass to exert himself and burn up calories, thus he has to feed to replace them. The slack tide will be a rest period and the bass will not move around as much. Another factor is that baitfish will move around more on the moving tide and thus will attract more attention from the bass.

Effects of the Wind   One key to fishing coves during the early and late season has to do with the direction of the wind. Water temperatures in the coves can rise very fast if you have a few warm days and a good breeze blowing up into them. It's during the cold water season that you'll find the outgoing tide to be more productive when waters are cold in the main river. Incoming tides carry water into the shallow areas and it is warmed up by the combination of the warm air and wind. This brings both warmer water and baitfish to the bass as the tides recede. Since the bass are not as active during the cold water season and will only feed sparsely, they wait for the warm water to bring the forage to them. The bass can be taken in the shallow water with the incoming tide, along the drop-offs with the outgoing tide. The side of the cove that the wind is blowing up against is usually the side where the fish are most active and you should take advantage of this anytime it avails itself.

The effects of the wind on the fishing is a double edged sword. Just as it can help the fishing, it can also slow it down if the air temperatures turn cold. In this case the wind will chill down the water that is pushed into the shallows with the incoming tide and carry it back along the drop-offs with the outgoing tide. When this happens, your best bet is to fish the drop-offs with the incoming tide, as the water temperature will be warmer than the water from the shallows which will come back with the outgoing tide.

Warm Water Fishing   During the warm water season, the river comes alive with all types of traffic. During daylight hours, power boaters, skiers, jet skies, etc. really churn up the water and force the fish under cover in some cases or into deeper water most of the time. Much of the better fishing for largemouth will be found in the back water areas where these disturbances are at a minimum and the bass won't be as spooky. So if you have to fish during the mid day hours, fish the out of the way places that offer a less disturbed environment.

Largemouth taken from a drop-off during the summer.

Fish the Dark Hours   Another thing you can do to cope with these problems is to fish after dark when the waters are much more quiet. Here, again, tides play an important part in the fishing. Since water temps will have climbed into the high 70's to mid 80's, the bass will become very active, feeding on both incoming and outgoing tides. The warmer the water gets the more prevalent this is since they will be burning up calories at an elevated rate. However, there are certain times when you will have several factors in your favor and these are peak times to fish.

Your best tides will be an incoming tide that occurs about an hour before dark or one that occurs several hours before it gets light. These tides are called evening and morning tides, respectively, and will be greatly enhanced if they occur from 2 to 6 days after the full moon. It's at this time when the effects of the moon's pull on the tides are the greatest and the waters will move their swiftest, obtaining their highest and lowest depths. This puts the tides, moon phases and time of day on your side of the equation.

Most flats and tidal marshes will have vegetation on them, and the best time to fish these areas is just before and after the water floods into them. Bass gather along the edges of drop-offs and scatter into the vegetation and shallow water that the incoming tide creates. Just before the water moves into the shallows, fish edges of these flats with crankbaits, swimming plugs and spinnerbaits. As the water floods the flats, fish over the submerged vegetation with buzzbaits and constant motion surface plugs. Bass move into these areas to feed on frogs, minnows and small snakes that come out after dark. Since forage that ventures into places like this will be dark in color, keep your lures dark for the best results.

Fish the shadows   Another factor you can use during the warm water season is the shadows and dark water haunts produced by sunken barges, wrecks, pilings and fallen trees along the main river, coves and tidal marshes. Since most coves and back water areas were once used for shipping, most still have some sizeable drop-offs remaining. Likewise, bulkheads and pilings are usually located along channels and deep water areas. All of the afore mentioned structures are usually found close to drop-offs, and forage fish move in and out of these areas with the tides. This gives the bass food and protection from the sun, making them an ideal place for the bass to hold up in during the day. Boat traffic will usually shy away from these places and this helps keep the disturbances down in these areas.

How you fish these areas depends largely on the depth of the water found there. If these structures are found in deep water, jigs, jig/rubberbait combinations and plastic worms will be your best bet. If they are found in shallow water, plastic worms, spinnerbaits, crankbaits and surface lures will give you better results. Remember, you are fishing on structures that are full of debris and snags, so you have to go as weedless as possible. It is also a good bet to fish on the side of the river that gives you the largest shadows.

The Fall Season   Once fall begins, the bass will start feeding on the schools of shad and herring that are making their way back down river. For several weeks the action will be best in and around these schools. On an average year these schools of small shad and herring move in and out of the coves and stream confluences, resting as they make their way back to the sea. On the main river, the schools gather around flats and points of land. When fishing these schools it's always better to lay back away from them and cast at them from a distance.

Once the schools of shad and herring are gone, the bass start heading into the coves and back water areas where they winter over. This is when these areas again come back into prime time. On an average year this happens about mid October, with the best fishing occurring during the first part of November. On a mild year the bass fishing can last into the Christmas season.

In water temperatures above 55 degrees, both lures and live bait will give you good results. Spinnerbaits, plastic worms and jig/rubberbait combinations will be your best bet in the lure department. Once the water drops below the 55 degree mark on a steady basis, the better fishing is on live bait.

Drop-offs, old pilings, wrecks and barges will have some good numbers of fish around them. Jigging live bait in these areas will give you the best results. All different types of fish school up here and it is not uncommon to catch bass, crappie, catfish, white and yellow perch and other fish from a small area. During the early fall, both incoming and outgoing tides will produce, and the amount of fish that you catch on the outgoing tide is usually about half of that which you catch on the incoming tide. You will find that during the early fall, fish found on a structure will be spread out all over it. As the water temperature begins to drop the bass will school up tighter in these areas. This makes them easier to miss if you are using a sonar set.

Nice-sized largemouth taken on a jig/minnow combination in the fall.

Once the water drops into the 40's and lower, the outgoing tide is the better producer. This is because bass lay along drop-offs and don't follow the baitfish into shallow water with the tide. Their body metabolism is slowed by the cooler water and they don't feed as often. They will remain along the drop-offs and feed as the baitfish come back into deeper water with the outgoing tide. Since the bass are schooled up tighter and will be holding tighter to the structures, you have to position your boat right on top of the structures and present your offerings as close to them as possible. You will also have to use a slower jigging motion, and dead sticking jigs and live bait will give you good results.

Spawning As water temps start to climb, the bass start making their way into their traditional spawning areas. Look for them in the deeper water and along drop-offs that border the shallow areas where they spawn. They will remain there until the water temperature attains the levels needed for spawning to begin. During this time the bass will be susceptible to both artificials and live bait. Once the fish begin to build their nest, which is the first part of their mating ritual, their eating habits become very erratic.

Bass fishing in tidal water during spawning time is much different than fishing in a lake or pond. Unlike waters that have consistent water levels, bass found in tidal areas spawn in shallow water as it relates to low tide. Shallow areas one to eight feet deep at low tide is where they will build their nest. This water will be as much as five to eight feet deeper when the tide comes in and these spawning bass will remain there. The most common mistake anglers make when fishing for spawning bass in tidal areas is that they fish in shallow water as it pertains to the incoming tide. As a result, they are fishing in dead water as the fish have remained in the deeper water where their nests are. You can get a good picture of this scenario if you travel into shallow regions of the river during spawning time; you can see the nests that the bass build in the shallow water as well as the bass themselves in many cases. Fish these same areas with the incoming tide instead of moving into the shallow tidal waters. Many anglers are of the school of thought that the bass fishing during the spawning time is better when tides are coming in and is deeper over the nests. This is because the bass will be less spooky in the deeper water and will be shielded from the anglers trying to catch them.

The mouths of the tributary streams that flow into the river in the tidal section are another place to look for bass during the early season and spawning time. Bass move into these areas earlier than in other areas because the water here will warm up faster. Thus spawning temperatures are reached sooner than in coves. This is especially true when we have had a mild winter and low water conditions. On the opposite side of the coin, if a year with excessive rain and cooler than normal temperatures presents itself, the reverse can be true. Rains will pour cooler water into these streams and they will remain cooler. Changes in water temperature in these areas is more common than in other parts of the river, whether for the good or the bad.

LURES

The wide variety of structures and conditions that you find on the tide water Delaware allows you to find a place for just about every lure in your tackle box. When considering the size of your lures, you should remember that most of the forage found in the river is on the small side and thus smaller lures will out produce their larger counter parts. When it comes to the color of your lures, the standard rule of bright colors for bright days and dark colors for dark days is appropriate. Natural patterns and natural colors are often the most versatile in the tide water river.

Using Spinnerbaits Spinnerbaits are most productive during the early and late parts of the year. They are ideal for fishing the shallow gravel type flats that warm up fast during these periods. Both single and double blade spinnerbaits can be used, and most anglers prefer double bladed models when the water is on the dirty side for the vibrations they give off and their better visibility. Spinnerbaits also make excellent lures for use along the weed lines and drop-offs where bass gather prior to moving into shallow water to feed. White and silver are your spring colors, while gold and darker colors make good choices for early morning and late evening summer fishing.

Surface Fishing Most surface fishing is confined to the flats, bars and shallow water areas both on the main river and the back water area. Constant motion surface lures make ideal choices for fishing these areas and are preferred over other types of surface lures. The best time to fish them is when evening tides flood the areas we have mentioned. Keep these lures about two to four inches in length. Many anglers prefer the double jointed versions of these lures. Black and dark colors make the best choices for night fishing and fishing on overcast days. Bright colors are better for the day time.

Crankbait Fishing Crankbaits are one of the main tools for fishing the numerous drop-offs found on the river. The best time to fish them is on the incoming tide, and casting them parallel to the drop-offs will keep them in the strike zone longest. They are good warm water baits, but do not produce as well when the water is cold. Your best sizes are two to three inches long and the depth of the water you are fishing will determine whether you use shallow or deep running models.

Jigging Most of the jigging that is done on the river is done with Jig N' Pig, jig/twister and jig/live bait combinations. Live bait is the preferred dressing during the cold water season and will produce around pilings, wrecks and along other types of objects located along drop-offs. These same areas are prime spots for jig/twister and Jig N' Pig combinations during the summer months.

Live-bait Fishing The best live bait fishing occurs during the spring and fall seasons. Although many types of live baits are used, minnows are the preferred bait.

78

Live-lining and casting and retrieving minnows will work well during the warmer part of the spring and fall season. Once the water cools down, jigging and dead sticking are the preferred methods.

Plastic Worm Fishing   These are one of the most versatile lures that the angler can use on the tide water river. The most often made mistake is to use too large of a plastic worm. Six inch worms are the preferred size, however, many anglers score good catches on four inch worms when the water is gin clear in the summer. For the most part, color is a matter of personal choice, although dark colors are preferred by most anglers. Plastic worms with twister tails also have an edge over plain versions.

REEL SUGGESTIONS

Spinning
Penn - 716Z, 714Z, 4200, 4300
Shakespeare - RT-835, RT-825
Daiwa - EL705, TD2HI, PS2L-5B
Quantum - SS2, SS3, SE3, LS2
ABU Garcia - Pro2, GM2, Pro3, GM3

Conventional
Quantum - 1420 MG, 1421 MG
ABU Garcia - 5500,5500C, 4600C
Daiwa - TD2HI, PS2L-5B
Shimano - B1000I

ROD SUGGESTIONS

Light & medium action spinning or conventional rods in 5 to 6 foot lengths for casting swimming plugs, spinnerbaits and crankbaits. For fishing jigs and rubber baits 5 to 6 foot medium action. For live-lining, medium light action conventional rods in 5 to 6 foot lengths. For trolling and vertical fishing, light and medium light action conventional rods. For fly fishing, light and medium action fly rods in 6 to 9 foot lengths.

LINE SUGGESTIONS

Spinning gear: Triline XL, XT & Tri-Max in 4, 6 & 8 pound test

Conventional tackle: Triline XL, XT & Tri-Max in 8, 10, & 12 pound test

LURES

Surface Lures

Popping Plugs
Trouble Maker (Gudebrod)
Pop "R" (Rebel)
Plunker (Creekchub)
Hula Popper (Arbogast)
Chugger Spook (Heddon)

Darting Plugs
Blabber Mouth (Gudebrod)
Darter (Creekchub)
Zara Spook (Heddon)

Constant Motion Plugs
Lucky 13 (Heddon)
Sinner Spinner (Gudebrod)
Zara Spook Pooch (Heddon)
Jitterbug, Sputter Bug, (Arbogast)

Buzzbaits
Triple wing Buzz Baits 1/4, 3/8 & 1/2
ounce (Strike King)

Swimming Plugs

Floating
Rapala Minnow (Rapala)
Rebel Minnow (Rebel)
Long "A" (Bomber)
Flatfish (Heddon)

Sinking
Countdown (Rapala)
Sinking Rebel Minnow (Rebel)

Crankbaits

Shallow Running
Fat Rap (Rapala)
Model"A" (Bomber)
Fastrac "R" (Rebel)
Crawfish (Rebel)
Balsa "B" (Bagley's)

Deep Running
Shad Rap (Rapala)
Deep Fat Rap (Rapala)
Deep "R" (Rebel)
Balsa Deep "B" (Bagley's)
Deep Crayfish (Rebel)

Rattle Plugs
Rattl'n Rap (Rapala)
Rat-L-Trap (Bill Lewis)
Spot (Cordells)

Spinners
Aglia, Elix, Back Fury,
Comet Minnow (Mepps)
Panther Martin
Vibrax (Blue Fox)
Diamond Back (Cabela's)
CP Swing
Swiss Swing
Rooster Tail

Spoons
Syclops (Mepps)
Slab Spoon (Bomber)
Dardevle
Kastmaster
Phoebe

Spinnerbaits
Little George (Mann's)
Single and double bladed in
1/4, 3/8 and 1/2 ounce sizes
Twister Spins (Mepps)
Mean Dude (Mepps)

Jig/Rubberbait
Twister Tail, Sassy Shad, Sassy
Shiner, Split Tail (Mr. Twister)
Foxy Jig, Vibro Tail (Blue Fox)
Rubber skirt jigs, plastic worms

Flies & Popping Bugs
Medium sized streamers in various
patterns, medium and large sized
deer hair bugs and popping bugs.

Author's selection of top lures used for largemouth on the tidal river.

Live Bait

Aquatic
Killies, fatheads (natural & golden),
shiners, dace, crayfish, frogs,
tadpoles, perch & small panfish, eels

Terrestrial
Hellgrammites, night crawlers,
large insects

#140-A Black Widow Eel, #1 & #11 Pork Frog, #800 Spring Lizard, #260 Split Eel, #12 & #14 Flippin' Frog, #50 Bass Strip

Hooks

Light wire shank preferred in sizes #8 through #1 (Mustdad- Long shank #37360, Short Shank #3892B) (Eagle Claw- Long Shank #214; Short Shank-#72), for use with plastic baits, weedless hooks- Mustad (#W3369A, #W3369AW) Eagle Claw (#249W)

Misc. Gear

Night lights for night fishing, hook sharpener, medium sized net, marker buoys for outlining structures.

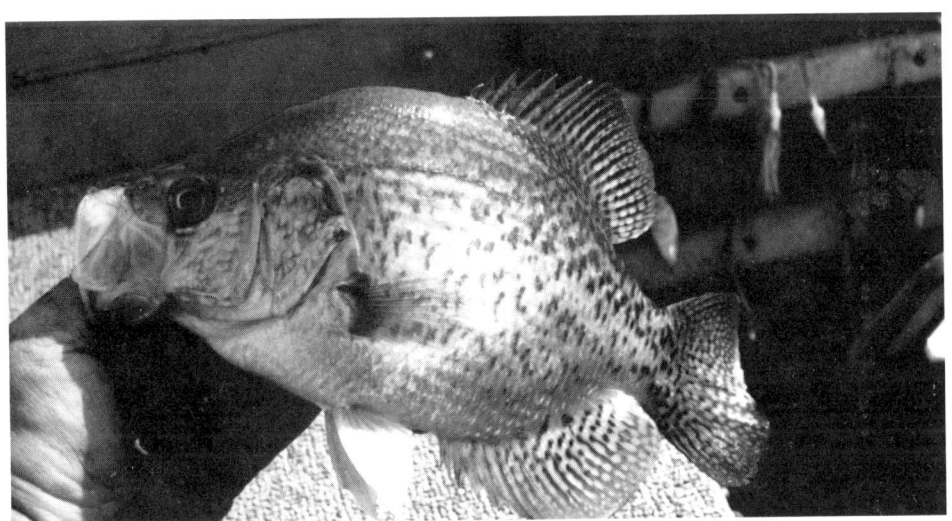

CRAPPIE
FISHING AND METHODS

Crappie go hand and hand with the largemouth found in the tidal river. They are found on the same structures, feed on the same forage, spawn in the same places and have most of the same habits. They are the major member of the panfish family found in the tidal river and are pursued by countless anglers throughout the year.

Even though these fish can be taken all year long, they are most abundant during the spring and fall. Summer finds the bulk of these fish roaming the main river. Once water temperatures start dropping in the fall they move back into coves and back water regions, remaining there through the winter and spring. After they spawn, they will again move back out into the main river, while their young will remain in the coves and back water areas.

Being school fish, they will follow baitfish populations and adhere closely to structure. Definite patterns develop with regard to their movements in relation to structure in certain areas and these are affected by seasonal weather and water conditions. The tidal river contains a multitude of structures that crappie prefer. At the top of the list are dock and bridge pilings, old wrecks, fallen trees and drop-offs.

Crappie are hardy fish, actively feeding in water temps down in the 30's, and this makes him a favorite of the hard core anglers who fish the river during the winter.

His preferred temperatures range between 45 and 60 degrees and spawning takes place when water temps reach 61 to 68 degrees on a regular basis. He is affected by quick water temperature changes and can really turn on during the cold water season after a few days of warm weather and good breezes. Likewise, he will be turned off under the reverse conditions.

Nice crappie taken from a drop-off in the early season.

Crappie taken from the river during the cold water season are some of the tastiest fish that the river produces. The average size of these fish ranges from a half to three quarters of a pound, with over a pound and a half fairly common on most years. One days catch can easily provide several meals for the fish gourmet. Crappie are not as adversely affected by pollutants such as PCB's, however, parasite worms are common among the larger fish found in coves and back water areas, especially in the spring.

It doesn't take much in the way of tackle to fish for crappie, and ultralight gear will give you the most fun. Being curious fish, crappie hit a diverse variety of baits and lures, and one of the most commonly made mistakes is to use baits and lures that are too big. I have studied these fish in the confines of the huge tank I have in my office and have observed that they have a distinct preference for very small minnows. Even larger crappie prefer super small minnows and this makes the key word in crappie fishing SMALL.

When crappie are in their active state they inhale bait and lures on impulse, however, most of the time they will move right up to a bait when it is cast into the water and observe it for a few seconds before hitting it. This is why lively minnows take more crappie than slower moving ones. Since crappie inhale their prey, you don't have to give them time to swallow the bait once you detect their hit if you are using the right size bait. Simply raise the rod tip, tighten the line and tap the rod tip to set the hook. Their soft mouth is easily penetrated by a sharp hook, making for an easy release if you choose not to keep the fish.

During the warm water season (late spring, summer and early fall), artificials produce the largest amounts of fish. The most deadly of all lures is a small jig/ rubberbait combination. Bright color twister tails and minnow imitations are the best dressings for your jigs. Yellow, white, chartreuse and green are the preferred colors and your best jigs sizes are 1/32 and 1/16. Whether or not you use painted jig heads is a matter of personal preference and doesn't make a noticeable difference in the amount of fish you catch.

During the cold water season, nothing out produces live bait. The natural action of a lively small minnow as he tries to elude a crappie is an irresistible combination. Wounded minnows, especially those trying to get away from a pursuing fish, emit a smell and give off vibrations that can really put crappie on the feed under the right conditions.

Killies are the number one forage of the crappies found in the tidal river, thus they are the best bait. A well stocked livewell or bait container with minnows in the 1" to 2" size is your ticket to some excellent fishing during the spring and fall. One tip when it comes to using live bait is to keep the bait in a container that allows you to keep it in the water. This keeps the minnows well oxygenated and lively while you are fishing. Since crappie inhale the bait and then turn it around in their mouth in a head first position, it's best to hook minnows through the lips.

There are three major ways of using live bait for crappie, the first of which is casting and retrieving them. This method is quite similar to live-lining in that a minnow is placed on a weighted hook or jig and then is cast into a likely looking spot and slowly retrieved. This method is excellent for checking a structure to see if any crappie are around.

The second method is jigging minnows, whether by hand holding your rod or by dead sticking it. It's an excellent way of fishing once you have located crappies. To employ this method successfully you should anchor your boat up wind and allow the wind to push you back over the structure you are fishing. The most crucial factor in this type of fishing is being able to get your baits down to the same depths time after time. Crappie will often be suspended in a thermocline layer of water commonly found around structures in the tidal river and this significantly narrows down the strike zone. A good way of making sure your baits get to the same depth time after time is to mark you line with a Magic Marker once you have taken your first fish. This allows you to lower your line down to the same depth by lining up the marked line with a certain spot on your rod.

The third way of using live bait is through the use of a sliding bobber. Small pencil shaped bobbers are preferred, as they offer the least resistance as the fish takes the bait. A small split shot can be placed about six inches above the hook to keep the bait down and stop the bobber from sliding down to the end of the line when casting. A bobber stop is used to preset the depth at which the bait will sit and is attached directly to the line.

Bank fishermen will find that the bobber method is an effective way of fishing because it allows you to cast your baits better and makes it easier to detect a hit from the shore. One trick many shoreline fishermen use is to substitute a jig for a plain hook when using this method. This allows the bobber to slide right up to jig, giving you better distance when you

Dead-sticking is a good method of catching crappie during the cold water season.

cast. You can also raise and lower you rod tip while retrieving, causing the bait to jig up and down below the bobber.

Most of the areas you will fish for crappie are full of hang ups and one way to cut down on your jig costs is to use a split shot jig. It is made by taking a small standard jig hook (size #10 or #12) and squeezing a small wingless split shot onto the bend of the hook. This makeshift jig can be dressed with bait or artificials.

A sonar unit is one device that can come in handy when crappie fishing. It will help you locate crappie that are found in coves and back water areas. During the early fall and late spring they will be more spread out than during the heart of the cold water season and are easier to spot on the screen.

If you don't have a sonar set there is one way you can pinpoint crappie once you have caught one. Take the first fish you catch and attach a small hook to it's top fin, then add a length of line to it; attach a small balloon to the line and release the fish. Once in the water he will return to the school and you will be able to see where they are and where they move to. When you are done fishing simply pull in the line and remove it from the fish.

One tip for crappie fishing in the cold water season is to try and fish after a few warm breezy days have occurred. Concentrate your fishing on the portion of a cove or back water area where the sun is on it the longest and the wind has been blowing up against it. These are the places where the water temps will warm up fastest and the crappie will be most active.

TACKLE

The use of ultralight tackle is the unanimous choice among crappie fishermen. Ultralight spinning rods in four and a half to six foot lengths will enable you to present the small baits in the river. Keep all lures and baits as small as possible. Full action rods are preferred for use with small live bait, and tip action rods are better suited for casting small artificials.

ROD & REELS

Fly Tackle

Use three weight fly rod and reel combos and different styles of three weight lines. The fly patterns which are used for trout are excellent for crappie. In addition, fly fishermen can use small popping bugs and deer hair bugs, along with small rubber baits and live bait.

Spinning Reel Suggestions

Shakespeare - RT 725, 2500 ULX, RT 825   Daiwa - UL 7, EL 705, BG10, PS705BL
Quantum - SS1 UL, EX2, SE2, LS1   Shimano - TX-1000F, SC-1000F, SO-1000FA
Penn - 4200, 716

Rod Suggestions

Use ultralight spinning rods in 4 1/2 to 6 foot lengths for casting swimming plugs, spinnerbaits and crankbaits. For surface fishing, 5 to 6 foot noodle type spinning rods. For jig and rubberbait fishing, 4 1/2 to 5 1/2 foot ultralight tip action rods. For live bait fishing, ultralight spinning rods in 5 foot lengths. For fly fishing, ultra light rods in 5 to 8 foot lengths.

Line

In the line department, 2, 4 & 6 pound test are the most commonly used line weights. Always choose small diameter lines, as they provide better casting distance with the smaller lures. Triline XL in 2, 4 & 6 pound tests, Tri-Max in 4 & 6 pound tests.

CHAPTER 7: SHAD & HERRING

SHAD

Steady improvements in water quality and record numbers of fish, coupled with the spectacular fighting antics of the shad, have combined to make the legendary shad run in the Delaware more appealing to increasing numbers of anglers each season. Considered to be the crown jewel of shad rivers, it's shad and the great come back they have made have been the subject of much research and study, so much so that fish from the river have been transported to other river systems in efforts to restore or create new shad runs in them.

Not only are shad important as game fish in the spring, their offspring are a substantial part of the river's food chain in the summer and fall as well. As the millions of small shad return down river, they provide predators with an excellent forage base on which to feed. This has helped the smallmouth and largemouth bass, walleye, striper and numerous varieties of panfish swell to abundant proportions.

KEY FACTORS

Shad are Current Fish   One thing that shad fishermen should always keep in mind is that shad are current fish and follow the river's current as they make their way upstream. The only time they will depart from the current is when they move into slow areas to rest for the night or when resting in calm areas prior to or after moving through a stretch of swift water. These facts about the current are a great influence on how productive certain sections of river are. Always look for areas where the current sweeps close to the shore, such as a river bend. This brings the shad closer to the shoreline and puts them within your reach.

Shad Time Table   Once the shad's natural alarm clock triggers their spawning instincts, the shad begin moving down the Atlantic coast towards the Delaware, making their way into the bay in late February and early March. By the end of March, the front runners will be as far up river as Trenton and by mid April they will be as far up river as Easton and even the Delaware Water Gap. The beginning of May finds them spread throughout the river all the way into it's head waters in New York state. Fishing will usually end in the Trenton area by mid May and be done throughout the river by mid June on average years.

Water Temperature There are several markers on the thermometer worth noting, most important of which is the 50 degree mark. Shad found in water temps below that level will be sluggish. This does not mean they won't hit a lure, but the numbers of fish anglers catch will be low. Once water temps hit the 50 degree mark they will become more active and strike lures more readily. Shad spawn when the water hits 65 degrees on a steady basis, and fly fishing will be best when water temps are in this range because the shad will move into shallow areas to spawn, making them easier to reach with fly tackle.

Water Color Although this factor does not keep the shad from traveling up river, it will affect their ability to see lures, thus affecting the amount of shad taken each year. It is governed not only by the amount of rain that falls in the spring but by how and where it falls as well. A simple rule to follow is when the water is gin clear use smaller lures and when it's dirty or off color use larger ones. In both cases use a good selection of colors to start with in order to see which is the most productive on any given day.

Water Levels This condition is governed by the amount of rain that falls in the spring and the amount of snow that fell in the upper regions of the river during the winter. The one thing that high water does is move shad closer to the shore and into relatively quieter waters. Low water conditions will cause the shad to move up river on the strongest current located in any give section. This makes anchoring or fishing a dominant current line of the most importance.

STRUCTURES

When looking at the structures that are productive for shad, it must be remembered that anywhere you can narrow down the water you have to fish, the more visible your lure will be to the shad. Another thing to remember is to always fish the current because that is what brings the shad the properties that they home in on while making their way up river and this is where most of them will be found when they are active.

Anglers fish for shad alongside a bridge piling.

Bridge Pilings   One of the most often fished places for shad is the water found around bridge pilings. Their high visibility to anglers is one of the reasons, however, the eddies found below their pilings make good resting places for shad. This, combined with the fact that the pilings change the currents found in the sections in which they are located, makes them a top spot for shad.

River Bends   As the river winds it's way through the mountains, it takes many bends that cause it's currents to swing from side to side. These river bends provide the angler with excellent fishing, since the shad follow the river's current and this situation will push them to one side of the river in good numbers and bring them within casting range of the shoreline fisherman.

Islands   Another top area is where the river passes by islands and it's waters are narrow between the island and shoreline. This situation forces shad to move through a smaller stretch of water, reducing the area you have to fish. Most islands have some deep holes where shad will lay over during the nighttime, and the river between the islands and shore will be first place they head for as day breaks. Both the boat and shoreline fisherman can take advantage of this condition by positioning themselves to fish this area to get at the shad.

Wing Dams   All three wing dams located on the river, Scudders Falls, Lambertville and Bulls Island, have always been prime spots and are heavily fished. On low water years, only the sluice way of these dams have water going through them and this forces the shad to pass through this small slot, making the current lines leading up to and out of the sluice top places to fish. Caution should be exercised when fishing these areas as they have some of the strongest currents on the river and annually take several lives.

Finger Structures   Finger structures are found in numerous sections of the river and are quite similar to wing dams. There are, however, two differences between the two. First, finger structures are natural structures, not man made, and second, they usually have more than one break in them which acts as sluices through which the water flows. Low water enables waders to come within casting range of these openings through which the fish pass. Boat fishermen can anchor along them to fish, and fingers have pools downstream from them where shad congregate and rest. When high water is present, shad will move up along the slower currents found on the sides.

Points of Land   Points of land are typical single current line structures that has a dead water pocket located downstream from them. Since the current is forced around them and shad follow the current, this gives them two excellent places for anglers to fish, the dead water pocket and the current line. Names like Point Pleasant eddy have become synonymous with shad fishing for this reason.

Warm Water Discharges   Some of the first places to produce shad in the spring are the warm water discharges that flow into the river. At one time these were more plentiful, however, only the Duck Island power plant at Trenton and the Met Ed power plant at Portland still have active discharges. Simply put, they make good shad spots because their warm water will attract the fish and will make them more active sooner then anywhere else in the river.

METHODS

Shoreline Fishing   Your best choice in rod and reel combos for shoreline fishing are eight to twelve foot light action noodle sticks. These rods, with longer surf rod type handles (commonly referred to as power handles), ceramic or polished aluminum guides and properly balanced with large spool graphite reels allow anglers to hit distances, current lines and shad hot spots he could only think about reaching with shorter light action gear. Longer rods give the angler better leverage, while the softness of the rod's action keeps the lure from pulling out of the fishes mouth.

Proper positioning is an important factor in shad fishing, and gaining it from the shoreline is much harder than when fishing from a boat. The high, fast waters of the spring can limit shoreline access, and waders or hip boots, accompanied with a pair of felt soles or spike shoes and/or a wading staff are necessities. When using the longer rods, these items allow you to get away from trees and other things that might interfere with casting.

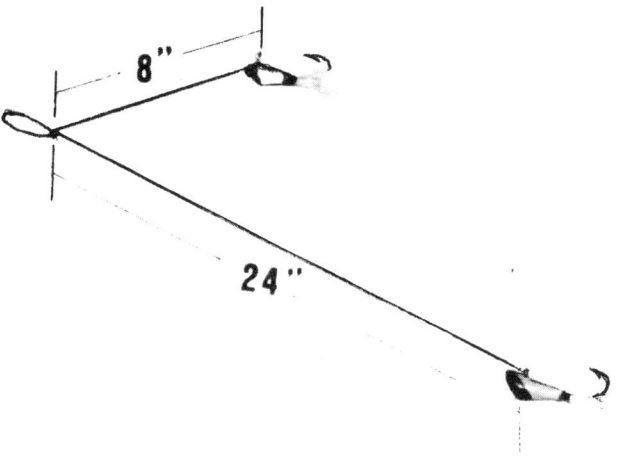

The Double Rig Method There are many plusses to using this type of rig, the first of which is that it allows you to use a larger lure to get a smaller one to where the fish are without using extra weight. For the shoreline fisherman it provides better casting distance, while boat fishermen find it allows them to cover more water than a single dart rig. The rig allows one lure to compliment the other, and shad will often be attracted by one and hit the other because it's closer or more aggravating. It is easily tied by taking a length of leader line about two feet long and tying the heavier or larger lure to one end and the smaller or lighter lure to the other. You then drop the smaller or lighter lure down about 6 to 8 inches and tie a double loop at the top of the rig. You then tie your main line to the loop. Some favorite lures for use with the double rig are: A large and a small dart, a dart/ spoon combination, a dart/flicker spinner combination, a dart/ streamer fly combination and limitless other combinations.

BOTTOM WALKING RIGS

Bottom Walking Rigs In recent years shad fishermen have begun adapting tackle and methods from other types of fishing for use in shad fishing. This is where the bottom walking rig comes in. The prime ingredients of this rig are a bottom walking sinker and a doctored up floating jig head which is shaped and painted to look like a shad dart. This rig can then be dead sticked or slowly cast and retrieved. It allows the floating jig head to ride about two feet above the bottom and is ideal for working slower currents and deeper waters. Some anglers substitute a flutter spoon for the floating jig head.

Narrow Down the Water You have to Fish   Shad traveling up the river to spawn have to pass through each section at one time or another, passing through wide and narrow as well as deep and shallow stretches of river. It only makes good sense that the less water you have to fish, the greater your chances are of placing your offerings within their sight, thus the better your chances are of hooking up.

Any time you can narrow down the water you have to fish, you increase your chances of taking shad. There are two basic ways of doing this, either by picking an area where the banks come close together or choosing a spot where the water is shallow across the entire river. This applies to fishing from a boat or from shore.

Working the Current   Whenever possible, choose the deeper side of a straight stretch of river. Even though shad spread out throughout the river, most of them travel along the deeper side. When fishing from shore, cast slightly upstream and across the current. You can then slowly move your rod tip up and down without reeling, working your lure with the current downstream. Once the lure is downstream from your position, retrieve it back with the same slow pulsating motion.

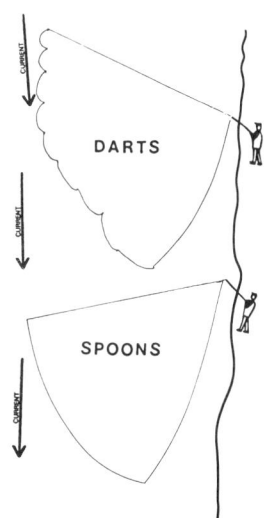

It's important to keep your lures in the current as long as possible. To do this, keep as much line out of the water as you can. This helps keep the current from sweeping your lure out of the strike zone. When fishing a current line from the side, keep your rod tip high while working your lure with the current, gradually lowering the rod tip as the lure moves downstream and then holding the rod close to the water as you retrieve it back.

Working Slow Water Areas   Shad hold up in areas of slow moving water to rest before moving back into the river's main current. These areas are among the most difficult to fish since most lures used for shad have weight to them and tend to sink quickly in such areas. When fishing quiet water with a dart, keep it as small as possible. A Flutter Spoon is another good choice as it is lighter than other shad lures. If you are a fly fisherman, a streamer fly works well when fishing these slow moving waters. As previously mentioned, bottom walking rigs are ideal for working slow water. These choices apply to clear water only.

Prime time for fishing quiet areas and the current lines next to them, such as pools and eddies, is first thing in the morning and just before night fall. This is when the shad move in and out of these places in the largest numbers. Just before dark, the shad begin moving into the quiet water to rest for the night. Most biologists believe that they remain there, resting throughout the night and, as day breaks, begin moving back into the river's current, resuming their journey upriver. It's at this time that the best fishing will occur where the current merges with the slower moving water. How many shad will be found in quiet water the rest of the day will depend on how many are moving through at any given time.

Trolling   Although trolling is a viable method of taking shad, there are several factors that make trolling non-productive or difficult at best. Most sections of the Delaware are not suitable for trolling and most of those that are, are heavily fished by anchored boats, making trolling difficult. In order to troll successfully, you must first locate a section where it is practical.

Conventional gear is your best choice for trolling; it will cut down on line twist, provide a smoother drag system to accept the hard hits you will get and is easier to deploy lures.

The river's current rules out the use of electric motors, making your outboard your mode of power. If the motor on your boat is too big to troll adequately, your next best bet is to mount a smaller motor on your boat to do the job. Getting your lures to the shad in a slow precise manner makes speed control a very important factor. Beaded sinkers are the best way of adding weight to your rigs when trolling because they not only add weight to your line but help prevent line twist as well. A Gapen's Bait Walker makes an excellent second choice.

Some anglers employ down riggers to troll for shad. They make a good way of deploying darts and other lures while trolling, however, the uneven bottom of the river, especially in shallow water, can create problems. Another reason why they are not used by more anglers is that most fishermen simply cannot afford one.

Dead Sticking   Of all the methods used for shad from a boat, none is more deadly when done right than dead sticking. Dead sticking is as easy or as complex as you yourself make it. Simply put, it is anchoring your boat in the river, casting your lures into the current and letting them sit there while the current gives them their action. The trick is to position your boat where the shad must come through, in other words, being in the right place at the right time.

Boat rigged for dead sticking.

When it comes to the tools of the trade for the dead stick shad fisherman, they, too, can be simple or complex. A good grappling hook type anchor with plenty of anchor line is a must to hold your boat in the current. Some type of rod holders or a dead stick pod will be needed to hold your rods.

Just about any well built spinning or conventional rod and reel will suffice, and even fly outfits can be used. In recent years conventional gear has made some deep inroads into this type of fishing. Largely because of it's dependability and smoother drag systems, coupled with an assortment of light action rods, from short five footers

90

to eight, ten and twelve foot noodle sticks, it has become the preferred choice in tackle among serious anglers.

The most efficient way of covering the water behind your boat by dead sticking is through the use of a dead stick pod or rod holders strategically placed throughout your boat. If you anchor your boat properly over a section of river were the shad must pass and spread out your rods so that they cover the widest section of water behind your boat, you will soon find out how deadly this method is.

Proper boat position is a must for dead sticking. When rigging your boat, place two anchor chalks on the bow a few feet from the tip of the boat, one on each side. This allows you to set your anchor line on either side of the boat, thus changing the position of the boat relative to the amount of anchor line you have out from one side to the other without picking up your anchor and moving. If you are anchored in a spot and all your hits are coming on one side of the boat all you have to do switch the anchor line from one side to the other, via the anchor chalks, so that the boat is pushed by the current more towards the side on which you are getting the hits.

If this fails to achieve the desired results, your next step is to change the angle of your motor as it sits in the water. If your motor is set so that it is pointed straight ahead, the motor will not have any effect on your boat. If you desire your to shift the boat either right or left of the center, all you have to do is position your motor in the opposite direction, right to shift left and left to shift right, and the current will do the rest. The motor acts as a rudder and the force of the current against it will move your boat.

Jigging   Many anglers prefer to impart their own action into their shad lures. When fishing from shore, jigging and dancing your lures is a prime way of fishing them. When fishing from a boat, dead sticking is recognized as the premier method of taking shad. Dead sticking does have a drawback, mainly when the shad are moving through in good numbers. If you are dead sticking four or more rods and get multiple hook ups it can become pure pandemonium, and the fish will often tangle lines. This is the time to start jigging. Jigging allows you better control when good numbers of fish are moving through an area because the angler must hand hold his rod instead of using a rod holder. When a shad strikes he will be able to instantly set the hook, and this doesn't give the shad a chance to foul any other rods that are out.

The shad dart is the primary tool for jigging, although in recent years other types of lures have become popular. Some of the new types of spoons that have come into more wide spread use have turned into excellent jigging tools. Bottom walking sinkers and floating jig heads have also become a favorite of many shad anglers.

Adding a small bright color twister tail to your dart is a good way of making them more visible to the shad, and this has become a common practice among shad fishermen when jigging and dead sticking alike. One of the most common mistakes made when adding a twister tail is using one too big. Since shad hit a lure out of impulse, too large of a twister will cause the shad to bounce off the rig or hit short. Some anglers have also begun tying a few strands of metallic ribbon to their lures to give them more flash. Another thing you can do is place a small spinner blade (0 or 00 blade size) on the hook of their lure to give it more flash and visibility.

SHAD TIME TABLE

The first place anglers see any number of shad in the non-tidal river is in the

Yardley/Scudders Falls area. Access to this area is from Yardley access, which is run by the PA Fish Commission and offers the angler access to the waters below the Route 95 bridge and Scudders Falls wing dam, both of which are April hot spots.

The next area that is heavily fished is the Lambertville area. Shoreline fishermen will find some excellent action along both sides of the fast moving river below the wing dam, with the top spot being Fireman's Eddy, located about a half mile below the wing dam on the Jersey side. Boat access is from the ramp on the Jersey side next to the water treatment plant and it provides access to the waters above the dam. Top spots here are the Lambertville bridge, the Route 202 bridge and the mouth of the Alexhauken Creek on the Jersey side.

The Bull's Island State Park ramp (located below the wing dam) and the Bryam access (located above the dam) are the principal areas for shad fishermen in the Raven Rock area. Shoreline fishermen will find good action in the Point Pleasant eddy on the PA side and the Devils Tea Table region on the Jersey side, which is located about five miles north of Bulls Island.

By late April and early May on a normal year, some of the best fishing is found in the Phillipsburg/Easton section. By this time the water temps have hit the 50 degree mark and the fish are very active. The one thing nice about this area is that there is plenty of access for both the shoreline and boat angler. From the shore your best spots are the Route 611 overlook and the waters just north of Standt's Eddy on the PA side. In this section the current sweeps up against this side, bringing the fish well within casting range. Boat access is excellent at Easton Front Street access and Standt's Eddy access on the PA side and the Phillipsburg access on the Jersey side.

As the month of May gathers steam, the better fishing is found in the Delaware Water Gap area. This section is one of the most picturesque areas and, as part of the Water Gap National Recreation area, it to offers the angler plenty of access. Wallpack Bend is located in this area and is a favorite of shoreline fishermen. One of the best known and most heavily fished shad spots is Dingman's Ferry, which is located in the northern most part of the Recreation Area. Over the years it has become synonymous with excellent shad fishing during the later part of May on into the first part of June. It has an excellent ramp and plenty of shore line fishing, and from here north is where the majority of shad will spawn on an average year.

TACKLE

When it comes to the tools of the trade for this sea run gamester, most anglers prefer light and ultra light gear. The fragile nature of the tissue that makes up their mouth is the reason most often cited for the use of light tackle. Current trends in recent years have favored the use

A shad's soft mouth makes light action tackle necessary.

of long eight and ten foot noodle rods saddled with suitable spinning and conventional reels packed with light line.

Shoreline fishermen, on the other hand, will find the afore mentioned rods combined with light action spinning reels a better choice. The combination of a noodle stick, spinning reel and light line enables you to get superb casting distance needs to put him in touch with the current lines shad follow.

Reel Suggestions

Spinning
Penn - 716, 714, 4200, 4300
Shakespeare - 2500ALX, RT 825
Daiwa - EL705, EL1305
Quantum - SS1UL, SS2LT, SE2, LS1
Shimano - TX1000F, SC1000F, SO1000FA
ABU Garcia - GMUL, GM2, UL, PRO 2

Conventional
Quantum - 1310MG, 381
ABU Garcia - 4600-C3, 5000C XLT2
Daiwa - PS2-5B, PS2-2B & PR1HI
Shimano - B110, BSM2201FS & B100 II

Rod Suggestions

When it comes to spinning tackle for casting darts, choose ultralight, light and medium light rods in 5 to 7 foot lengths. Another excellent choice are 8 1/2 to 10 foot light action noodle sticks. Conventional tackle makes a better choice for dead sticking with light and medium light action rods with full handles in lengths of 5 to 7 feet. Conventional noodle sticks in lengths of 8 1/2 to 10 feet of the type used with down riggers for salmon in the Great Lakes are an excellent option. In the fly rod category, 7 to 9 foot steel head rods with extended butts and reels with drag systems are the favorite.

Line Suggestions

Recommended line weights include 4, 6, & 8 pound tests, however, many anglers choose to test their skills with two pound test, and with the use of a noodle stick rod and reel combination with a smooth drag system, the use of two pound test is gaining in popularity with each passing season.

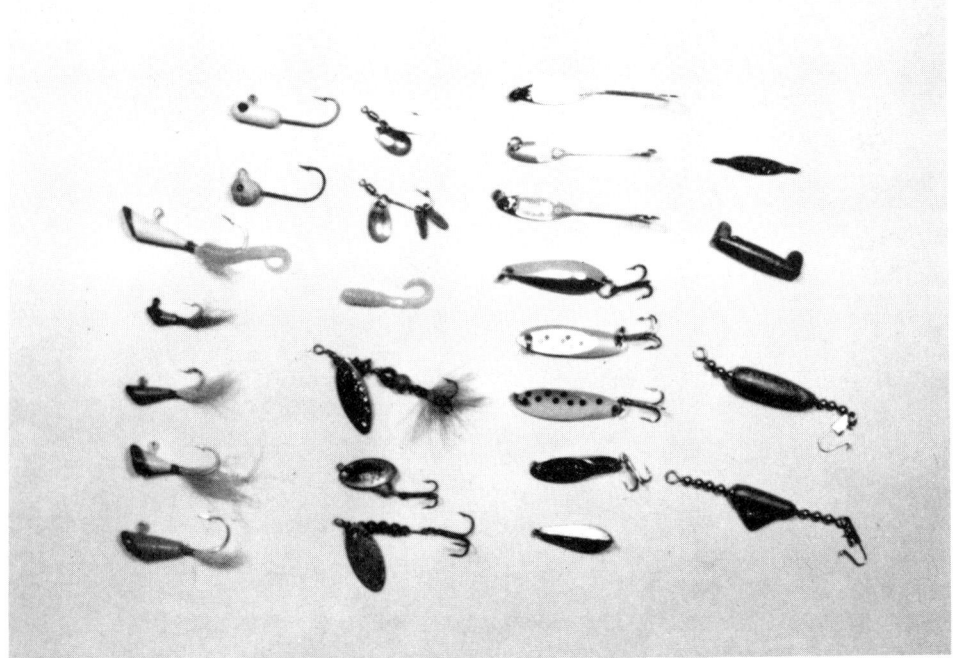

Floating jig heads, darts, flutter spoons, flicker spinner, spinners, twister tails and spoons used for shad, along with the inline sinkers that get these lures down best.

Lures

Darts: A well rounded selection of weights, sizes and colors. Floating jig heads fished with bottom walking rigs.

Towards the end of the run when the water temperatures are in the 70's, shad can be taken on small spinners and spoons.

Spinners: Aglia, Elix (Mepps), Rooster Tail, Panther Martin, Vibrax (Blue Fox) CP Swing, Swiss Swing.

Spoons: Dardevle, Kastmaster, Phoebe, Shad Spoon, Flutter Spoon

Flies: Bright color streamer flies.

Rubberbaits: Small twister tails in various colors

Weights: In-line sinkers, pencil lead, egg sinkers, split shot

Misc. Tackle: Large net (preferably with an extendable handle), water temperature gauge, dead stick pod, rod holders

Rules & Regulations   Fishing privileges in the river, whether fishing from a boat or from the shoreline, are reciprocal between Pennsylvania and New Jersey, and Pennsylvania and New York. As of this printing Pennsylvania has a six per day bag limit. Legislation had been introduced into the New Jersey legislature to impose the same limit on the New Jersey side, however, as of this printing it has not been enacted. There are no size regulations anywhere on the river.

Herring are smaller members of the shad family.

HERRING

Herring are smaller members of the shad family and migrate up the Delaware river in order to spawn in the spring. They make excellent sport on light tackle and are a good way of breaking the younger generation into fishing. Fishing for herring takes place during the month of April, through May and into June.

Besides being an excellent light tackle sport fish, they are more important as forage for every predator in the river. During the spring, stripers follow the herring up river, feeding on them. Once the herring are done spawning they move back down river, taking a good part of the striper population with them. During the summer and fall, the small are forage for all types of fish, and are a significant part of the food cycle in the river.

The majority herring spawn as far up river as Frenchtown and some will go even further under certain conditions. Herring spawn on the numerous flats found along shorelines and islands, and how far up river they spawn is determined by where they are when water reaches their spawning temperature, which is the mid 60's. Most tidal streams that flow into the river will have herring spawning in their waters, and fishing is available in them as well.

Just about any rod and reel combination will do, however, ultralight spinning tackle is the best water to fish for them. Some anglers also enjoy fishing for them with light fly tackle.

When fishing the tidal river from a boat it's best to anchor along the channel edge and vertically fish the waters under the boat. Some gold hooks and bank sinkers are all that is needed in the way of terminal tackle. Herring, like shad, do not feed while they are spawning and will hit a gold color hook as a reflex action. Some anglers place gold sequins on the hook to make them more productive. Herring are so cooperative that if you tie on three hook you will catch three at a time.

Gold hooks are not the only thing that will take herring. Small gold spinners, flicker spinners and spoons also make excellent choices for them and are most productive when the fish are found spawning in shallow water when the water temps are warmer.

Herring are excellent baits when live lined for stripers, musky, and other large game fish, however, they are difficult to keep alive, and a well aerated container or live well is needed for this purpose. They make very good cut baits for catfish, and many anglers stock up their freezers with herring during the spring and use them for bait later in the year. Many anglers will trap small herring during the summer and fall and use them for bass, walleyes, crappie, and panfish.

CHAPTER 8: SMALLMOUTH BASS
(MICROPTERUS DOLOMIEUI)

Even though smallmouth are called bass, they are not a true member of the bass family. In reality, smallmouth are actually one of the largest members of the sunfish family (Centrachidae), the same as the largemouth. The only true bass are striped bass, white bass and white perch.

The growth rate of the smallmouth in the river is between four and seven inches the first year and two to four inches each year thereafter, with a smallie of four pounds or more being considered a trophy fish.

Although smaller in size than the largemouth, most anglers agree he is a far superior fighter. River smallmouth are stronger, more aggressive and have more stamina because they live in a current environment.

When it comes to his aggressive nature, here, too, the current is the culprit. Because the current brings the smallmouth his food in most cases, he has to be ready to grab it or the current will take it away from him. Smallies are school fish and are often found in small groups or pods. When bass stack up on a current line and a piece of forage moves their way, he has to get it before another fish beats him to it. The oxygen rich water of the river boosts the smallies metabolism so that they burn up calories more quickly and thus have to feed more often.

KEY ELEMENTS OF DELAWARE RIVER SMALLMOUTH

As with any fish, *water temperature* is one of, if not the, most important factors that affects their behavior. Smallmouth found in the river can tolerate higher water temperatures because of the higher amount of dissolved oxygen that is present in the water. Water temperatures in the Delaware often climb well into the 80's without any adverse effects on the smallmouth. Basically, the warmer the water in the river gets, the more active the smallmouth will be. The easiest way of seeing this is to compare him to a car engine. An engine takes in fuel just as a smallmouth takes in forage. The car engine unites the fuel with oxygen and produces power to run the car. Smallies digest forage and unite it with oxygen to form calories, which in turn power the smallmouth. The faster an engine goes the more fuel it uses. Likewise, the warmer the water gets, the faster the smallies burn up the calories and the more they must eat. On the opposite side of the coin, the cooler the water gets, the slower and less often they feed.

Water temperature not only regulates how heavy the bass feed, as well as the speed control at which an angler uses his lures, but it can change his forge base and way of feeding as well. During the summer, the Delaware has huge bug hatches, and the smallies forage base shifts to them over the other types of forage 50% to 80% of the time. Another example is the fall feed when cooler water starts the shad and herring fry moving down river and they become the largest part of the smallmouth's diet.

Smallmouth spawn in the river when water temps are between 60 and 70 degrees and this usually takes place in the river during the months of May and June on an average year.

One thing that makes the Delaware such a great fishing spot and keeps it's fisheries healthy is the *rich oxygen levels* that the river has. Ripples, rapids and other river structures act as circulators, constantly mixing air with water. These high oxygen levels greatly influence smallmouth.

A good sized smallmouth taken from a fast section of river.

Because the Delaware receives high amounts of oxygen through it's moving waters, weather conditions have a quicker and more direct effect on it. If weather patterns are favorable then they affect the river's water in a positive way. Of course, the reverse can be true.

One of the main things that high oxygen levels do is allow smallmouth to tolerate high water temperatures, and one of the keys to fishing for smallmouth in the Delaware is knowing how to play these oxygen levels.

In the spring, an angler should concentrate on areas of the river where the oxygen causes the water to warm up quickest. Small eddies, ripples and other shallow areas are some top choices.

During the summer, the best fishing during the mid day hours is in the ripples and rapids, as well as the portions of river structures where the oxygen counts are the highest.

Rich oxygen levels are also responsible for large bug hatches and this gives both forage fish and smallmouth an excellent forage base and enhances the food cycle.

Once the water cools down in the fall, concentrate on the areas that offer a more stable environment such as pools and deep eddies.

Another key factor that affects the smallmouth is the *amount of light that penetrates the water*; the Delaware offers many different ways of coping with this. Ripples which defuse the light, deep water, shadows from mountains, fog, etc. can have a direct effect on the smallmouth fishing, both in the amount of fish you catch and how you go about it.

Shadows cast onto the river by the mountains through which it flows cause the fishing to last longer in the morning and start earlier in the afternoon, thus giving the angler more time to take the feeding smallmouth.

Another way shadows can help you is if you fish the shady side of bridge pilings, rocks and other obstructions. The bass hold in these shadows during the day light hours and they are a prime place to fish.

A good sized smallmouth taken on a foggy morning.

One of the best ways of coping with the effects of light penetration is to fish on **overcast days**, because once the bass begin to feed on a cloudy day, they will often feed throughout the day and do so close to the surface, making them easy to get. They aren't as spooky and you don't have to worry about casting shadows on the water. Keep in mind that overcast days serve you best during the warm water season when the effects of the sun are not so desirable.

Another weather related condition that increases your chances of taking good numbers of smallmouth is the *fog* that is common on the river during certain weather changes and is most common during the changing seasons when the difference between the water and air temperatures are more distinctive.

There are two scenarios that are conducive to fog. The first is in the spring when the water temperature is cooler than the air. The second is when water temps are warmer than the air in the fall. Fog occurring during the early fall is usually more productive than that which occurs in the spring.

As with overcast conditions, fog causes smallies to feed closer to the surface and be less spooky. As the sun breaks through they begin to move into deeper water or under cover, so you will have to change the way you fish.

If the water is warm enough to support lure fishing, surface and shallow working lures will be your top choices. Since much of the fog occurs when conditions are prime for live-bait fishing, live-lining will work well.

Water color is one element that can change very quickly and you should think of it on a weather related basis, in relation to the amount of rain fall and how quickly it falls, along with current water levels.

During the summer, local rain fall can cause small streams to rise and get muddy. This water flows into the river and creates a muddy water breakline, carrying all types of forage with it. Bass stack up in the color change where the clear water meets the dirty water and pick up the forage as it passes by.

When the entire river is dirty, the first places that clear up are the small streams that flow into it. This is the reverse scenario and smallies move into this clear water for the better oxygen levels and forage they hold. Some of the biggest smallmouth are taken from the river as it starts clearing up after a dirty water period; when the water starts to turn green in color, visibility starts to improve and the bass begin to feed more. In gin clear water, big smallies tend to roam much less, and the clearer the water gets, the more spooky they become.

The Delaware goes through long periods when the water is *gin clear* and this usually goes hand in hand with low water conditions. This is when anglers must use extra caution when wading and using a boat and learn to take advantage of the opportunities that a river offers to allow him to cope with these conditions. *(See Light Penetration section of this chapter.)*

A smallmouth taken from gin clear water during the summer.

Whenever possible, camouflage the bottom of your boat to cut down on any glare when the water is extremely clear. If you are wading, wear dark colors and camouflage patterns, as they don't stand out as much as brighter colors. No matter how you fish, keep from making fast or sharp movements, as they are more visible when the water is clear.

A simple rule to follow when smallies are found in **high water conditions** is to fish structures that offer them a place to get out of the river's swifter currents. Smallies move in along shorelines and stay out of the river's main current and this makes for some easy fishing during high water.

How high water levels affect smallmouth fishing can be influenced by when they occur. As an example, if you have had low water conditions throughout the summer and into the fall, a heavy rain can raise water levels, changing water temperatures too quickly, turning off the smallies. Simply put, drastic differences between the temperature of the rain and the temperature of the river can have adverse effects on the smallmouth fishing.

Under low water conditions, smallmouth tend to spread out more, relate to a wider variety of structures, roam more and chase lures and bait much further. Low water conditions allow water temps to go higher since the sun has less water to warm up. This pushes the bass into areas of decreased light and high oxygen and greatly enhances surface fishing because the lures are more visible and closer to the fish.

FORAGE

The diet of the smallmouth found in the river is very diverse. Most forage in a river is on the small side and smallmouth feed similar to the way trout feed in a stream, feeding on numerous small pieces of forage instead of one or two large pieces as a muskie would.

The *seasonal forage* population is made up of the small shad and herring fry that are born in the river each year. From mid July and into the fall they are a major part of the smallmouth's diet.

After a good rain, ***terrestrial forage*** such as worms, grubs and hellgrammites wash into the river from the numerous streams that flow into it. The Delaware also has massive insect hatches during certain times of the year. As a result, insects will be a large part of the smallie's diet during the warm water season.

FISH THE SHADOWS

The Delaware is a hard, rock base river that flows through mountains and hills which cast their shadows on the river and it's structures. These shadows have a direct effect on the fish's movements.

Structures with shadows on them in the morning have fish movements that last later into the morning, while those with shadows on them in the afternoon have fish movements which begin earlier. You should choose the structures you fish accordingly to put the odds in your favor.

One tip to fishing structures with shadows has to do with the color of the fish that you catch. Smallmouth change color; when found in shallow water they are pale and when found in deeper water or under cover they will be dark in color. If you take a bass that is dark in color from a shallow structure, chances are he has just moved there from deep water or out from under cover, and there will usually be more bass moving on that structure. The reverse is true if you catch a pale color fish in deeper water.

TOP STRUCTURES FOR DELAWARE SMALLMOUTH

Flats   Flats are the most exciting places to fish for smallmouth, since there is nothing more spectacular than a bronzeback taken in shallow water as he goes airborne in an effort to throw the hook. Smallies hooked in only a few inches of water, whether on a surface lure, other lure or even live bait, will explode out of the water. There is simply no place for them to go.

Smallmouth found on the flats are there to feed and certain times of the day will be more productive. Water temperature plays an important part in the fishing on the flats and will govern your choice of a productive flat. *(See section on Flats in Chapter 3.)*

Flats are typical evolving structures during the summer. As such, start fishing them in close with surface lures prior to sun up. Once the sun gets on the water switch to swimming plugs and spinnerbaits in slightly deeper water. During the mid day hours, fish the deep waters found around them with jig/rubberbait combinations. Likewise, a fly fisherman can have a ball using streamers, popping bugs and dry flies. Live-lining minnows is a good way to fish them during the early fall when the bass are feeding on the shad fry that are found there.

Points of Land   The first place to look for smallies on a point of land is the upstream pocket, which is a good bet in the early morning and afternoon. During the

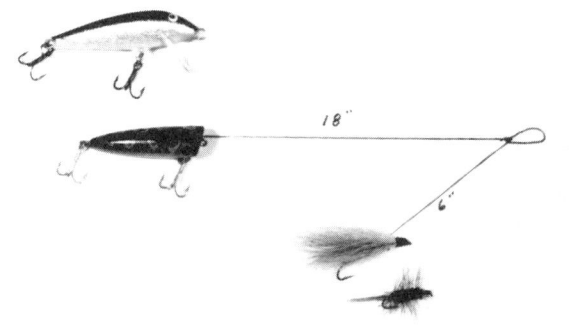

summer, small surface lures, swimming plugs and crankbaits will produce best. Live-lining and jigging minnows and other live bait is best during the early fall. Smallies frequent this pocket because the current sweeps forage into it as it moves along the shoreline.

Plug/teaser combination is a good bet during the morning hours on shallow structures.

When low water conditions are present, fish will be found along where the current line that sweeps around the point comes into contact with the dead water pocket. This is where the fish will be holding, waiting for a meal to come their way. It is also a good place to look during the mid day hours.

The most productive time to fish a point of land is when the water is high. High water forces the bass to school up in the dead water pocket in order to get away from the rivers swifter currents. These concentrations are usually easy pickings for jig fishermen. During the warm water season, jig/rubberbait combinations will work best. On the other hand, jig/live bait combinations are tops for the cold water season.

Bridge Pilings   Bridge pilings are classic two current line eddy structures, and the amount of eddies, their size and the swiftness of the currents that flow around them will vary with each bridge.

Many bridge pilings have upstream pockets at the head of the piling. This is another prime spot, as smallmouth gather there feeding on insects and the baitfish that feed on them.

Finger Structures   They are some of the best places to wade along the river.

Single Finger Structures have one set of eddies located below the rock ledge. *Multiple Finger Structures*, on the other hand, have numerous eddies and current lines located below them. Both will have an upstream pocket, a sluice or several breaks in the rock pile where the water flows through them.

Multiple-finger structure.

Summer low water periods will find the bass close to the surface during the early morning and afternoons. The upstream water of a finger structure is very similar to that on a wing dam and is best worked with surface lures and swimming plugs.

Bass found in the eddy below a finger will move from the bottom of the eddy to the top during low light periods to feed on insect life and other forage that is washed through the breaks in the finger.

During the summer, smallies migrate into the eddy portion during the mid day hours for the better oxygen contents and the diminished light penetration they possess. Digging them out with jig/rubberbait combinations and deep running crankbaits will be the way to go.

Under high water conditions, the majority of the smallies will school up in the eddies found along the shoreline close to the finger. When the waters are warm, fish jig/rubberbait combinations, swimming plugs and crankbaits; when the water is cold, jig minnow combinations will work best.

One of the top ways of fishing finger structures during the late season is to concentrate on the deeper eddies that have slower currents. These eddies will hold water temperatures longer and be more stable later in the year.

Tributary Streams   Most smaller streams have silt bars or deltas at their confluence with the main river and this bar is a prime feeding area.

During the low water in the summer months, the bar gives you some early morning and late afternoon action, since water from the smaller stream is usually cooler and better oxygenated than the main river, making the fish found here more active. Surface lures, spinnerbaits and swimming plugs are the top choices here.

Muddy Water Break lines   These are a product of high water conditions that can give you some big numbers of smallies. Bass stack up along the water coming from a small stream after a rain to feed on forage being washed into the river. When the river is dirty after rainy periods these streams will clean up quickest and the bass will migrate there for the cleaner, better oxygenated water and abundant forage. In either case they are prime spots to fish. Jig/rubberbait combinations, crankbaits and small spinner baits will work when the water is warm, and live-lining or jigging is best when the water is cold.   Because the Delaware has so many small streams flowing into it, heavy rains along an individual stream can result in the river being dirty from that point down. A good look at the current weather map or a call to some tackle shops can often tell you if the water will be cleaner upstream. In many cases you will be able to fish a river by fishing above where the dirty water comes in.

Drop-Offs   The majority of the drop-offs on the river are situated on river bends and can hold some of the deepest water in any specific section of river. They are not as productive when high water is present because of the swift currents that accompany high water periods. The key to fishing them is to find some type of object or secondary structure along them. A good sized rock, log, fallen tree or other object located along the drop-off will block the current and cause an eddy to form. Smallies lay behind these objects and grab forage as the current carries it downstream and then dart back to their haunts.

How you fish a drop-off is governed by how deep it is and how swift the current is. If the drop-off is of considerable depth and the current is moderate, trolling deep running plugs makes a good choice. You can also fish a drop-off by slow drifting it, casting jig/rubber bait combinations, jig/live bait combinations and crankbaits.

Wing Dams   Wing dams are not like dams used to back up water into a reservoir.

Instead of a fast sloping dam face, they have a gradual sloping side up river that provides some good surface fishing on early summer mornings. The bass can be found there, picking up small baitfish and insects as they are pushed over the dam.

Rising water levels will drastically change wing dams and the position of the smallmouth. Swifter currents will force the smallies up close to the shoreline or further downstream from the dam. Fish any slow water areas such as eddies, pockets or coves that may have formed as a result of the higher water.

There are numerous smaller dams found on the tributary streams that flow into the river. The spillways located below these dams make great places to fish during high water periods. As the river rises, the waters will back up into the tributary streams as far as the dam. Smallies seeking refuge from the faster currents will feed on the forage that is washed over the dam.

During the fall, the returning shad and herring fry move in and out of these places, giving the smallies some excellent forage on which to feed. These areas are some of the first to warm up in the spring and some of the first to cool down in the fall. In both cases, the dam spillways become the first places that the water temperatures will reach the preferred ranges of the smallmouth.

Islands   There are two basic types of islands found on the river. The first is an island located on a straight stretch of river and the second type is one that is located on a river bend. Both types of islands are typical evolving structures. Their bars, upstream flats and other shallow areas will produce some excellent surface fishing during the early morning and late afternoons during the warm water season.

During the cold water season, the downstream deep water pockets that are located below islands located on a river bend will provide anglers with some of the better live bait fishing. Smallies will gather there to winter over.

Rising water can drastically change smallmouth positions on both types of islands. The bass will usually move into any quiet eddies found below the island or along any secondary structures found adjacent to the island. In many cases the secondary structures found around an island will make or break the smallmouth fishing found there. *(See Islands section of Chapter 3.)*

TACKLE

Ultralight tackle is preferred for smallmouth.

Rods & Reels

Ultralight and light action spinning tackle are preferred for smallmouth on the river. Ultralight rods in the five and a half to six and a half foot lengths are best suited for surface lures such as poppers, darters and propeller plugs. Small buzzbaits will require a slightly stiffer rod and the preferable lengths are between five and six feet.

For swimming plugs and crankbaits, five to five and a half foot ultralights will give you better control in small eddies and along current lines. The same is true of small spinnerbaits, spinners and jig/rubber bait combinations.

When using live bait, light action rods in the five to six and a half foot range will give you better hook setting power. Choose full length action rods because they are easier on the bait when casting and give you better distance and control.

For fly fishing, three to five weight rod and reel outfits will give you the best results. The fly lines that you use will be determined by the type of flies or poppers you will be using, and carrying several spare spools filled with different type lines will serve you well.

Reel Suggestions

Penn - 716Z, 4200, 4300
Daiwa - UL 7, EL 705
Zebco - Micro Spinn

Shakespeare - 2500ULX, RT825, RT725
Quantum - SS1 UL, LS1, SE2, EX2
ABU Garcia - Pro UL, GMUL

Line

Four and six pound test are the most commonly used line weights, although some anglers go as low as two pound test to get better distances.

Line Suggestions: Triline XL in 2,4,6 pound tests Tri-Max in 4 & 6 pound tests

Some of the top smallmouth lures used on the river.

Lures

Surface Lures

Popping Plugs
Trouble maker (Gudebrod)
Pop "R" (Rebel)
Plunker (Creekchub)
Hula Popper (Arbogast)
Chugger Spook (Heddon)

Darting Plugs
Blabber Mouth (Gudebrod)
Darter (Creekchub)
Zara Spook (Heddon)

Constant Motion Plugs
Lucky 13 (Heddon)
Sinner Spinner (Gudebrod)
Zara Spook Pooch (Heddon)

Buzzbaits
Triple wing Buzz Baits 1/4 ounce
(Strike King)

104

Jitterbug (Arbogast)

Swimming Plugs

Floating
Rapala Minnow (Rapala)
Rebel Minnow (Rebel)
Long "A" (Bomber)
Flatfish (Heddon)

Sinking
Countdown (Rapala)
Sinking Rebel Minnow (Rebel)

Crankbaits

Shallow Running
Fat Rap (Rapala)
Model"A" (Bomber)
Fastrac Wee "R" (Rebel)
Crawfish (Rebel)
Balsa "B" (Bagley's)

Deep Running
Shad Rap (Rapala)
Deep Fat Rap (Rapala)
Deep Wee "R" (Rebel)
Balsa Deep "B" (Bagley's)
Deep Teeny Wee Crayfish (Rebel)

Rattle Plugs
Rattl'n Rap (Rapala)
Rat-L-Trap (Bill Lewis)
Spot (Cordells)

Spoons
Kastmaster, Phoebe (Acme)
Syclops (Mepps)
Slab Spoon (Bomber)
Dardevle

Spinners
Aglia, Elix, Back Fury, Comet (Mepps)
Rooster Tail
Panther Martin
Vibrax (Blue Fox)
Diamond Back (Cabela's)
CP Swing
Swiss Swing.

Spinnerbaits
Little George (Mann's)
Twister Spin (Mr.Twister)
Road Runner (Blakemore)
Horse-Fly (Cabela's)
Beetle Spin.

Jig/Rubberbait

Twister Tail, Sassy Shad, Sassy Shiner, Split Tail Teeny, Can'n Dad (Mr. Twister) Foxy Jig, Vibro Tail (Blue Fox) Hellgrammite, Cricket, Catalpa Worm (Burke)

Live Bait

Aquatic: Killies, fatheads (natural & golden), shiners, dace, crayfish, leaches, tadpoles

Terrestrial: Hellgrammites, reed worms, garden worms, night crawlers, grubs, toads and frogs, crickets

Pork Baits: #CL42 Pork Grub, #32 Crawdad

Hooks

Light wire shank preferred in Sizes #8 through #1 (Mustdad- Long shank # 37360, Short Shank #3892B) (Eagle Claw- Long Shank # 214; Short Shank-#72)

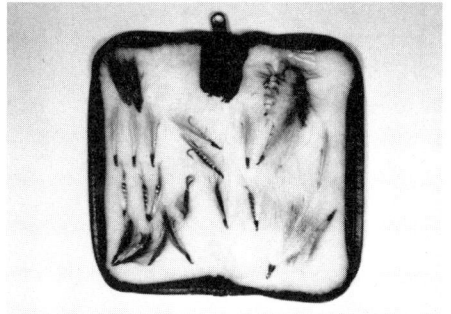

Rubberbaits used for smallmouth.   *Typical streamer flies used on the river.*

CHAPTER 9: STRIPED BASS

THE STATISTICAL FACTS ON THE DELAWARE STRIPERS

The resurgence of the striped bass population in the Delaware river has been a blessing for anglers who live in or in close proximity to the Delaware Valley. It has also spun the wheels of the rumor mill as to the number of fish, the number of fishermen catching them and the health of the striper population in the river. Here's the plain facts as compiled by myself in a log that I have kept for some thirty plus years and studies done by the states of New Jersey and Pennsylvania. Of the three states which border the river, the state of New Jersey has done the most research and has

Author with a striper taken while surface fishing.

amassed a significant amount of statistics. For several years I supplied statistical information and scale samples for some of the work that was done in New Jersey.

Striped bass are not the only migratory fish calling the Delaware river home. Shad and herring are the others, and the resurgence in these two species are closely related to the increase in the stripers. If you look at studies done on the shad population, you will quickly realize that it wasn't long after the pollution began to abate that these fish began increasing. Both are a major part of the striper's forage base, herring in the spring and small shad in the summer and fall. By the mid 80's, shad and herring stocks started exploding, and the striper population began to climb as well, and it doesn't take a rocket scientist to see the relationship between the two.

I would like to dispel a rumor that has begun to surface with regard to the relationship between stripers and shad. Some so-called experts say the striper population is depleting or will deplete the shad population. It's obvious that these people don't understand the food chain in the river. The bulk of the forage in the tide water river is made up of herring during the summer and early fall. In the fall the stripers feed on the shad fry as they move down river. Both fish are very prolific and millions are born in the river every year. The stripers have been feeding on them since the beginning of time and this is the natural way of things. The decline of the shad and herring in the river during the 50's was due to pollution, not the predatory nature of fish such as striped bass. In fact, biologists believe that it is the sign of a healthy river when the predator population grows in proportion to the forage base.

To sum up the point we are trying to make, every predator in the river feeds on small shad and herring. Stripers naturally feed on shad and herring as part of their life cycle and the river is better off for it.

Another myth is that the stripers are eating the smallmouth. One look at the recent explosion of smallmouth in the river, (the smallmouth have had six record years out of the last seven starting in 1986) and you can see that this isn't so.

Stripers have also been blamed for the decreases in walleye and muskie stocks as well. The PA Fish Commission has halted the stocking of these fish in the lower river because they believe stripers are eating the young fish after they are stocked. I find fault with this on three counts. First, the Commission stocks the fish in the spring and summer when the river is full of stripers. It makes better sense to stock these fish in the fall when stripers are not as numerous. Second, they put the young fish in the main river at a time when the striper population is at it's high. A better choice is to stock them in coves and back water areas so they can have time to settle in to the river. Finally, with all the soft finned forage in the river, which is preferred by stripers, why would they eat a spiny finned walleye?

Migratory stripers make up 70% of the rivers population. The difference is made up by a combination of 25% to 27% native fish which spawn and live it's entire life in the river and a 3% to 5% hybrid population which have gotten into the river from streams which flow from lakes that are stocked by both PA and Jersey. These stats are based on logged catches over the past seven years.

Another fact that points to a healthy, growing striper fishery is the male to female ratio. Of the fish that where sampled in the springs between 1986 and 1988, the ratio of female to male fish is decreasing. (1986: female 85.6% to male 14.2%; 1987: female 83.2% to male 16.8%; 1988: female 79% to male 21%) The general consensus among biologists is that since male fish take a shorter time to mature, they are more likely to stay in the river system longer than the female.

In 1980 New Jersey began it's yearly Young of the Year index. This was done to get an idea of the numbers of stripers in the river and in an effort to determine if stripers in the river were a separate strain of bass unique to the river. Biologists at that time believed that stripers migrated up the river from the Hudson or Chesapeake stocks which migrate along the Atlantic coast. Serious river fishermen who spent a good number of years on the river disputed this and the latter's beliefs proved to be true. Let's face it, a two inch fish doesn't migrate from either of the two afore mentioned places. These small fish that were being taken by bottom fishermen and in bait traps were obviously born in the river.

Once data from the Young of the Year index began to pile up, this theory began to assert itself. In the mid 80's, a scale collecting program was started to add to the data base. A number of seasoned anglers who fish the river regularly were asked to collect scale samples from the stripers they caught, and a huge bank of data was built up. Identifying one strain over another is a very difficult task and requires complex and expensive DNA studies. Studying scale samples, although not as accurate, can be used to determine many things about the fish and was used to help reinforce the separate strain hypothesis.

The Young of the Year index is complied by biologists through sample netting, which is done in the same areas year after year. When you look at a chart and see a 1.05 figure, this means that an average of 1.05 stripers were taken on each haul of the net during the corresponding year. The index was started in 1980 with an average of .07 and slipped to an all time low of 0 in 1981. Beginning in 1986, the Young of the Year index began a climb, and according to biologists that I have spoken with it hasn't peaked yet. There have been some ups and downs over the years and these can be attributed to the different weather and water conditions. The Young of the Year index for 1992 has been put at 3.83, which will be a new record, far above any previous year.

The fishing log I have kept since 1962 coincides very closely with the Young of the Year index which is kept by the biologists. In fact, if you were to graph both you can see how closely they match up.

Statistically, the striper stock is better than 300% larger than it was in 1980. In the last 5 years, it is almost 8 times what it was in 1988. The year 1992 was the highest Young of the Year index ever recorded and there is no reason for this trend not to continue.

The largest numbers of stripers are found in the tidal river, however, good numbers of striped bass travel as far up river as the Phillipsburg/Easton area. Smaller numbers of fish have been taken as far upstream as Port Jervis and into New York.

Hybrid striper.

These catches have been increasing each year and there are plans to extend scale samplings north of Scudders Falls. Pennsylvania started taking Young of the Year samples in the non-tidal river in 1993.

The outlook for the striper fishery in the Delaware is excellent. Unless a drastic change in the river's general water quality occurs or weather and water conditions cause several back to back years of poor spawns, striped bass will become an even larger part of the river's fishery in years to come.

KEY FACTORS

Water Temperature Of the key factors that affect striper fishing, water temperatures is at the top of the list. It triggers migratory and spawning instincts and controls the type of structures they frequent, how fast they move up river, whether or not they feed on the surface and more. Stripers winter over in the river, the bay and the many tributary streams. When the water temps are in the 40's, stripers begin moving up river to spawn. Spawning temperatures are between 55 and 67 degrees in the river. Most of the fish taken when the water temps are in the 40's are caught on live bait.

When the water is in the high 40's to low 50's, stripers begin taking jig combos, such as jigs dressed with Twister Tails, Sassy Shads, plastic eels, etc. Once water temps begin to rise into the high 50's to low 60's, trolling swimming plugs will pay off, both as a way to find the fish and as a method of taking them. The high 60's and into the 70's will find the fish beginning to chase surface plugs and readily taking swimming plugs. When water temps are above the mid 70's, surface plugs will pay off in shallow areas during the dark and just after day break. Trolling both shallow and deep diving plugs is a good bet along channel edges and over deeper flats.

THE TIDES & MOON PHASES

Striped bass are not only creatures of their environment but creatures of habit as well. In both cases tides play an important part in their movements on a daily and seasonal basis. The effect tides have on striper movements are influenced by external factors such as water temperature and moon phases, and knowing how to come up with the right equation can mean the difference between taking and not taking fish.

Stripers like rough water even when found in the ocean. A good example is the good fishing that is found in the rips along a beach and in inlets where the currents are very swift. The same is true of Delaware river stripers. Since full and new moons exert the most force on the river's tidal flow, this is when the fishing will be best.

One structure where tides have a definite effect on the fishing are bridge pilings. Stripers hold up behind bridge pilings, retreating from the river's main current, especially when high water conditions are present. Bridge pilings located in the tidal river have their eddies shifted with each change of the tide. On the incoming tide stripers are found on the upstream side, because this is where the eddy will be located. On the outgoing tide, the reverse is true.

One place where tides make a big difference is in the Trenton area where the tides end. This is a rocky, swift moving section where knowing how the tides move and when they occur not only helps you with the fishing but it can save you some peril and grief as well. When fishing from a boat you can follow the incoming tide into the waters above the bridges; once the tide starts to turn you have to know when to get out or you will be faced with running swift moving water through treacherous rocks or sitting above the tidal drop until the tides once again come in.

You can also wade into the river in this area with the outgoing tide. The drawn out tide creates some excellent eddy and white water fishing. Once the tide starts coming in you will have to know when and where to start moving towards the shore. More than one angler has become trapped on the rocks after having failed to pay attention to the tide.

Tides in this area are also affected by the water levels in the non-tidal river. High tides that fall on the full and new moons will, under normal water levels, be about a foot above normal. On high water years the tides can be as much as three to four feet above normal during the new and full moon phases.

Another thing worth mentioning about tides in this area is their speed. Under normal summer conditions the waters of the river move at a 6 to 8 mile an hour clip. In the Trenton area, this normal flow rate is increased by 3 to 5 miles an hour with the outgoing tide under normal water conditions. This can be greatly increased when there is a lot of water coming from the non-tidal river on a full or new moon period.

Water Levels   The next factor that the angler must consider is water levels. Although these do not affect the tidal river directly, they can be the underlying cause that will affect fish movements. Heavy amounts of water pouring in from feeder streams can change the oxygen levels, Ph factors and water color. Often when the non-tidal river is dirty from heavy rains there is a block of clean water that will move back and forth with the tides. This will give the striper fisherman good water to fish when other areas are unfishable. In the non-tidal river high water conditions will affect the position of the stripers and how you fish for them.

Water Color   This is another key factor and, surprisingly enough, stripers have a tolerance for muddy water, especially in the tidal portions. Water color is affected by rain fall each year, and as we mentioned earlier dirty water pouring in from the tributary streams will form a clean water block which is very productive. Trolling plugs with rattles in them is a good way of coping with the off color water.

When the water is super clear, the stripers will be less spooky when the water is cool. Once the water warms up the stripers will get real spooky in clear water and your best bet is to fish during the dark of the night. Stripers are well know as nocturnal feeders, and when the water is warm and clear most major movements occur in the dark in the river.

TOP BAITS

When it's dinner time for these members of the bass family, they are linesided killers. Size is not a real concern, as they will readily attack other forage fish as big as they are. They do, however, have some preferences when it comes to dinner time.

Herring   The most important forage fish in the Delaware river is the herring. The abundance of herring and shad has contributed significantly to the striper explosion. The migration of the stripers up river is closely tied to that of the herring. They are also the key to many of the structures on the lower river; if herring are present the stripers will also be there. During April and the first part of May they make excellent bait for the stripers which feed on the schools of spawning herring.

When it comes to rigging herring, there are several ways you can fish them. The first way is to liveline them by snelling a hook directly to your line and hooking the

herring through the back just below the top fin. You can jig them by snelling a length of leader and a hook to a jig and then placing the jig hook through the head of the herring and the second hook in the tail. You can cast and retrieve herring once the liveliness has left them by using a double hook rig made from two hooks snelled to a length of leader and hooking the back hook in the tail and the top hook in the head of the herring. It is also possible to troll herring by rigging it on a diamond jig or spoon.

Herring make excellent bait for striper and muskie.

Blood Worms   Blood worms are one of the most popular baits for stripers and are sold by many tackle shops along the river, ranging in price from a couple of dollars a dozen to as much as $60 a flat. The most common way of fishing them is on a standard fish finder rig. In recent years, however, many anglers have taken a page out of the walleye fisherman's book and fish them with Lindy rigs and floating jig heads. You can also use them as dressing on a jig, which has become very popular with light tackle fishermen. The one draw back when it comes to using blood worms is that they often catch more junk fish than they do stripers.

Eels   Eels are another popular bait for linesiders, and some of the bigger bass taken each year are the victims of live or rigged eels. You can trap your own eels by placing funnel traps in a tidal stream baited with chicken necks. Many river bait shops carry eels, however, they carry a good price tag. The one good thing about them is that they are very durable. Most anglers liveline them while they are fresh and after they are done using them, rig and freeze them for later use. As with herring they can be rigged in combination with jig heads for jigging and with diamond jigs and spoons for casting and trolling. The best lengths are between six and fifteen inches.

Killies   One of the most over looked baits is the killie. He is native to the river and is a forage fish for the stripers. During early spring they make excellent baits for the light tackle fisherman. Killies can be livelined or used as a dressing on a jig. They are best worked in and around the mouths of feeder streams and warm water discharges.

Cut Baits   All types of cut baits are commonly used for stripers. Chicken livers, cut herring and shad, as well shrimp, are a few of the more popular baits. Most of these baits are used by catfishermen and because of the large numbers of stripers in the river many catfishermen began catching stripers while fishing for cats. This has led to the use of these baits for stripers.

Although livebait is excellent for stripers, it does have several drawbacks. Of all the tools the angler uses, it is probably the most damaging to the fish, especially during the warm water season. Stripers are very fragile when they are found in fresh water. They are a hard fighting fish and loose valuable body salts and enzymes when hooked in fresh water. Stripers will often get gut hooked and even when they are released they will die because of damage done by the deep hook. Mortality in larger fish is especially high. Live herring and eels are two of the most damaging baits used and it's for this reason many veteran river fishermen would like to see them banned. If you choose to use live bait cut your line and leave the hook in a gut hooked fish; the price of a hook is not worth the life of a trophy fish at a later time.

TOP LURES

Stripers are creatures of their environment, and water conditions and other external factors will dictate what lures will produce and when to use them. Delaware stripers offer anglers a chance to use just about every lure in his tackle box, however, certain lures have proven themselves to be deadly for Big "D" linesiders.

Surface Lures   Once the water jumps above 70 degrees, the stripers will start chasing surface lures in shallows and flats in the tidal areas. There are three main surface lures that allow you to cover the different types of shallow water. On slow moving tidal flats, popping plugs such as the Striper Swiper, Adams, Pencil Popper, etc. and darting plugs such as the Wood Eye, Jumping Stick, Zara Spook, etc. will serve you best. Casting and retrieving them back with an erratic motion (walking the dog) is the best way of using them.

Swimming Plugs   These are perhaps the most versatile of all lures. You can cast them, troll them and even use them as a surface plug. There are some, however, that work better than others when you fish in a river's current. Of the swimming plugs that are on the market, the Bomber Long "A" and the Red Fin are the best. Both lures will run true in a current and each has plenty of wobbling action on their own, which makes them ideal for trolling. When casting them in a current it's always best to retrieve them with a stop and go motion. This causes them to dive deeper and run truer than if you retrieve them with a steady retrieve.

Deep Diving Plugs   This one area where your choice in lures can really make a difference in the number of fish you take. Most of the time you will be trolling this type of plug instead of casting it. The plug you choose will have to have a good natural action and be one that allows you to feel the it's vibrations. Feeling the plugs vibrations is very important while trolling, as it will allow you to adjust your boat's speed by how fast or slow the plug is vibrating. Of all the plugs on the market, the best is the Rebel Spoonbill and Deep Red Fin. These lures have excellent vibrating motions and run true at fast speeds.

Crankbaits   Of the wide variety of crankbaits that are available, the Shad Rap, Rattle Trap and Rattle-N-Rap are the most commonly used. Keep them on the large side. the best colors are the black and silver, and blue and silver; these most closely imitate the herring.

Spoons   Many anglers are now trolling spoons with good success for suspended stripers. They are also a good jigging tool when stripers are suspended and stacked up in the late summer and early fall. The most popular are the Kastmaster, Hopkins and Silver Daredevil.

Jigs and Rubberbaits   There are several jig/rubberbait combinations that are very popular in the river. The first of these is the jig/twister combination in four to six inch lengths and jig sizes ranging between 1/4 and 1 ounce. Although many anglers prefer painted jigs, most catch as many fish with unpainted ones. The same holds true for jigs dressed with bucktail. Having used all different combinations I have found them all to work equally well as long as they are used at the right time and place. When it comes to the best colors, white and yellow are the two top colors, with chartreuse a close second.

Another dressing used with jig heads are minnow imitations such as the Sassy Shad and Sassy Shiner. They make excellent choices for jigging behind bridge pilings and places where you need good depth and speed control. When it comes to color, natural colors, mainly black and white or silver, which closely imitates small shad and herring are best.

Rigged Plastic Eels   They make an excellent choices for casting and trolling. Two of the best and most durable are produced by J.T. and Banker's Fishing Specialties.

STRUCTURES

Islands   Islands found in the tidal river all have the same basic characteristics, however, each has some minor details that give them their own identity. Names like Tinicum, Burlington, Chester island, etc. are well know to the striper fisherman.

If you are not familiar with an island, the best way to locate stripers is by trolling. Normal depths around the islands can range between 0 and 20 feet when the tide is high, and incoming tides are usually the most productive. This is because shallow areas that are devoid of water during low tide will come alive with baitfish as the tide come in.

In many instances the stripers will be found on the down side of the island with the outgoing tide and on the upriver side with the incoming tide. Water temperature comes into play here and you will find that water in the mid 70's or above can put the stripers on the surface feed. When water temps are between 55 and 70 degrees, trolling swimming plugs is best; below that point jig/combinations and live bait will be most productive.

Bridge Pilings   Bridge pilings, even on the same bridge, can be very different from each other. Their position in relation to the channel and shallow water will often determine their productivity. Some bridges have pilings, located on a side that is shallower than the other.

This is usually productive as the stripers will hold in the slack water behind the deeper pilings when the tide is low and then move into the shallower water with the incoming tide to feed.

The basic tools used to fish these waters are jig combinations and live bait. In many cases the waters swirling around the pilings will be swift and the tools we mentioned give you the speed and depth control to get

Striper taken from a bridge piling on the incoming tide.

your bait to the stripers.

Stream Confluences   These come in various sizes, ranging from the confluence of the Schuylkill to such small streams as Pennypacker and Rancocas creek. The main place to fish is the bar or delta located at the mouth of these streams and they will be best on the incoming tide. With the exception of the confluence of the Schuylkill, which has been dredged over the years, the bars will be very shallow and have a deeper side along them. This deeper side is a good place to fish jig combinations with the outgoing tide, as the swirling water will trap baitfish.

Underwater Bars and Humps   The Delaware river has a well defined channel. One of the top spots for the deep water fisherman is along the under water humps and bars that offer the stripers a contour change in the norm of the bottom. In some cases these will be silt bars that have built up because of some twist in the current that deposited silt in a specific section. In other cases, and the more productive of the two, these humps will be rocky lumps along the bottom where the current keeps silt from forming over the rocks.

The depth of the water we are talking about will be the determining factor on how we fish them. If these structures are in deep water, say 15 feet or more, trolling is the way to find the stripers and a good sonar unit and the skills to work it properly are a big plus in this type of fishing. Once you have pinpointed the depth at which the fish are holding you can choose the proper lure to get down to the fish. In most cases the stripers will be suspended in these areas, making vertical jigging a top way of fishing.

If these bars or humps are positioned in shallower water, there is a good chance that you can cast swimming and diving plugs to the fish with the outgoing tide. Vibrating plugs such as Rattle Traps and their many variations are a favorite tool for this type of fishing. The shallower bars and humps are excellent for live-lining with eels and herring.

Pilings and Buoys   Compared to the other structures we covered, they are not as productive most of the time. This does not mean that they should be over looked, as they can be very productive on occasion.

Striper taken from a bar on a swimming plug.

Dock pilings found on the main river will usually hold school stripers and small fish. The closer these pilings come to the channel, the more productive they will be. They are prime targets for the bottom fisherman using live bait, and some anglers have had success fishing jig combinations.

When it comes to buoys, each buoy is anchored with a huge anchor and chain. This anchor is often the only break in the uniform contour of the bottom and thus is a gathering point for stripers. Because they are located in deep water, it is easier to check them out with a sonar unit to see if any fish are close to them. Trolling deep running plugs, fishing live bait rigs along the bottom and jigging are the best methods for the stripers found here.

Tidal Flats   If I had to pick one structure that I considered to be the most productive and my personal favorite, it would have to be a tidal flat. It's a basic tenet that stripers spend most of their time in deeper water and feed in shallow water and this is the reason flats are so productive.

A flat is a shallow water area, sort of a dinner table for the stripers. In the Delaware they serve up large helpings of herring, killies and other forage thus meeting one of the basic needs of the stripers, FOOD.

First let's take a look at where we find productive flats. Most islands have at least an upstream flat. No matter whether they are found in the tidal or non tidal river they will be productive. As the current pushes water over the flat it carries with it insects which the forage fish feed on, thus good the forage fish will attract the striped bass. Flats are also spawning places for herring and this is a definite plus. Since stripers follow the herring to feed, flats are a gathering place for them.

The moving tide will always be more productive than slack water and since flats are shallow water areas, they are only productive for certain portions of the tide. Since there is no way of telling just when a flat will become active because of the external influences exerted on them, a well kept log is a valuable tool isolating seasonal patterns on each of them.

During the warm water season flats can be more productive after dark. One way to determine this is by taking the moon phases and tides into consideration. If the tide is incoming on a good portion of the lunar cycle during the dark hours, then the fishing will be better after dark, as long as the water temperatures are reasonably warm.

The size of the flat has a very definite influence on how you fish it. On large flats, flat line trolling will be a prime method with shallow and deep running swimming plugs as well as spoon combinations your principle tools.

When trolling, the amount of line you let out is very important. Your first inclination is not to deploy your plugs too close to the boat because motor noise will spook the stripers. Once you have done enough trolling you will realize that some of your best action comes very close to the boat, in fact right in the prop wash. I have done some experimentation and have found that the fast whine of a motor will spook fish, but the slow gurgling noise of a motor when trolling will actually attract schooling stripers. This is even more pronounced when trolling shallow water.

There are two basic ways of holding your rods while trolling. You can use rod holders or a pod, or you can hand hold them. Over the years, hand holding the rods has proven to be the more productive way, since holding the rods will allow you to feel the vibrations of the plugs which is very important for speed and depth control when flat line trolling.

Stripers found on uniform flats will roam around more than they will when the flat has objects located along it. If the flat is uniform in lay out, trolling consistently, will be the most productive way of fishing. On the other hand, if the flat you are trolling is broken up or has objects located along it, you can troll to find the fish and then stop and cast to take fish holding next to the objects.

In early spring, trolling is not as productive since the stripers are not as active. This is when live bait is a better choice and drifting is the method that you should use to get it to the stripers. On a uniform flat stripers might be scattered, drifting without stopping is the best choice. When fishing flats which have objects along them, drifting until making contact with the bass and then anchoring is a better way to fish.

A simple fish finder or Lindy rig in combination with a floating jig head baited with blood worms are excellent tools for drifting a flat. During the spring and summer season live eels, herring and small white perch make good baits. These traditionally take some of the bigger fish each season.

One last thought on fishing flats. It is not uncommon to see surface feeding stripers when large schools of herring are present and this can mean some fine surface action for short periods of time. So don't overlook the possibility of surface action, especially when the water starts to warm up.

Channels   One place most anglers overlook and one that holds both sizable fish and good numbers of them is the river channel and it's surrounding waters. These areas are complex and difficult to fish but are well worth the effort.

The two main methods of fishing channel edges and the waters around them are trolling and jigging. In many cases a combination of both will be your best bet. (Example: Trolling against the current and jigging while drifting back.)

Electronics   A good graph and water temperature gauge are your basic needs. Most serious deep water fishermen prefer the use of a paper graph because of the better definition they offer as well as the record they provide. A temperature gauge helps you define temperature changes that may affect the fishing and one look at it before starting will give some idea the speed control you will need.

Night Time Stripers   The tide water river, which stretches from the bay to Trenton, is entirely different from the non-tidal river, which goes from Trenton north to it's head waters in New York state. The tide water regions are characterized by deep channels, tidal streams, deep coves and plenty of marsh land. River traffic from pleasure boats, ocean going vessels, tugs and barges, etc. will push the stripers into the deeper regions during the day time. This makes the night time hours the most quiet time on the river and the time when the stripers can roam around freely.

One tip for fishing at night is to use plugs that have a rattle in them and make a noise when retrieved. The noise they produce gives stripers something to home in on. One plug that falls into this category is a Rattle Trap and it's many imitations. These plugs don't make good trolling tools since even when the smallest piece of vegetation, leaf or any other debris gets caught on them they will cease to work right. Swimming plugs are a better choice.

One thing you will find is that dark moonless or overcast nights are some of the best fishing for stripers on the river. Many anglers feel that this is so because when the full moon is up and bright there is too much light on the water. Overcast nights are usually accompanied by low pressure systems and this also causes stripers to move more freely. So many of the more experienced anglers prefer to fish on the darkest of nights.

TACKLE RECOMMENDATIONS

Rods & Reels   If you have fish for stripers on the jetties or in the surf, you'll find that much of the tackle used there can be employed for river stripers. Five to seven foot spinning rods in medium, medium/heavy and heavy actions will allow you to present the larger baits and lures that you need. Since you can use a variety of lures for the stripers, you will find that different types of rods allow you to use certain lures more effectively, so having several rod and reel combinations with you will help you get the most from your lures.

Fishing for stripers requires the use of heavier lines, so choose reels that are capable of handling larger line capacities. Strong gearing, smooth bearings and a smooth drag system are a must for reels used for stripers.

Trolling is a major way of fishing for stripers and the use of conventional tackle is better suited for this purpose. Conventional reels employ a system which puts line rolls on the spool directly. Spinning reels use an offset system to put line on the spool and this will cause plenty of line twist when trolling. If you choose conventional reels for trolling this problem is all but eliminated, making conventional tackle better choice. Here, again, keep the rod actions in the medium, medium/heavy and heavy class.

In recent years, many anglers have taken to using fly tackle for stripers in the river. For this purpose fly rods used for salmon fishing make excellent choices. Fly reels with a drag system are better suited for this type of fishing, since most anglers choose to fight the fish from the reel directly.

Reel Suggestions:

Spinning
Penn - 4200, 4300, 440 & 450SS
Shakespeare - RT835, RT740, RT80
ABU Garcia - GM3, Pro 3
Daiwa - BG13, BG15 & PS2005
Quantum - QG20, QG40 & QG50
Shimano - PSX300Q & PSM-III Q

Conventional
Penn - 920 & 930
Quantum - 381 040 & 040SW
Daiwa - PR33SH
ABU Garcia - 5500C, 4600C &
500XLT
Shimano - B1000II

Rod Suggestions: Spinning: Medium, medium heavy and heavy action in 5 to 8 feet lengths for use with swimming plugs, crankbaits and jig/rubberbait combinations. Surface fishing- medium and medium/heavy rods in 6 and 7 foot lengths. Another good choice for surface plugs are 8 to 9 foot noodle rods. Conventional rods for trolling and vertical fishing in 5 to 7 foot lengths.

Line Suggestions: Trilene XL, XT & Tri-Max in 8, 10 & 12 pound test.

Lures

Surface Lures
Striper Swiper, Atoms Popper,
Zara Spook (Heddon)
Troublemaker, Blabbermouth & Sinner
Spinner (Guidebrod)
Jumping Stick, Boy Howdy (Cordell's)
Pop "R" (Rebel)
Devil Horse (Smithwick)
Large Buzzbaits

Swimming Plugs
Floating Rapala, Count Down (Rapala)
Long "A" (Bomber)
Rebel
Red Fin (Cordell's)
Hellcat (Heddon)
Spitfire (Poe's)

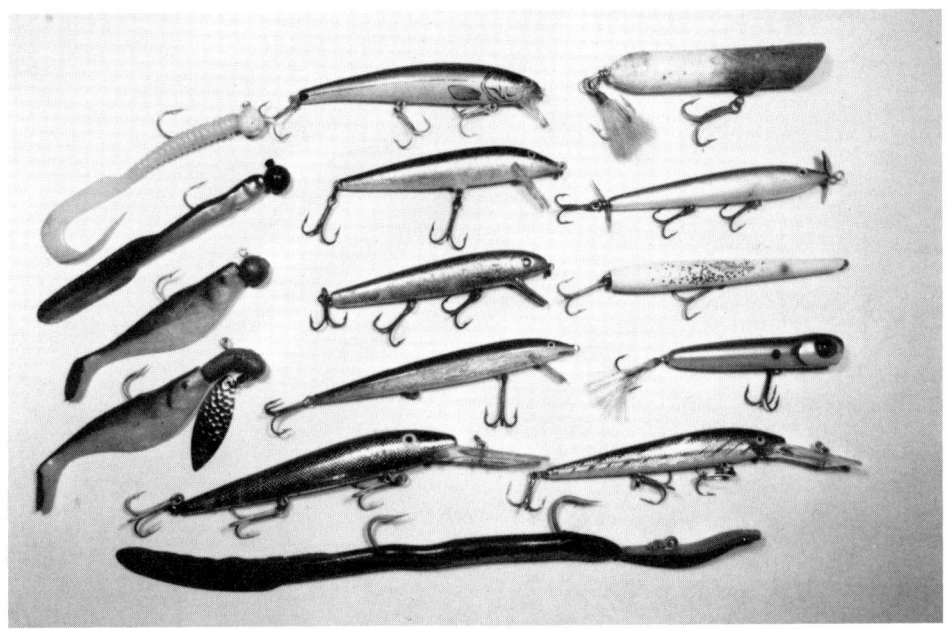

Some of the top lures used for stripers on the Delaware.

Deep Diving Plugs
Shad Rap, Fat Rap (Rapala)
Deep Long "A" (Bomber)
Spoonbill Minnows (Rebel)

Vibrating Plugs
Rat'L'Trap (Bill Lewis)
Ratt'l Spot Minnow (Cordell's)
Rattl'n Rap (Rapala)

Spinners
Musky Killer Lusox (Mepps)

Jig/Rubberbait Combinations
Jig Weights 3/8, 1/2, 5/8
Twister Tails, Sassy Shads,
Sassy Shiners (Twister)
in 4 & 6 inch Lengths

Flies & Poppers: Large streamer flies tied on 1/0 & 2/0 hooks and tandem tied hooks. Preferred colors- white, white/black, yellow, yellow/black.

Many anglers prefer to add silver or gold tinsel to their streams as an added attraction. Large deer hair bugs and balsa wood poppers are the preferred surface lures for the fly rodder.

Live Bait:	Large shiners, live herring, live and rigged eels, blood worms, small white perch
Pork Baits:	#70 Striper strip in white & yellow
Hooks:	Heavy gauge, short shank and galvanized steel preferred in sizes 1/0, 2/0, 3/0.
Misc. Gear:	Nets - Large nets with telescoping handles are preferred.
	Down Riggers - Basically used for trolling the tidal portions.

Kosher Salt - When migratory stripers are taken in fresh water they will loose the salt in their system and must be revived when released. Placing amounts of salt (one tablespoon per gallon) in your live well and holding the fish in it for several minutes before releasing him will help replace this necessary mineral in his system, thus giving him a better chance to survive after being released.

**WATER SHED ASSOCIATION
OF THE
DELAWARE RIVER**
Box 753
Lambertville, NJ 08530
(609) 397-4410

To report Pollution call:
1-800-8 DELAWARE

CHAPTER 10: MUSKIE AND WALLEYES
MUSKIE

Author with a nice muskie taken from the tidal river.

As recent as ten years ago, the tiger muskie population in the Delaware river was producing some exciting fishing. There's an old saying that "all good things must come to an end" and with the recent decision to discontinue stocking of these fish in the Delaware's tidal portions by the state of Pennsylvania, muskie catches are now on the decline. These fish are still being taken in the northern reaches of the river, however, and there is still hope for the future in the lower river.

The majority of the muskies that are in the river are tiger muskies, which are a hybrid fish and cannot reproduce. Now that they are no longer being stocked, these fish will simply die out. The hope for the future is that the state of New Jersey has embarked on a program to refurbish it's old Charles O'Hayford hatcheries for the reproduction of fish other than trout. This option is available to them because of the great success the new Pequest trout hatchery has been. Although the possibility of stocking muskie on a regular basis in the Delaware may be years away, it is being considered and does offer hopes for the future of this fishery in the lower river.

CHARACTERISTICS Before we cover places to fish and some of the methods that are used to catch muskie, we should first take a look at what makes him tick in a river. First, *muskies are quiet water fish*. They shun fast moving water and tend to migrate into the quiet stretches of the river or will be found in the quiet water portions of river structures. A good example would be a point of land where the fish are always found in the dead water pocket of the eddy that forms below the point.

Another fact that is well known about muskies is that *they are territorial fish*. Once settled into a certain area of the river they won't stray from it as long as water conditions remain stable and forage is available. As a result, once you have located a good sized muskie it's a good bet that he will remain in the area where you made contact with him, and patience and persistence will be the keys to taking him. Let's face it, he's not known as "the fish of a thousand casts" for nothing.

Although muskies are often spotted sunning themselves in shallow water or near the surface, they do have a *preference for deep water*. As we previously stated, muskies are lazy fish, preferring slow moving water. Deep water is generally slow moving water and offers a big fish such as a muskie shielding from the sun, forage, and a more stable environment. Shallow areas are more susceptible to quick changes in weather, water levels, temperatures, etc.

One of the things about the muskie which makes him difficult to catch is that *he is a cycle feeder*. By this we mean that he will take a large piece of forage and then take several days to digest it. This is especially true during the cold water season. He does not feed in small bites like a bass nor does he feed constantly, even during the warm water season like many other fish in the river. What this means to the angler is that his infrequent feeding habits give you less opportunities fish for him when he is active.

Muskie also have *definite preference in the type of forage* they eat. Contrary to what many people believe, muskies do not feed on anything that moves. They prefer soft finned fish such as herring, suckers, fall fish, shiners, etc. and will only feed on other fish when this type of forage is not available. What this means to the fisherman is that it will determine which baits are better for muskie, as well as which places he will be fishing during certain times of the year.

Twenty pound plus muskie taken on live bait.

METHODS   Unless you have spotted a muskie working a certain area, you will have to hunt for them. The best way of doing this is to troll for them if possible. Even if you don't take any while trolling you sometimes spot fish following lures or miss a few hits indicating there are muskies present. If you spot a fish you can stop and cast lures or live bait in an effort to get him to hit. If this fails, your next step is to fish the area where you have spotted the fish over a period of time until you either get the fish or feel he is gone.

Trolling is best done with more than one person, since the more lines you put out, the better your chances are. Whenever possible, vary the depth at which your lures run to cover the water as completely as possible.

Since you are fishing a river and you have to deal with the current, your best bet is to slow troll against the current. Speed control is a very important factor. This means you would have to troll more slowly than you would in a lake, and you should be sure that your motor operates efficiently at slower speeds.

Another method that works is slow drifting. You may have noticed that I said "slow drifting". Anglers often drift too fast to completely cover the area they are fishing. The best way to solve this problem is through the use of a drift anchor. (See "Equipment" section of this book.) You use it to drag along the bottom off the front of your boat, slowing down your drift, allowing you to place more casts in an area, thus covering the water more completely.

When drifting, you have two choices. First, you can cast and retrieve lures. Your second choice is to liveline large baits. This allows you to cover the area you are fishing at a slower rate. Many anglers combine the use of live bait with that of lures for a type of one, two punch for muskie.

One of the top places to look for good sized muskie in the spring is around the mouth of a feeder stream. Suckers and fall fish move into these areas to spawn and the muskie won't be far behind, looking for an easy meal. Live-lining good sized baits in these areas will take these fish. These areas are usually sheltered from the spring winds and this greatly enhances their appeal to the early season angler.

TACKLE

In most cases I disagree with the theory that you need big lures to catch big fish. When it comes to muskies, however, bigger lures and heavy tackle increases your chances. Every year, large muskies are taken by anglers fishing for trout, small-mouth and other fish on light tackle. In many cases the angler will tell you that the fish fought like a log. Well, I have had this happen and the reason for it is that muskie taken on light tackle many times don't realize they are hooked. If that same fish was taken on medium or heavy action tackle he more than likely would have put up a better tussle.

As far as lures are concerned, keep your plugs in the six to ten inch class for the best results. Swimming plugs, jump baits and constant motion surface lures such as big jointed Jitter Bugs are some of the favorites. Jumbo sized in-line spinners, spinnerbaits and buzzbaits, along with large spoons, are your top choices in the metal lure department. And oh yes! It doesn't hurt to have a good sized net, just to be on the safe side.

Reel Suggestions

Spinning
Penn - 714Z & 712Z, 4300, & 440SS
Shakespeare - RT835, RT740, RT80
Daiwa - EL1605, BG15, PS1605BL
Quantum - SS3, EX4, SE4, LS3
Shimano - TX-2000F, SC-2000F, SO-2000FA
ABU Garcia - GM4, Pro 3

Conventional
Quantum - 1420 MG, 1421 MG
Daiwa - TD2 HI, PS2L-5B
ABU Garcia - 5500C, 4600C
Shimano - B1000I

Rod Suggestions

Spinning- Medium, medium heavy and heavy action in 5 to 8 feet lengths for use with surface lures, swimming plugs and crankbaits. Conventional- Preferable for trolling and live lining in 5 to 7 foot lengths.

Line Suggestions

Triline XL, XT & Tri-Max in 8, 10 & 12 pound test. The use of 20 & 30 pound test is recommended for leader material.

A collection of large muskie lures used on the Delaware.

WALLEYE

Walleye taken while trolling plugs.

The walleye is one of the most fickle fish that swims the Delaware river and is well known as a light hitter. He is a bottom feeder who prefers live bait over lures most of the time and favors cooler water temperatures and deeper waters. The bulk of this fishery is found in the non-tidal waters, however, in recent years efforts to introduce these fish into the tidal waters have met with moderate success.

In view of these characteristics, some of the tackle that you will find effective for him will be different from that which is used for most other river fish.

Although these fish can be taken the year round, prime time for them is during the spring and fall seasons when the water is on the cooler side. Most of the better fishing is during the dark hours of the night, as these fish are nocturnal feeders, however, occasional fish can be taken during the daytime.

Whether fishing from a bank or from a boat, it will be necessary to have a good lighting source. Lighting for your boat is best placed so that it shines on the floor of your vessel. If you stop to think about it, whether you are tying on a lure, rigging a line or baiting a hook you are, for the most part, looking down on the subject. Likewise, light that shines on the floor of the boat will not show itself over the water. So it's best to place your lights in an out of the way place close to the floor.

The bank fisherman has an altogether different problem to solve. He has to be able to shine light on what he is working on, yet still keep his hands free. This is best accomplished through the use of a miners light, which can be placed on his cap or hung around his neck. They are relatively inexpensive items produced by numerous companies and will do the job very efficiently.

BAIT & LURES

For the most part, live bait will out produce artificials for these fish, especially during the cold water season. Over the years, *night crawlers* have probably taken more walleyes than any other bait, not because they are the best bait, but because they are the easiest to obtain and use. Most tackle shops stock a good supply, and a trip out into the back yard after a good rain will usually get you more than you need.

Minnows are also a good choice and are very easy to obtain. They are easier to keep during the cold water season, as cold water will hold oxygen better than warm water. Also, the cooler the water is, the less oxygen they will need.

Leeches and eels are usually the hardest to get, however, they are very effective for old Marble Eyes. Eels in particular can be pre-rigged and kept frozen until they are needed.

Leeches are, for the most part, a spring bait and many tackle shops do not carry them during the summer or fall. They can be easily kept in a small container of cool fresh water for long periods of time.

Walleyes are current feeders. They rely on the current to bring them their food. Ultimately, your best structures will be those that will have some type of current around them. Some favorites are points of land, bridge pilings, drop-offs and bars that are located around islands. One other structure that can be a real hot spot if it is present will be a warm water discharge from a power plant or other source.

During the *spring season* the walleyes migrate into shallow areas to spawn during March and will remain there until they finish spawning, which usually ends in late April or early May, depending on water temperatures and water conditions.

Structures with slow moving currents, or the slower currents of any given structure, can be best fished with a bait and jig combination. When fishing a worm and jig combo, choose a jig with a long shank hook. You must hook your night crawler from the tip of the head down through the body and out below its collar. The use of a stinger hook snelled on a small piece of line and tied on to the jig so that the second hook can be placed in the worm in the mid section is recommended. Walleyes are fickle hitters and many times they will hit the worm in the mid section and tear the worn off without getting the jig hook. The use of a stinger hook will help you take these hits and help keep the bait on the hook while casting.

Always position yourself, whether wading or fishing from a boat, along side of the current so that you can use the current to take your jig/bait combination to the fish. This is the same path that the forage will take, and the walleyes will be facing upstream, looking for an easy meal.

If you choose to use a leech with your jig combination, you should hook it through its mouth and down its back about a quarter to a half inch (depending on the size of the bait) and out the top. This will allow the tail to stretch out and provide a good enticing action as it waves in the current.

Minnows should always be hooked through the lips for the best results. Hooking them that way will offer less resistance to the current and will put the hook in the business end of the bait, as walleyes will usually swallow their prey head first.

Hop, skip and jumping a bait and jig combination with the slower currents can put some nice marble eyes on your stringer, but once you get into the faster currents, this type of rig will not be so effective. Swifter currents will often keep your rigs from getting into the strike zone. Deeper sections of water will also create some problems for a jig and bait combination, so a different course of action is in order.

Of all the different types of bottom walking rigs you can use, the most effective and most widely used is the Lindy rig. For many years, this rig has been the back bone of the walleye fisherman and affords better control over your bait in deeper water and swifter currents. The basic rig consists of a bottom walking sinker (specifically, the Lindy design, a curved sinker with most of the weight towards the bottom) placed on your line above a swivel, to which an 18" to 2' or longer leader is attached. There are several different choices to place at the business end of the leader.

A plain long shank wire hook is one option and is the better choice in faster currents such as those found around points of land, finger structures and warm water discharges. All four of the previously mentioned baits will work well with this Lindy rig option. This rig will keep your bait several inches off the bottom, which is a prerequisite for fishing the areas about which we are talking.

In deeper water, the Lindy rig can better serve you when combined with a floating jig head, or by injecting your bait with air. This will keep them higher off the bottom than the previously mentioned combination. Walleyes found in deeper water are more likely to pick up a bait farther off the bottom than those found in a faster current. The reason for this is that in faster currents, the current will be slower along the bottom, and most river bottoms will have small rocks with eddies behind them in which the walleye can seek refuge. This means he will be looking closer to the bottom for his food.

A floating jig head works exceptionally well with minnows and eels. The latter should be kept in the 6" to 8" size, and is best rigged with an extra hook about half way down its length. The leader from the hook can be secured to the eye of the floating jig head.

Worms and leeches will be better used with the air injection method. Air injectors are sold at many tackle shops and through most mail order catalogues. After you have hooked the bait, you can inject small air bubbles under its skin, causing it to float. Both the baits mentioned will have a more natural action when rigged this way.

Drop-offs found in the Delaware, can also be fished with a Lindy rig. You can either drift slowly along their edges, or anchor your boat at different points along the drop-off and cast your bait downstream, working it back to the boat. In both methods, the crucial part is maintaining contact with the bottom. If drifting, you may have to slow up your boat with your trolling motor through the use of a drift anchor or by varying the weights of your sinker to compensate for the depths you are fishing.

When working your Lindy rig from an anchored position, there are two ways of doing so. You can cast it downstream, allowing it to sink to the bottom. You can then move the rig along the bottom by raising and lowering your rod tip, bringing it off the bottom and then allowing it to drift back down, taking in a little line each time you do this.

You can also walk your sinker along the bottom by dropping it straight down over the boat until it hits the bottom. Then, lifting your rod tip so that when the sinker comes off the bottom it is moved downstream by the current, you play out a small amount of line with each lift of the rod tip. Once you have worked it out as far as you want, you can then walk the sinker back in the previously described manner. Working it this way will keep it on the bottom for longer periods of time, thus keeping it in the strike zone longer.

STRUCTURES

Drop-Offs   Drop-offs can also be effective worked with jig/rubber bait combinations and deep running crankbaits. When fishing from a boat you should position it away from the drop-off and cast your jig combination upstream and work the lure along the drop-off with the current.

The best way of fishing deep running crankbaits is to position your boat right on top of the drop-off, cast them downstream and retrieve them back along the base of the drop-off. Super slow speeds and an occasional twitch of the rod tip to drive the lure downward is the most effective way of fishing them.

Bridge Pilings & Eddies   Bridge pilings and the eddies that are located below them are another good bet for walleyes. When using bottom walking rigs with live bait, anchor right by the base of the bridge piling and work you rigs by casting them downstream and bringing them back to yourself. The reason for this is that there is usually plenty of debris that has drifted in the eddies below bridge pilings, and you will get less snags by slowly working your rigs to the boat against the current. Working jigs and crank baits in these eddies should be done by positioning yourself along side of the eddy and casting you jig/rubberbait combinations and crankbaits towards the top of the current lines and working them along them with the current and through the slack water sections of the eddy.

Warm Water Discharge   When fishing a warm water discharge during the cold water season you will sometimes find that the water is warm enough to make lures effective. One of your best bets during this time will be the jig and twister combination. Walking it slowly along the bottom can give you some good results. You can also fish a twister tail with a floating jig head on a Lindy rig.

Deep diving plugs can be made to produce for you in and around warm water discharges. Likewise, small spinner and bait combinations have long been the favorite of many walleye anglers. When fishing a warm water discharge, you should always remember that warmer water rises, and the farther you get away from a discharge point, the more it will dissipate. The most productive area to fish in a situation like this is where the warm water merges with the main river; it is here that

125

the warm water will be trapped. Likewise, most of the available forage will gather here, making it a prime feeding area for old Marble Eyes.

Walleyes are the most challenging fish on the Delaware. It will suffice to say that the population is not as large as those that are found in mid west river systems but it is adequate enough to offer the angler a good shot at these fine fish. The walleye is one fish that varies in their numbers each season and how many fish are taken on any given season will depend on how well these fish spawned two to three years previously.

The walleye population is in good shape in the Delaware river, however, this fishery could be further enhanced with a good supplemental stocking program from the states on both sides of the river.

TACKLE

Reel Suggestions

Spinning
Shakespeare - RT835, RT825
Daiwa - EL705, TD2HI, PS2L-%b
Quantum - SS2, SS3, SE3, LS2
Penn - 716Z, 714Z, 4200, 4300
ABU Garcia - Pro2, GM2, Pro3, GM3

Conventional
Quantum - 1420MG, 1421MG
ABU Garcia - 5500, 5500C, 4600C
Diawa -TD2HI, PS2L-5B
Shimano - B1000L

Rod Suggestions

Ultralight spinning rods in 5 to 6 foot lengths for casting swimming plugs, spinnerbaits and crankbaits. For fishing jigs and rubber baits, 5 to 6 foot ultralight tip action rods. For live bait fishing with Lindy Rigs and other bottom walking rigs, light action spinning rods in 5 to 6 foot lengths. For trolling and vertical fishing, light and medium light action conventional rods.

Line Suggestions

Triline XL, XT & Tri-Max in 4, 6 & 8 pound test.

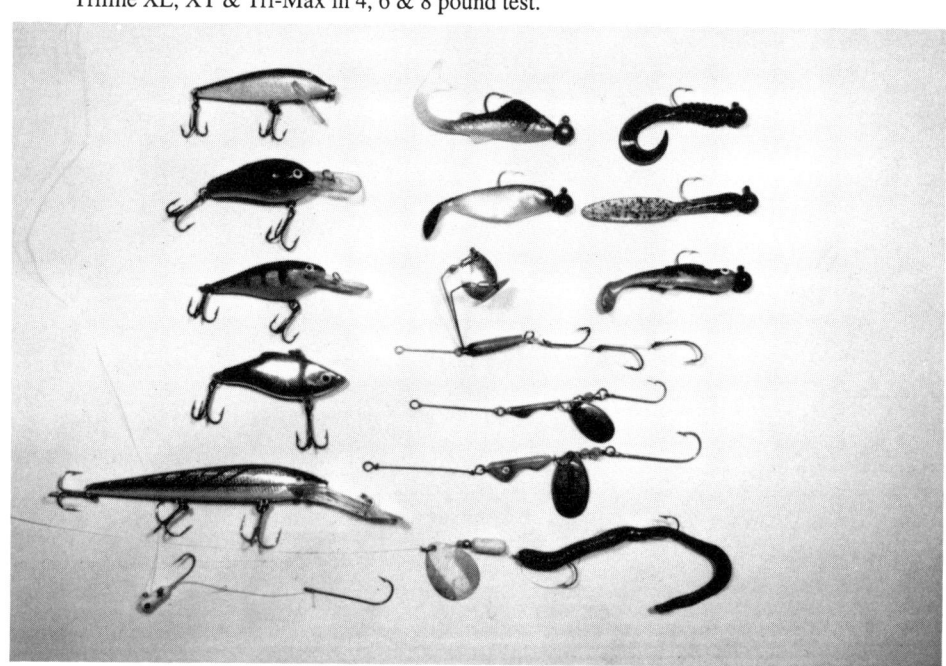

A collection of walleye lures and rigs.

Lures

Swimming Plugs: Floating Rapala & Countdown (Rapala) Rebel Minnow (Rebel) Long "A" (Bomber) Spitfire (Poe's)

Deep Diving Plugs: Shad Rap & Fat Rap (Rapala) Stretch + (Mann's) Shadling (Lindy) Wally Diver (Cordell's) Spoon Bill Minnows (Rebel)

Vibrating Plugs: Rat-L-Trap (Bill Lewis) Rattl'n Rap (Rapala) Rattlin' Spot (Cordell's) RC 3 (Poe's)

Jigs: Vibro Tail and Foxee Jig (Blue Fox) Fire Ball, Whistler jigs, Airplane jigs (Northland)

Rubberbaits: Sassy Shad, Sassy Shiner, Twister (Mr. Twister) Marsh minnow (Toledo Tackle)

Live Bait

Aquatic: Killies, fatheads, shiners, dace, crayfish, leaches, small eels, lamprey

Terrestrial: Hellgrammites, night crawlers

Miscellaneous Tackle

Pork Baits: #50 Pork Strip, #140-A Black Widow Eel

Hooks: Short shank O'Shaughnessy style hooks in sizes 4 through 1/0 (Mustdad # 94150 & 9174) (Eagle Claw # 318N)

Weights: Lindy sinkers, egg sinkers, catapillar sinkers, pencil lead

Other: Swivels, leader lines for rigs, spinner blades and clevises, air injector, floats and floating beads, different color and sized beads.

GUIDE SERVICES

J.B. KASPER
Fresh Water Fishing Instructor
Member Professional Guides Association, Lectures and Seminars
Guide Services for Smallmouth, Largemouth, Shad, Trout,
Stripers, Crappie and Down River Trips on the Delaware
215-295-1502

400 Hillside Avenue   Morrisville, PA 19067

CHAPTER 11: PANFISH AND FORAGE FISH

BLUEGILLS & SUNFISH

Both the tidal and non-tidal portions of the river support good numbers of bluegills and sunfish, as well as some good sized fish which provide excellent light tackle action. During the spawning season (May and June) and when they are on the

fall feed, fish of a pound or more are not uncommon. These two portions of the year are two of the prime times to take these fish. The most common varieties in the non-tidal river are the red breasted and pumpkin seed sunfish; the dominant sunfish in the tidal river is the bluegill.

Sunfish and bass are members of the same family and as such have many of the same habits and haunts. In the non-tidal river they frequent the same structures and feed on the same forage as the smallmouth and in the tidal river they haunt the same structures, feed on the same forage and move on the same portions of the tide as the largemouth do.

During the summer the best fishing for them is just after day break when they readily hit small surface baits and popping bugs, providing excellent action on ultralight spinning tackle and fly rods. Once the sun gets on the water they will retreat into eddies, ripples and shaded areas where they will hit small jig/rubberbait combinations. The use of a double rig jig (two jigs and rubberbaits tied in tandem or in teaser style) will allow you to catch two at a time.

June and early July can provide the fly fisherman with some excellent action if he fishes along the banks where there are over hanging trees, for this is the time when the inch worms are falling on the water in good numbers and the sunfish feast on them throughout the day. Anglers using ultralight spinning tackle can also take some good numbers on small spoons, spinners and jig/rubberbait combinations.

During the fall season sunfish will go on the fall feed like the other inhabitants of the river, feeding on the small shad and herring that are making their way back down the river. Jigging or live-lining small minnows, hellgrammites, crickets and other types of live bait will give you some excellent numbers of fish.

Here's one last trick for taking sunfish. During the summer months some really great action can be had by injecting small worms with air via an air injector or syringe, casting them into the current and allowing them to float on the surface. A can of small worms, an air injector, and some light tackle can provide some exciting action and make a good way to get kids excited about fishing.

TACKLE

The fly fisherman will find some top-notch action for panfish on the Delaware, and the fly patterns that are used are consistent with those that are used on trout streams. Small popping bugs and deer hair bugs, along with small rubber baits, are also top producers for the fly fisherman.

Reel Suggestions

Penn - 4200, 716
Daiwa - UL 7, EL500H
Shimano - PSM-ULS

Shakespeare - 2500ULX, RT 825
Quantum - SS1 UL, SE2 150

Rod Suggestions:

Ultralight spinning rods in 4 1/2 to 6 foot lengths for casting swimming plugs, spinnerbaits and crankbaits. For surface fishing, 5 to 6 foot noodle type spinning rods. For fishing jigs and rubber baits, 4 1/2 to 5 1/2 foot ultralight tip action rods. For live-bait fishing, ultralight action spinning rods in 5 foot lengths. For fly fishing, ultra light rods in 5 to 8 foot lengths.

Line Suggestions

Triline XL in 2, 4 & 6 pound tests, Tri-Max in 4 & 6 pound tests, Hi Seas Tournament Line in 4, 6 & 8 pound tests.

Lures

The lures used for panfish are the same as those that are used for smallmouth and trout. Keep them on the small side for the best results.

TROUT

Trout fishing in the Delaware takes on two different perspectives. The first is the nationally known native populations of the east and west branches of the river. The second is the fishing that takes place near the confluences of the small streams that are stocked with trout by their respective states. Trout in the tidal Delaware are all but non-existent.

In the northern most regions of the river, brook, rainbow and brown trout are found. Native reproduction takes place in this part of the river and many of the streams that flow into the river have native as well as stocked trout populations. Many of the trout from these streams wind up in the river and this makes for some better than average trout fishing.

The upper Delaware has more than it's share of bug hatches and these provide fly fishermen with plenty of challenging fishing. For the fisherman who prefers spinning tackle, small spoons and in-line spinners are his meal ticket. The river is very wadeable and scenic in it's upper reaches.

Angler fishes for trout on the upper Delaware.

Most of the trout fishing in this area, however, is done with live bait. Hellgrammites, grubs, salmon eggs and various other forms of natural baits fished both on spinning and fly tackle take a good amount of trout each year.

TACKLE

Reel Suggestions

Penn - 220GR
Sigma 025 Daiwa - UL
Shimano - PSM-ULS

Shakespeare - 2200
Quantum - QSS2

Rod Suggestions:

Ultralight spinning rods in 4 1/2 to 6 foot lengths for casting small spinners, spoons and jig/rubberbait combinations. For live bait fishing, ultralight action spinning rods in 5 foot lengths are recommended. For fly fishing, ultra light rods in 5 to 8 foot lengths with matching reels.

Line Suggestions

In the line department, two and four pound test are the most commonly used line weights. Triline XL in 2 & 4 pound tests.

Lure Suggestions

All types of small spinners, spoons and small jig rubberbait combinations.

Fly Patterns For Delaware River Trout Streamer Flies: Black Ghost, Gray Ghost, Golden Shiner, Muddle Minnow, Black Nose Dace, Coachman Bucktail, Mickey Finn

Wet Flies: Brown Woolly, Black Woolly, Dark Cahill, Lady Beaverkill, Black Gnat, Coachman, Light Cahill, March Brown, Brown Hackle, Blue Dun, Black Ant, Quill Gordon, Olive Quill

Nymphs: Black May Fly Nymph, Light Cahill Nymph, March Brown Nymph, Yellow May Fly Nymph, Dark Olive Nymph, Green Caddis Fly Nymph, Hellgrammite

Dry Flies: Adams, Light Cahill, Royal Wulff, Coachman, Black Gnat, Dark Hendrickson, Blue Dun, Ginger Spider, Adams Midge, Quill Gordon, March Brown

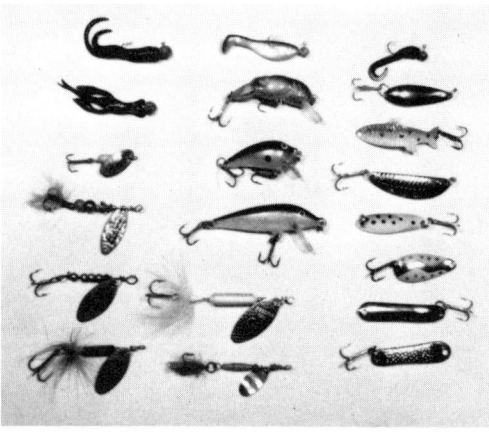

Live Bait

Killies, fatheads (natural & golden), shiners, dace, crayfish, leeches, hellgrammites, reed worms, garden worms, night crawlers, grubs, manure worms

Other Baits

Velveeta cheese, Berkley Power Baits, salmon eggs

Hooks

Light wire short shank preferred in Sizes #8, #10, #12, (Mustad - #3906, #94150, #7958) (Eagle Claw - #80, #59, #159, #58) For use with salmon eggs sizes #8, #10, #12, (Mustad - #9479, #9651, #9522S, #94842) (Eagle Claw - #38 #479, #227)

Tiny rubberbait, plugs, spinners and spoons used for trout on the upper river.

MISCELLANEOUS SPECIES

Fallfish

BOWFIN - This fish is a prehistoric relic that is taken from time to time in the river, mostly in the tidal section around Trenton. There is no significant numbers of these fish and most are caught by anglers searching for other fish. They are bottom feeders and frequent the deeper regions of the river.

FALLFISH - Jokingly referred to as river tarpon, these fish are large members of the minnow family, similar in appearance to a large chub. Commonly taken by anglers on live bait and lures,

130

they are found throughout the non-tidal river. They make excellent bait for stripers, muskie and other large gamefish.

STURGEON - Another prehistoric fish that is found in the Delaware. In recent years, several studies have been done on these fish and they have revealed a good population in the river as well as off the coast near the mouth of the bay. They are bottom feeders with feeding habits similar to catfish and carp and are sometimes caught by shad fishermen in the spring. The short nose variety is on the endangered list and it is illegal to take or kill these in the waters of the Delaware.

Sturgeon

NORTHERN PIKE - This fish is still a question mark in the river. Even though some fish have been stocked in the river by New Jersey, there is still no program for building a viable population in the river. There has been some interest in stocking them in the tide water river but this still has not come about.

PICKEREL - In the last few years anglers have started to see more of these fish in the tidal river, especially in the back water areas. Both chain barrel pickerel are found in most tributary streams. Very few are found in the non-tidal river and those that are taken come from the slower moving quiet water sections.

Pickerel

PERCH

WHITE PERCH - One of the most prolific fish found in the tidal river is the white perch. Their numbers decline the further you travel into the non-tidal portions of the river. They will hit small lures and live bait throughout the year, however, the prime time for these fish is during the cold water season when they school up and move into coves and back water areas. During spawning time they can be taken in good numbers by bottom fishermen using worms and other natural baits.

White Perch

Although not the biggest member of the panfish clan found in the river, they do reach weights of a

131

pound or more. They make an excellent table treat when they are taken from the non-tidal reaches of the river, however, there is a consumption warning for white perch taken from the river below Trenton because of PCB contamination.

YELLOW PERCH - In the last several years the numbers of these fish have been increasing in the river, especially in the tidal river. Historically, the Delaware at one time had one of the best yellow perch populations on the east coast. The worlds record came from Crosswicks creek, a tributary of the river, in the 1800's by Dr. C.C. Abbot. Their numbers reached an all time low in the late 50's and early 60's, just as most other fish did.

Like the white perch, spring and fall are the prime time for these fish. They migrate into the coves and back water areas in the tidal regions off the river and school up with the white perch, crappie and bass, haunting the same structures and feeding on the same forage.

Nice yellow perch taken from the tidal river.

FORAGE FISH

The one thing that there is no lack of in the Delaware is forage. The excellent supply of both seasonal and natural forage is responsible for the premium stocks of stripers, smallmouth, largemouth, crappie and other fish.

SEASONAL FORAGE - Herring and shad make up the seasonal forage population in the river. During the spring as these fish make their way up river to spawn, herring are the main forage for the stripers that also migrate up the river to spawn, along with the bigger walleyes and muskie. Starting in mid July and on into the fall, the shad fry are the main forage for the smallmouth, walleye and panfish in the non-tidal river. In the tidal river, the herring fry are the forage for the stripers, largemouth and crappie. During the late fall, the returning shad fry are forage for the same fish in the tidal river as they pass through it.

Both of these fish are hard to keep alive as bait since they need well oxygenated, moving water. In the spring, many anglers catch herring while they are fishing and then liveline them for stripers. Many anglers also catch good amounts of these fish and freeze them for late use as catfish baits and for crabs and as chum for salt water fishing.

NATIVE FORAGE - In the tidal river, the main forage fish is the killie. These fish are found in the main river, tributary streams, coves and back water areas. In recent years, good numbers of alewives have been seen in the tidal river.

In the non-tidal river, killies, chubs, dace, fallfish, stone catfish and shiners make up the forage fish. There are numerous large bug hatches that take place on the non-tidal river each day during the warm water season and these hatches form a good part of the forage for smallies and panfish, as well as the trout populations in the far northern sections of the river.

There are several type of forage that are common to both the tidal and non-tidal river. Small panfish, leeches, hellgrammites, crayfish and eels are some of the forage that is common in both sections of the river.

There are several methods that can be used to take baitfish from the river. In the case of the killies that are found in the tidal river, funnel traps placed in tributary streams and back water marshes will do the trick. Both a throw net and seine can be used to net small shad or herring.

CARP

Both the tidal and non-tidal portions of the river have good carp populations. Even though these fish are not found in the numbers they once were (due to the increases in the game fish populations in the river), there are still enough to provide some excellent fishing.

These fish are more popular among shoreline fishermen than they are with boaters. Bottom fishing corn meal baits, corn and dough balls is the common way of fishing for them. Anglers also snag a good number of them while herring fishing, and occasional fish are taken on lures by bass fishermen. Another place these fish are taken by accident is in the coves and back water areas by crappie fishermen during the spring and fall. Carp move into these places and winter over on the same structures as the crappies and bass do.

Another part of this fishery that attracts ever increasing numbers of anglers each season is bow and arrow fishing for them. Bow and arrow fishing is permitted by all the states bordering the river both from the shore and in a boat. Most bow and arrow fishing is done during the spring when the carp are spawning in the shallow water weed beds. In the tidal river, some good bow fishing can be had among the pilings and wrecks found in the tidal coves and marshes. Carp spawn later than most fish in the river because their spawning temperatures are between 68 and 82 degrees, and these temperatures usually are not reached until June.

Because carp prefer quiet water, the tidal river offers the angler the best fishing for them. Each year the tide water river produces some huge carp in the 20 and 30 pound range. One of the best places for

Carp

133

them in the early season is in a warm water discharge from a power plant or industrial plant. They gather there during the months of March, April and May, and bottom fishing corn meal, corn and worms are the favorite way of taking these fish.

Once spawning is over carp will take up their normal warm water patterns, feeding along the bottom in the deeper sections. They are excellent fighters and use their powerful bodies and sucker-like lips to root through the silt looking for food, and the tell tale trail of air bubbles that they leave makes a good way of tracking them.

Carp have a very sensitive sense of smell and it's the reason that dough baits spiked with anisette oil, maple syrup, vanilla extract and other sweet smelling substances are good baits. A couple of fishing rods, some triple hooks, bank sinkers and some dough baits are the tools of the carp fisherman.

TACKLE

Both spinning and conventional tackle can be used for carp fishing. Medium, medium heavy and heavy action rods in 5 to 7 foot lengths will serve you best. Since you will be using heavier lines, your choice in reels should lean towards medium sized reels with larger line capacities. Strong gearing and smooth bearings, along with a smooth drag system, are a must for these fish.

Reel Suggestions

Spinning
Penn - 4300, 440S, 714Z, 712Z
Shakespeare - RT 835, RT 735,
Daiwa - BG13, BG15 & EL 1305
Quantum - SE4, LS3, EX3
Garcia - GM3, GM63, Pro 3

Conventional
Quantum - 381, 1311 MG
Daiwa - TD2 PI
ABU Garcia - 5500C, 4600C & 500XLT
Shimano - PSX300Q ABU

Rod Suggestions

Spinning and conventional with full handles in medium, medium heavy and heavy full length action rods in 5 to 7 feet lengths.

Line Suggestions

Triline XL, XT & Tri-Max in 8, 10 & 12 pound test.

Bow Fishing

The use of a bow and arrow for carp fishing is becoming more and more popular each season. During the spawning season, the angler can wade the river or fish from a boat, using a long bow or compound bow for carp with good results. For the best results, bow pull strength should be at least 35 pounds. Aluminum or fiberglass arrows with twist out heads will serve you best.

Miscellaneous Gear

Nets - Large nets with telescoping handles are preferred.

Baits

Corn meal and dough baits, worms, corn, peas, potatoes, cotton seed meal.

Hooks

For use with dough baits, Mustad #D3551 and Eagle Claw #374SB

SUCKERS

Suckers are one of the most underrated fighting fish that swim the river. They are bottom feeders and are found in both the tidal and non-tidal sections of the river,  although their numbers are greater in the non-tidal river and it's there that they are mostly fished for. They feed along the bottom on vegetation, insects and other forage in eddies and slower sections. The best sucker fishing occurs in the spring when they make their way into tributary streams to spawn. They start moving into these areas during March and spawn when the water temps reach between 54 and 67 degrees, staying there into the month of May. It's during this time that muskie will also move into these areas to feed on them.

Suckers differ from carp in that they will readily take worms, hellgrammites and other terrestrial forage. During the summer, these fish are found in deeper well oxygenated pools that are preceded by rapids and ripples. Even though they prefer cooler water they will tolerate warmer water as long as good oxygen levels are present.

Suckers in the Delaware attain weights of five pounds or better, however, the average fish is about two to four pounds. Light

Suckers

action spinning tackle, some hooks, sinkers and a good supply of garden hackle are all you need to take them. They are a light hitter and possess excellent fighting qualities. Suckers are important to the river not only as sportfish but as forage fish as well.

TACKLE

Reel Suggestions

Penn - 4200, 716Z Shakespeare - RT 825, RT 725
Daiwa - UL 7, EL 705   Quantum - LS1, SS2

Rod Suggestions

Ultralight and light action spinning rods in 4 1/2 to 6 lengths. Light action fly rods in 5 to 8 foot lengths with compatible reels and sinking lines.

Line Suggestions

In the line department, 2, 4 & 6 pound test are the most commonly used line weights. Triline XL in 2, 4, & 6 pound tests, Tri-Max in 4 & 6 pound tests, Hi Seas Tournament line in 4, 6 & 8 pound tests.

Live & Other Baits

Hellgrammites, reed worms, garden worms, manure worms, night crawlers, grubs, corn, Berkley Power Bait, corn meal baits.

Hooks

Light wire shank preferred in Sizes #8 through #1 (Mustad - Long shank #37360, Short Shank #3892B) (Eagle Claw - Long Shank #214, Short Shank #72)

CHAPTER 12: FLOAT TRIPS

One of the best ways of gaining an education on the Delaware River, it's structures and it's fisheries, not to mention it's scenic beauty, is to do a float trip. A Huck Finn adventure will put you in touch with more types of structures under a bigger variety of conditions than any one day trip to one spot on a river. Getting away from it all will allow you to concentrate better on the fishing you are doing, and you will retain more of what you learn on such a trip. Besides, a Huck Finn trip tends to bring out the little boy in us all and it's just plain fun.

Canoe packed for a float trip.

It's hard to compare a float trip to any other type of fishing venture, and when done properly it will have you chomping at the bit in anticipation of your next such trek. Seeing the sun rise over a desolate mountain top as you cast your lures to the waiting smallies, the snap, crackle and pop of a camp fire after a long days fishing, waking up to the morning birds and the taste of a cup of coffee cooked over an open fire are the things that you can't put a price tag on. A float trip is even better when done with a few friends to make it more interesting.

PACKING

One of the most crucial elements that goes into the making of a successful down river float trip is packing properly for it. You will need some rudimentary knowledge of the outdoors, and common sense is something that you should not leave at home. It's important not only in knowing how to pack, but what to pack, as well as making sure that your gear gets where you are going in good, serviceable condition. Let's face it, crawling into a soggy sleeping bag is not the way to get a good night's sleep.

As odd as it may seem, packing for a down river float trip is one of the simplest chores you will have on such a trip. Keeping your tents, sleeping bags, camping gear and other necessities as dry as possible is your main concern. One thing that you should remember when packing for a float trip is to choose items that can serve more than one purpose. A pocket knife that has a fork and spoon attached will save you the need of taking along separate eating utensils. A coffee pot can be used to hold smaller containers of spices, matches, drink mixes, etc., thus safe guarding them and keeping them out of the way. Clothing and cloth items can be packed in plastic and used as cushions to protect more fragile items.

The first step is choosing the proper container in which to pack your gear. There are many good commercialy produced water proof bags and containers. Some are available in local sporting goods and department stores, however, the best way to

Dinner time on a down river trip.

obtain them for a reasonable price is through an outfitters catalog. Prices can range from twenty dollars and up. When choosing one, make sure that the bag is water proof and not water repellent. The latter will not withstand getting dumped overboard if the unthinkable should happen. Water proof bags float in most cases, depending on how much weight they have in them. For many of us our wallet is a prime consideration, and even though the money is well spent, there are less expensive ways of protecting your gear.

Heavy duty plastic garbage can liners are a universal antidote of sorts when it comes to storing gear on a float trip. It will solve the damp sleeping bag problem for you no matter what your finances are. (For the best results, choose a bag of 5 mil thickness or heavier.) Plastic five gallon buckets with water proof lids are another way of storing your gear. When sealed, they will float if dumped out of a canoe and their handles can be tied to your canoe to keep them from being lost if you should tip over. They also make it easy to get at eating utensils, snacks and other necessities while in your boat or canoe.

Zip Loc plastic bags can be purchased at most supermarkets and they have limitless uses on a down river float trip. Besides the obvious job of storing food, they can be used to seal up any other small items, soap, clothes, towels, wallets, paper work, etc. that you need to protect from getting wet.

The first step when packing for a float trip is to take proper care of your wallet, drivers license or any other important papers that you normally carry with you. It's too easy to hop out of a canoe and start wading, only to remember when it's too late that you have forgotten to safeguard these important perishable items. Protecting on a permanent basis is not all that hard to do. For a few dollars you can purchase a roll of clear contact paper and cover every item in your wallet with a coating of thin plastic that will secure them no matter where you are. This type of protection also works well on items such as maps, instructions, etc. which may not be water proof but you might want to take along on your trip.

Most all your individual personal needs such as soap, towels, spare clothing, toilet paper, a first aid kit, etc. can be sealed up in Zip Loc bags. Always choose heavy duty freezer type bags, as their extra thickness will hold up better. You should compress the bag and the ingredients inside and force or suck out the air whenever possible. This will compact them and save you space. You can also place breakable or fragile items in with your clothing, removing the air so that the clothing will act as a cushion to protect them.

A float trip has much in common with a back packing trip. The two share the same space and weight considerations, though a float trip gives you much more leeway. Although a pack frame can be used to store the majority of your gear on a float trip, it is of little value in keeping it's contents from getting wet. A heavy duty plastic bag can be placed in the main compartment, as well as the other smaller compartments, to keep their contents safe and dry. After placing your gear in each compartment, you can seal the bags up with a small piece of string or a rubber band to make them air tight. Always wrap pointed items such as eating utensils, combs, etc. in a wash cloth or an item of clothing to keep their sharp points from puncturing the plastic bag. Most items that are placed in your main compartments should also be placed in a Zip Loc bag as a double protection.

CAMPING GEAR

Space on a float river trip is always at a premium, and the camping equipment you choose for your trip should be of the compact type used for back packing. Most major equipment manufacturers produce this type of gear, and even though it is a little more expensive, it is well worth it in the space it saves you. Small lamps and their propane cylinders can be stored in a plastic container for their protection and safety. You can use an empty 35 mm film container to store extra mantels and matches along with them. Mantels are easily damaged and in most cases you will have to replace them each time you use your lamp.

Angler sets up camp on an island on a down river float trip.

No matter what type of container you use to store you gear on a float trip, there are some items such as lamp globes or other breakable items that should be stored securely to prevent them from being damaged. You can achieve this by using the clothing items that you packed in Zip Loc bags as cushions between the items, as we have mentioned, or you should store them in their own plastic or metal container before being packed.

When it comes to choosing a tent for a float trip, modern nylon back packing tents are ideally suited for our purpose; they are light in weight, compact when packed properly, dry out fast should they get wet and many need not be staked down to the ground to be set up.

Always choose a slightly larger tent than needed as it will be more comfortable. (Ea. a two man tent for one person, a three man tent for two persons, etc.) You should always use a tent that has a fly over it because camping along a river bank produces a lot of moisture in the form of dew, and the fly will keep it from forming on the top of your tent.

A tent fly also has other uses on a float trip. It can be used to cover up canoes and gear to keep the dew or the weather from getting at them. If foul weather should come on you suddenly you can beach you canoe and cover it up with a nylon fly, as well as use a fly to set up a temporary shelter to keep dry under.

In the sleeping bag department just about any well made one will do. The best way to pack them for a trip is to place a plastic bag inside of a stuff bag and pack the sleeping bag in it. This will keep the bag in better shape over the long haul and will keep it dry on a float trip. One item that comes in handy at sleeping time is an air mattress or a foam mat. Even though most river islands have plenty of soft silt to camp on, they still can get pretty hard and damp, and some type of protection will make them a better bedding for the night.

Speaking of camping on damp ground, most river islands and banks have plenty of moisture in their soil and you should always use a piece of plastic as a ground cloth to keep moisture from the bottom of your tent.

FOOD

Of all the things that you will have to pack on your trip, none is more important than the food you take with you. This is especially important during the warm summer months when the heat can prove to be your worst foe. Once you begin your trip, you can't stop at a supermarket or convenience store to replace anything you might have forgotten. So choose your food properly and prepare it so it takes up as little space as possible and creates as little waste as possible. The less waste you have the less you will have to pack out when leaving. It goes without saying that leaving your trash at your campsite for someone else to clean up is not right.

I don't know about you, but dehydrated food never turned me on, especially after a long days fishing on a river. Steak and potatoes cooked over an open fire is more to my way of thinking. What food you choose and how you pack it is often dictated by how many days you intend to spend on the river. The longer you intend to stay on a river, the less you will want to depend on perishable food. For instance, you will be able to sustain a two day trip for four people with only a good sized ice chest and couple of one or two gallon drink containers if done properly.

You can start out by filling a couple of gallon plastic milk containers with water and freezing them. You can use them to keep your ice chest cool and they will give you a source of cool water whenever you need it. When empty you can compact them to save space while being packed out. On the average three day trip (3 days & 2 nights) you will need three breakfasts, three lunches, and two dinners. Choosing the proper foods will get you through all three days without wondering when it's time to eat again.

Main entrees such as steak, chicken, sausage, bacon, etc. should be frozen prior to the trip and placed in the ice chest in a frozen state. This will preserve them for a longer period of time and will add to the efficiency of your cooler, thus you will have to take along less ice and you will have more room for food. Canned or raw potatoes make excellent home fries for breakfast and can be roasted in a Dutch oven for the evening meal. Any canned potatoes or other vegetables should be taken from the can and drained, then placed in a Zip Loc bag and left in the refrigerator overnight. Raw potatoes and vegetables can be transported whole or sliced up and treated the same as canned vegetables. This will take up less space and weight, and being already cooled they will last longer and draw less from your ice supply. Fresh vegetables such as lettuce, tomatos, etc. should also be cooled down prior to being placed in the ice chest.

You can pre-cook items such as chicken, turkey, steak, etc. to extend their life and these can be eaten cold as lunch or heated on the open fire for dinner. Lunch meats can also be frozen to extend their life and you can use them as they thaw out.

Fragile items that are easily damaged (ie: eggs and butter) should be placed in separate containers, not only to prevent damage but to prevent them from damaging other items if they should get broken or spoiled. Plastic containers used for this purpose can be purchased from camping supply or department stores or from outfitters catalogs. Small amounts of spices, sugar, seasoning and powered cream can be placed in small separate containers (an empty 35 mm film container is a good choice) and packed in your coffee pot. The amount of these items that you take along with you will be determined by the length of your trip.

Powdered drink mixes are your best bet when it comes to something to drink on a trip. Your second choice are drinks that are stored in paper containers. Powdered drink mixes can be mixed in the same drink containers each time you make them and you can burn paper containers after their use in the evening camp fire. Empty cans from soda and other drinks will have to be packed out and are more difficult to store.

The best way of doing it is to make up a couple of gallon thermoses for use on the first day or two and then as you need more you can drain water from the gallon containers you froze for your ice supply and mix them as you need them. Spare drink mix can be carried in separate containers in dry form and what you don't use you will have for another time.

BOATS & MOTORS

There are several types of vessels that are suitable for this type of trip. Over the years, I have used both canoes and wide body flat bottom prams for such trips and both will do the job. A flat bottom pram is a very stable vessel that allows you to carry more gear than a canoe, however, if you have to carry one around a dangerous set of rapids you will quickly learn their one drawback, that of weight.

A canoe, on the other hand, is not as comfortable, nor does it have as much space, but it is better for running rapids and is easier to transport if you choose not to run them. It is also easier to transport on a vehicle.

The best all around choice is a square back canoe with a light horse power motor. It is sort of a compromise between the two previously mentioned vessels. It's well suited for use in rivers where you come in contact with a lot of rapids, especially those around which you will have to carry your canoe. On the

Always put safety first on the river and never underestimate the river's current.

other hand, if you will be traveling on a slow stretch of river or want to return to a spot through which you have drifted, the small outboard will give you the power to accomplish both feats. Some canoes such as the Coleman Scanoe are almost as stable as a wide body pram and can hold almost as much gear and weight.

You may have noticed that we chose a small outboard as the method of propulsion. Since fishing is our main concern, it will enable you to cover much more water by using a motor in the stretches that you don't want to fish and moving right into water that looks more productive. The use of muscle power should be used only to position your vessel for fishing. Besides, if you are not in the best of physical shape it can save you some aches and pains around the evening camp fire and make your trip more pleasurable.

It goes without saying that the size of the motor you choose for your boat should be one that your vessel will be able to handle. Since speed is not your prime objective, you will not need a lot of horse power. Besides, smaller engines are more fuel efficient on a trip such as we are discussing and it is easier and quicker to lift out of the water if you have to pass through some rapids or shallow water.

One special note when using smaller motors for such a trip. Since most small motors use some type of shear pin arrangement, always carry spare shear pins and the tools to replace them. It doesn't hurt to carry a spare prop as well.

Some anglers choose to use electric motors for this type of fishing and although they can be used, they do have some draw backs. They are not strong enough to move back up against the current of most rivers for starters. Second, the battery or batteries you have to carry add plenty of weight to your vessel and most batteries will wear down long before the trip is over, so you will have to use them sparingly.

TACKLE

Your rod and reel concerns for a float trip are best addressed by taking several different action rod and reel combinations. The tackle you take will largely be determined by the type of fishing you will be doing. *(For some insight into what tackle to take, consult the chapters on the different fish and the tackle used for each).* In any case, it is always wise to take a few extra rods along, packed in hard containers, as insurance should anything happen to the ones you are using. The cases should be tied to your vessel for obvious reasons. Some velcro strips will come in handy to secure your rods to the boat quickly when you will be paddling through rapids. Some extra spools of line are also a good addition in case you lose a lot of line while fishing.

Always pack your tackle wisely, including several lures from each of eight different lure groups: spinners, spoons, surface plugs, shallow running crankbaits, deep running crankbaits, swimming plugs, jigs and rubberbaits. Since you will have to cope with a variety of structures and conditions on a float trip, you will more than likely have a chance to use just about every piece of tackle you take along with you at one time or another. Remember, once you are on the river there are no tackle shops for you to replace anything that you might lose or not have, so pack accordingly.

Big tackle boxes don't go with the compact space you will have in a canoe. A better choice is to use several smaller ones that will fit into a wading bag or a sealable canvas bag. You can keep the ones you are fishing out of open in your boat where you can reach them and the tackle they hold. When it comes time to jump out of the boat and wade, you simply tuck them into the wading bag and start fishing. You can use the belt that holds the bag to tie the bag to the cross piece of a canoe when you are not using it and you'll still be able to get at the tackle while in the boat.

The Delaware in most parts is shaded by the mountains through which it passes, and tree lined shores with over hanging trees are very common. They offer you many opportunities to cast at the fish that will hide in the shadows with swimming plugs, spinners and crankbaits. Flat shallow stretches are ideal for surface plugging in the early morning and late evening hours, especially during the hot summer. During the daylight hours, good amounts of the fish can be taken in the white water and ripples which defuse the light from the sun and put good amounts of oxygen into the water, keeping the fish active. Swimming plugs and jig/rubber bait combinations will do the trick here.

As you can see, a down river float trip puts you in touch with every type of structure found in the river and you will have to change the way you fish based on the type of structure and the current conditions you are fishing. So a variety of tackle will spice up your float trip.

MISCELLANEOUS GEAR

A first aid kit is a must. Most store bought first aid kits are usually missing some key items that you will find useful on a down river float trip. Additions to your kit should include brown soap, anti-bee sting medication, antihistamines, poison ivy lotions, and a snake bite kit. Water purification tablets are another item to have, along with a disinfectant rinse for your cooking and eating utensils to sterilize them after washing them.

A spare parts kit can help you out in a pinch and is a good safety precaution since most outside help won't be available. Include some sewing thread and needles, duct tape for temporary boat repairs, spare spark plugs and other items for your motor, tools to fit the screws and bolts of your motor, and wood matches and wax, which will enable you to start a fire even in foul weather.

In addition to your spare parts kit, a battery operated weather radio, a CB style walkie talkie (there are several on the market that have built in weather bands), flares and a set of spare batteries make useful additions.

PLANNING SUGGESTIONS

Besides a trip of two or more days duration, the angler can elect to float through different sections of a river one day at a time. A one day float trip will allow him to cover sections of the river that he can't cover with a larger boat. Planning for this type of trip is not as complex, however, some planning is necessary to get the most out of a trip like this. It doesn't matter if you intend to spend one, two, three or more days on a river, there are several factors that you have to consider on any float trip.

Your starting and pick up point will, in many of cases, be determined by how many days you have to spend on the river. You should try to learn as much about the section of river you will be traveling before you start. Pick up maps that are available and scout it whenever possible. Since fishing is your main concern and not canoeing, you will want to get the most amount of fishing time that you can from the section you are fishing. Naturally, the amount of water you will be able to cover will be determined by your mode of transportation, mainly if you are using a motor or not. The use of a motor will greatly increase your distance and will allow you to cover larger amounts of water as well.

Another thing that affects the amount of water you cover and how fast you will be able to cover it is the speed of the current in the river or in any given section. This can also vary with the amount of water that is present at the time you are on it. A trip during the summer months will usually put you on it when the waters are at their lowest and slowest. The weather, of course, will have something to say about the water level. The average current during the summer months at normal levels will allow you to cover between 10 and 15 miles a day, depending on whether you are paddling or using a motor. In either case, it will give you enough time to get out and fish several productive spots, along with fishing productive areas from a boat.

You will, however, need to set a time table for yourself on any type of float trip. You can do this through the use of a map or by advance scouting, choosing certain points to be at during certain points of the trip. It's always wise to give your itinerary to someone not on the trip so in case anything should happen they will know when you are over due and approximately where to start looking.

On trips of two days or more, you should add the extra amount of water you will be covering by adding the distance covered on the first day for each additional day.

PICK YOUR OVER NIGHT STOPS WISELY

When traveling close to cities and other so-called centers of civilization, camp whenever possible on an island. This will ensure you the most privacy and security. In many cases, shorelines are private, and this can also cause you some problems.

When traveling in areas away from civilization, choose well sheltered places like islands, coves, shorelines with high banks, etc., for your stopping point. This will keep your campsite secure if foul weather should set in. Most shoreline and islands will have ample supplies of fire wood, and the first thing you will want to do when reaching your site will be to gather a good supply for cooking and the evening fire. Always choose dead fall over live wood for obvious reasons. You should always get an advanced weather forecast whenever possible prior to your trip and this should also help influence your choice in camp sights. If you are on a two day trip, choose a sight that is past the halfway mark of your trip. This ensures that if something unforeseen happens, you will have less of a journey on your second day. If everything goes right you will have more fishing time.

Camping on a quiet island makes a nice way to spend a few days on the river.

If you are on a trip of longer duration, always pre-plan your overnight stops and include them in your time table. Make them flexible enough so that they will allow

143

you to compensate for any delays that you might experience. Another good thing to do is to choose alternate sites in advance so that if you don't get to your main site or find it already occupied, you can camp at one of your close by alternates without throwing your schedule off or changing the general area in which you want to camp.

Since your main reason for doing a float trip is fishing, it's best to pick campsites that are located close to good morning and evening structures to maximize the fishing time during these prime periods. Your choices in overnight campsites should also be governed by the time of the year your are doing your trip. First, a well sheltered site is better for camping during the spring and fall when the nights usually are cooler. Likewise, areas closer to deeper water and deep eddies will be a better choice during the spring and fall when the water is on the cooler side. During the summer, a more open, shaded spot will be a cooler choice on a warm summer night and shallow flats and eddies are more conducive to good early morning and late afternoon fishing, as we have already pointed out.

ONE DAY TRIPS

LAMBERTVILLE to TRENTON - The starting point for this trip is the car top access located downstream from the Lambertville wing dam (Belle Mountain Access). Your pick up point will be either the Yardley access or City of Trenton access (formally the Mercer County access). The rapids at Scudders Falls and Trenton are the two sections on the river where rapids may cause some degree of difficulty. If you choose Yardley access as your pick up point you will eliminate the rapids at Trenton. Pick up at Trenton approx. 17 miles; pick up at Yardley 14 1/2 miles.

RAVEN ROCK to LAMBERTVILLE - Byram access or Bulls Island give you two excellent points to start this trip. Both accesses are located on the New Jersey side. Bryam access is located above the Bulls Island wing dam and if you choose to launch from Byram you will have to run the sluice way at the dam or carry your canoe around it. If you choose Bulls Island access to launch from you will not have to run the sluice at the Bulls Island wing dam. Your pick up point will be the Lambertville access, and the only rapids you will have to contend with are those located at Stockton. Approx. 6 miles.

FRENCHTOWN to LAMBERTVILLE - As a starting point for this trip you have the option to launch from either Tinicum access on the Pennsylvania side or Kingman access on the Jersey side. Your rapids in this section are located at the Devils Tea Table, Bulls Island wing dam and Stockton. Approx. 14 miles.

UPPER BLACK EDDY to FRENCHTOWN - Although this section is not a long section it makes an excellent area to stop your canoe and wade. The section has numerous eddies, flats, points of land and other structures which make it an excellent fishing area. Either Kingman or Tinicum access can serve as your pick up point. Approx. 4.5 miles.

HOLLAND CHURCH to UPPER BLACK EDDY - Holland Church access is a shore line/car top access that is a Fish and Wildlife Management Area owned by the New Jersey Division of Fish and Game. Several sets of rapids and deep pools are located in this section, offering the angler a variety of structures to fish. This section is ideal for stopping and wading. Approx. 7 miles.

RAUBS ISLAND to UPPER BLACK EDDY - There is no launch ramp located in this section, however, there are several places to launch canoes or car toppers from the shore line in this area. It is excellent for stop and go fishing during the summer months and it is excellent for live bait fishing during the fall season because of the many deep pools which offer some stable conditions to fish. The Eagle Generating Station located on the Milford, New Jersey side often pumps warm water during the fall, winter and spring months, giving the angler a warm water discharge to fish. Approx. 10 miles.

EASTON/PHILLIPSBURG to UPPER BLACK EDDY - Because of the distance to be covered on this trip it makes a good full day trip. You will have to watch your timing, and the amount of time that you will be able to spend in any one place fishing will be greatly reduced because of the distance you have to cover. This area holds as good a variety of structures found anywhere on the river and because this section of the river is very inaccessible, some great, out of the way fishing is available to the angler. Launch areas are located on both the Jersey side (Phillipsburg access) or on the Pennsylvania side at the mouth of the Lehigh River (Easton Front Street Access). Approx. 17 miles.

MARTINS CREEK to PHILLIPSBURG/EASTON - Your starting point is Martins Creek access and there are several choices for your pick up point. Typical structures found in this area are eddies, drop offs, deep pools and points of land. There are also several sets of passable rapids found in this section. If you end your trip at Standt's Eddy access your trip distance will be approx. 5 miles. If you choose to pick up at one of the ramps between the bridges at Phillipsburg/Easton your trip duration will be approx. 11 miles.

PORTLAND to MARTINS CREEK - This trip passes through another section of river that is very inaccessible. Several deep pools, islands, and rapids with plenty of eddies make for some good stop and go fishing. Foul Riff, one of the most dangerous sections on the river, will be your major set of rapids in this section, and caution should be used when attempting passage. Novice canoers should scout this section before attempting to go through or carry their canoes around these rapids, especially during times of high water. Approx. 11 miles.

WORTHINGTON to PORTLAND - This section is one of the most scenic areas on the river to fish. The legendary Delaware Water Gap with it's tall mountains and deep waters is located in this section. Your two choices in starting points are Smithfield Beach access on the Pennsylvania side or the access at Worthington State Park on the Jersey side. Your pick up point is the Met Ed access on the Pa. side. Approx. 10 to 11 miles.

BUSHKILL to THE WATER GAP - The prime place to fish on this trip is the waters of the scenic Wallpack Bend. Some of the best smallmouth fishing on the river is found here and this trip is excellent for the autumn season when the fall foliage makes this one of the most picturesque places on the river. Bushkill access is your starting point and you have several options for ending your trip. If you choose Poxono access as your pick up point, your trip will be approx. 11 miles. If you opt for Worthington State Park access, your trip duration will be approx. 16 miles. Picking up at Kittatinny access gives you a trip of approx. 20 miles.

DINGMAN'S FERRY to BUSHKILL - This secluded section passes through the largest part of the Water Gap Nation Recreation Area and gives the angler some banner surface fishing during the warm water season. You have several different points of pick up. Eshback access, which is car top/canoe access on the Pennsylvania side, gives you a trip of approx. 7 miles. The duration of your trip when picking up at Bushkill access is 11 miles. For a longer trip you can pick up at Poxono access for a trip duration of approx. 18 miles.

MILFORD to DINGMAN'S FERRY - Even though this trip is of short duration it passes through some excellent areas to fish during the summer months. Numerous flats, shallow water sections and large islands supply the ingredients for some good surface fishing. Your starting point is the Milford access on the Pennsylvania side and your pick up point is the Dingman's Ferry access, also on the Pennsy side. Trip distance is approx. 8 miles.

MATAMORAS to MILFORD - The fly fisherman will find this section of river to his liking for a float trip in the late spring. This is a major spawning area for the shad, and fly fishing for them is excellent during the late spring here. Your starting point is the Matamoras access. If you opt to pick up at the Milford access your trip will be approx. 8 miles. If you pick up at Dingman's Ferry your trip duration will be approx. 16 miles.

POND EDDY to MATAMORAS - This area makes for some excellent stop and go smallmouth action during the warm water season. Rapids, river bends and shallow areas give the angler numerous structures to fish. Route 97 runs close to the river along the New York side and you can put in anywhere off the road that is not posted as being private property. Your pick up point will be the Matamoras access, giving you approx. 10 miles, depending on where you put in.

BARRYVILLE to POND EDDY - Starting in the area of Shohola Creek, the angler can fish plentiful eddies, rapids and some deep pools. This trip is an excellent full day excursion for the summer months. You can pick up anywhere along Route 97, and the duration of your trip will depend on where you pick up. If you opt to pick up in the Pond Eddy area your trip duration is approx. 8 miles. If you pick up at the confluence of the Mongaup River your trip distance is approx. 12 miles.

NARROWSBURG to MINISINK - Abundant rapids and shallow areas make this area ideal for surface and spinnerbait action. Either launch ramp at Narrowsburg Eddy can serve as your starting point. If you opt to pick up at Lackawxen access your trip duration will be approx. 13 miles. For a slightly longer trip you can pick up at Barryville for a trip length of approx. 17 miles.

DAMASCUS to NARROWSBURG - Since much of this area is made up of fast rapids and shallow water, caution should be exercised when canoeing this area. Skinners Falls, which is noted as one of the most dangerous set of rapids on the river, is located in this area and should be scouted before attempting to pass through them. Either of the ramps at Damascus or Cochecton can serve as your starting point. Likewise, either of the Narrowsburg accesses can serve as your pick up point. Trip duration is approx. 8 miles. For a longer trip, you can choose to start at Callicoon and pick up at Narrowsburg for a duration of approx. 13 miles.

LONG EDDY to CALLICOON - An excellent section for surface fishing during the summer months, it's many shallow water areas and rapids give the angler plenty small structures to fish shallow water. You can launch anywhere along Route 97 where it is not posted, with your pick up point being Callicoon. Trip duration is approx. 11 miles depending on where your launch.

BUCKINGHAM to LONG EDDY - Buckingham access, located on the Pennsylvania side, is your starting point. The shallow waters of the summer months can make this section a bumpy ride as numerous rapids and shallow areas are located here. Picking up in the Long Eddy area will give you a trip duration of approx. 10 miles, depending on where you launch.

BALLS EDDY to EQUINUNK - The Balls Eddy ramp is the furthermost ramp up river and is located on the Delaware's West Branch. This trip is excellent for the spring when the water is higher. During the summer months low waters can make for a bumpy ride, however, some excellent surface fishing is available and fly fishing is excellent. Trip distance is approx. 7 miles.

TWO DAY TRIPS

MILFORD to YARDLEY - Overnight stop: Bulls Island. Approx. 28 miles.

EASTON/PHILLIPSBURG to BULLS ISLAND - Overnight stop: Lynn Island. Approx. 29 miles.

STANDT'S EDDY to FRENCHTOWN - Overnight stop: Raubs or Lynn Island. Approx. 27 miles.

PORTLAND to RIEGLESVILLE - Overnight stop: Keifer Island or shore line north of Phillipsburg/ Easton area. Approx. 32 miles.

WATER GAP to EASTON - Overnight stop: Dildine or Macks island. Approx 27 miles.

BUSHKILL to MARTINS CREEK - Overnight stop: Attins Island or shore line south of the Gap. Approx. 31 miles.

DINGMAN'S FERRY to PORTLAND - Overnight stop: Poxono, Tocks or Depew Island. Approx. 32 miles.

MATAMORAS to BUSHKILL ACCESS - Overnight stop: Minisink or Namanock Island up river from Dingman's Ferry. 24 Miles.

BARRYVILLE to MILFORD - Overnight stop: shore line camping in the area of the confluence of the Mongaup River. Approx. 27 miles.

NARROWSBURG to MATAMORAS - Overnight stop: shore line upstream of Barryville. Approx. 53 miles.

LONG EDDY to NARROWSBURG - Overnight stop: several available islands between Callicoon and Cochecton. Approx. 25 miles.

BALLS EDDY to COCHECTON - Overnight stop: New York State Forest Preserve north of Long Eddy. Approx. 32 miles.

THREE DAY TRIPS

PHILLIPSBURG/EASTON to YARDLEY - Overnight stops: first night- Lynn Island, second night- Bulls Island. Approx. 45 miles.

MARTINS CREEK to LAMBERTVILLE - Overnight stops: first night- Raubs Island, second night- Marshall Island. Approx. 47 miles.

WATER GAP to BULLS ISLAND - Overnight stops: first night- Keifer Island, second night- Raubs or Lynn Island. Approx 46 miles.

DINGMAN'S FERRY to MARTINS CREEK - Overnight stops: first night- Hamilton Cane Campsite, second night- shore line south of the Water Gap. Approx. 45 miles.

MATAMORAS to THE WATER GAP - Overnight stops: first night- Namanock Island, second night- Buck Island or Wallpack Bend. Approx. 42 miles.

BARRYVILLE to DINGMAN'S FERRY - Overnight stops: first night- island south of the Mongaup river confluence, second night- Mashipacong Island. Approx. 34 miles.

CALLICOOON to MATAMORAS - Overnight stops: first night- shore line camping south of Narrowsburg, second night- shore line camping north of Pond Eddy. 48 miles.

BALLS EDDY to NARROWSBURG - Overnight stops: first night- shore line camping at New York State Forest Preserve, second night- islands between Callicoon and Cochecton. Approx. 40 miles.

CHAPTER 13: MISCELLANEOUS INFORMATION
(Campgrounds, Tackle Shops, Marinas, Motels & Lodging, Canoe Rentals)

PHILADELPHIA/CAMDEN

Hotels and lodging in this section of the river are too numerous to mention because of it's location close to the metropolitan Philadelphia area. Just about every major motel and hotel chain has several facilities located on the outskirts of the city, and reservations can be made by calling one of their toll free numbers.

Tackle Shops

Taylor's Bait & Tackle - 6633 Buist Avenue - Phila., PA 19142 (215) 365-2697
Bryant's Gunsmithing - 4570 Bristol Rd. - Oakford, PA 18047 (215) 357-3064
Brinkman's Sp. Goods - 4999 Linden Ave. - Phila., PA 19114 (215) 632-0674
Kelly's Tackle Shop - 806 Third St. - Croydon, PA 19020 (215) 785-4783
Mike's Sporting Goods - 1414 Hwy. #38 - Hainsport, NJ 08036 (609) 267-7978
Yardley Landing - 15 Canal St. - Yardley, PA 19067 (215) 321-9121
Outdoor Haven - Rt. 206 - Columbus, NJ 08022 (609) 267- 0119
Bob's Bait & Tackle - 4863 Ridge Ave. - Phila. PA 19129 (215) 487-0887
Londahl's Live Bait - 424 State Hwy. 156 - Yardville, NJ 08620 (609) 585-4060

Marinas & Boat Repair Shops

N & B Marine - Route 130 - Bordentown, NJ 08505 (609) 298-3658
Big "D" Marine - Route 130 - Bridgeboro, NJ 08302 (609) 461-3550
Neshaminy Marine - 100 River Rd. - Croydon, PA 19020 (215) 785-5213
Jack's Marine - 3995 Bristol Pike - Bensalem, PA 19020 (215) 638-0484
Ed's Boat Yard - 900 Haunted Lane - Bensalem, PA 19020 (215) 639-8546
Clark's Landing - Dredge Harbor - Delran, NJ 08075 (609) 461-2700
Green Cove Marina - 351 N. Delaware Ave.- Phila., PA 19106 (215) 922-0357
D & S Boat Sales - 110 Main Street - Tulleytown, PA 19007 (215) 949-2100

TRENTON/MORRISVILLE to FRENCHTOWN
Tackle Shops

Andy's Sp. Goods - 1528 S. Clinton Ave. - Trenton, NJ 08611 (609) 394-8388
Brunswick Sp. Shop - 1177 Brunswick Ave. - Trenton, NJ 08648 (609) 393-3446
Yardley Landing - 15 Canal St. - Yardley, PA 19067 (215) 321-9121
Sportsmen's Center - Route 130 - Bordentown, NJ 08505' (609) 298-5300
Riverside Sp. Shop - Box 219 River Rd.- Pt. Pleasant, PA 18950 (215) 297-0989
Harry's Sp. Goods - Route 130 - Yardville, NJ 08620 (609) 585-5450
H & L's Live Bait - 78 E. Bridge St. - Morrisville, PA 19067 (215) 295-1400

Boat Dealers & Repairs

Trenton Marine - Lamberton Rd. - Trenton, NJ 080611 (609) 392-7275
Buttel's Marine Repair - 220 Elmwood Ave. - Feasterville, PA (215) 364-0858
Ross Marine Supply - 2445 Lamberton Rd. - Trenton, NJ 08611 (609) 393-2546
Art's Draw-Tite Hitches - 344 Newkirk Ave - Trenton, NJ 08609 (609) 586-6880

Motels & Lodging

Holiday Inn - Route 202 - New Hope, PA 18938   (215) 862-5521
Lambertville Sta. Inn - 11 Bridge St.- Lambertville, NJ 08530 (609) 397-4400
Tattersall Inn - Caffery & River Rd. - Pt. Pleasant, PA 18950 (215) 297-8233
Woodhill Farms Inn - Greenwood Dr. - Washington Cr., PA 18977 (215) 493-1974
New Hope Motel - 400 W. Bridge St. - New Hope, PA 18938 (215) 862-2800
White Hall Inn - Pineville Rd. - New Hope, PA 18938 (215) 598-7945

Campgrounds

Bulls Island State Park- Sanitary facilities, reserved sites, no hook ups, boat launch, laundry facilities. Location: 3 miles north of the town of Stockton, NJ along Route 29. (609) 397-2949
Washington Crossing State Park- Group camping only. Route 29, Washington's Crossing, NJ (609) 737-0623

FRENCHTOWN to PHILLIPSBURG/EASTON

Tackle Shops

Nockamixon Sport Shop - Rt. 313 - Perkasee, PA 18944 (201) 257-3133
The Owl's Nest - Rt. 519 - Springton, NJ 08865 (201) 995-7903
Dave's Sporting Goods - 1127 Easton Rd. - Doylestown, PA 18901 (215) 766-8000

Boat Dealers & Repairs

Lentine Marine - Route 31 - Flemington, NJ 08822 (201) 783-2077
Aquetong Marine - Route 202 - New Hope, PA 18938 (215) 794-7166

Motels & Lodging

The Bridgetown House - Route 32, Upper Black Eddy, PA 18972 (215) 982-5856

Campgrounds

Dogwood Heaven Cmpgrds. - Lodi Hill Rd. Upper Black Eddy, PA 18972 (215) 892-5402
Ringing Rocks Cmpgrnds - Woodland Drive, Upper Black Eddy, PA 18972 (215) 982-5552

PHILLIPSBURG/EASTON to DELAWARE WATER GAP

Tackle Shops

Bill's B & T - 246A Filmore St.- Phillipsburg, NJ 08865 (201) 859-5729
Muller's B & T - Rd #4 - Easton, PA 18042 (215) 252-2905
Pro Am Fishing Shop - RD #8 - Allentown, PA 18103 (215) 395-0885
Doc's Baits - 2400-1/2 Freemansburg Rd. - Easton, PA 18042 (215) 253-9974
Dave's Custom Tackle - 4321 Hewburg Rd. - Bethlehem, PA 18017 (215) 759-7371
John's Gun & Tackle Room - 2604 Freemansburg Road - Easton, PA 18042 (215) 253-1111

Boat Dealers & Repairs

Peter's Marine Ser. - 1402 Union Blvd. - Allentown, PA 18103 (215) 433-1606
Dinbrowitz Marine - 2946 MacArthur Rd. - Allentown, PA 18103 (215) 434-7400
Parch Marine Service - Rt. 611 - Easton, PA 18042 (215) 258-7754
Highway Marine - 875 West End Blvd. - Quakertown, PA 18951 (215) 536-4721
Lou's Marine - Rt. 378 - Bethlehem, PA 18015 (215) 868-5700

Motels & Lodging

Chalet Motel - Route 611 North, POB 596 - Portland, PA 18351 (717) 897-6498
Howard Johnson - Route 22 - Phillipsburg, NJ 08865 (201) 454-6461
Commodore Motel - Route 22 - Phillipsburg, NJ 08865 (201) 454-9771
Sabella's Motel - RD #1 - Easton, PA 18042 (201) 253-8764
Sheraton Inn - 3rd Street & Larry Holmes Dr - Easton, PA 18042 (215) 253-9131
Day's Inn - 25th & Route 22 - Easton, PA 18042 (215) 253-0548
Hotel Easton - 140 Northampton Street - Easton, PA 18042 (215) 253-6181

Campgrounds

Shady Acres of Portland - Hook up, laundry, camp store, cable TV, pool. Turkey Ridge Road, P.O. Box 417, Portland, Pa. 18351 Off Route 611 south (717) 897-6230
Jugtown Mountain Campgrounds - Hook ups, camp store, 279 Route 173, West Portland, NJ (201) 735-5995

DELAWARE WATER GAP to PORT JERVIS/MATAMORAS
Tackle Shops

W.A.G. Sport Shop - Rt. 46 - Columbia, NJ 07832 (215) 496-4641
Family Bait & Tackle - 624 N. Courtland Rd. - E. Stroudsburg, PA 18301 (717) 421-6981
Sportsmen's Shack - Rt. 209 - Marshall's Creek, PA 18335 (717) 454-1166
Dunkelburger's Outfitters - 6th & Main Street - Stroudsburg, PA 18301 (717) 421-7950

Outfitters

Delaware River Canoes - Delaware Water Gap, PA 18327 (717) 476-0398
Shawnee Canoes - Box 189 - Shawnee-on-the-Delaware, PA 18256 (800) 742-9633 or (717) 424-1139
Chamberlain Canoe Rentals - Shawnee River Road - Minisink Hills, PA (717) 421-0180
Adventure Tours Canoe Trips - Box 175-G - Marshalls Creek, PA 18335 (717) 223-0505
Kittatinny Canoes - Dept. PM - Dingman's Ferry, PA 18328 (800) 356-2852

Motels & Lodging

Delaware Water Gap Motor Lodge - Exit 53, I 80, Route 611 North - Delaware Water Gap, PA 18327
    Shawnee Inn - Shawnee-on-Delaware, PA 18356 (800) 742-9633
Glenwood Hotel & Resort - Delaware Water Gap, Pa. 18327 (800) 833-3050 Pa.
    (800) 822-2054 or (717) 476-0010
Howard Johnson's Motor Lodge - Exit 53, I 80 - Delaware Water Gap, PA 18327
    (800) 228-4897 or (717) 476-0130
Eagle Rock Lodge - Bed & Breakfast - River Rd - Shawnee-on-Delaware, PA 18327 (717) 421-2139
Fernwood Pocono Mountian Resort - Route 209 - Bushkill, PA 18324 (800) 233-8103 or (717) 588-9500
Black Walnut Country Inn - Bed & Breakfast - RD 2, Fire Tower Rd - Milford, PA 18337 (717) 296-6322
Cliff Park Inn - Milford, PA 18337   (717) 296-6491
The Historic Tom Quick Inn - 411 Broad St - Milford, PA 18337 (717) 296-6514
Tourist Village Inn - Routes 209 & 6, Box 487 - Milford, PA 18337 (717) 491-4414, 4178 & 4179
Best Western Inn at Hunt's Landing - Box 900 - Matamoras, PA 18336 (717) 491-2400
Mountain Lake Resort - Marshalls Creek, PA 18335 (717) 223-9224
Ceaser's Pocono Palace Resort - Marshalls Creek, PA 18335 (800) 233-4141 or (717) 588-6692
Minisink Acres Housekeeping Cottages - Minisink, PA 18341 (717) 421-9182 or (717) 476-0475
Pocono Environmental Education Center - RD #2, Box 1010 Dingman's Ferry, PA 18328 (717) 828-2319

Campgrounds

Worthington State Forest - Sanitary facilities, reserved sites, boat launch, no hook ups.
    5 miles north of the Route 80 Water Gap bridge off Mine road. (201) 841-9575
Delaware Water Gap KOA - Pool, Firewood, rec. room, snack bar, hook-ups, cabins.
    RD #6, Box 6196, Hollow Road, East Stroudsburg, PA 18301 (717) 223-8000
Ken's Woods Campground - Hook-ups, laundry, dump station, snack bar.
    Box 506, Bushkill, PA 18324 off Route 209 (717) 588-6381
Dingman's Campground - Hook-ups, dump station, camp store, firewood.
    RD #2, Box 20, Dingman's Ferry, Pa. 18328 off Route 209 (717) 828-2266
Otter Lake Camp Resort - Pool, laundry, rec. hall, hook-ups. Marshalls Creek, PA 18335 (717) 223-0123
River Beach Camp Sites - Sanitary facilities, reserved sites, dump station, firewood, showers.
    Milford, PA 18337 (717) 828-2700
Tri-state Campground - Riverfront sites, cottages, sanitary facilities, reservations.
    Shay Lane, Matamoras, PA (717) 491-4948

PORT JERVIS/MATAMORAS to NARROWSBURG
Tackle Shops

Jim's Sporting Goods - Route 97 - Sparrowbush, NY 12780 (914) 856-5646
Curt's Sport Shop - Route 97 - Sparrowbush, NY 12780 (914) 856-5024
Sportsmen's Rendezvous - 113 W. Harford St. - Milford, PA 18337 (717) 296-6113

Outfitters

Tri-State Canoe & Boat Rentals - Shay Lane - Matamoras, PA 18336 (800) 562-2663 or (717) 491-4948
Indian Head Canoes - Route 97 - Barryville, NY 12719 (800) 874-2628

Motels & Lodging

Eddy Farm Hotel - Route 97 - Sparrowbush, NY 12780 (914) 856-5266
Narrowsburg Inn - North Bridge Street - Narrowsburg, NY 12764 (914) 252-3998
Ten Mile River Lodge - Rd #2 - Narrowsburg, NY 12764 (914) 252-3998
Narrowsburg Holiday Inn - 90 Route 17 K - Narrowsburg, NY 12764 (914) 564-9020
Imperial Motel - 80 Broadway - Monticello, NY 12701 (914) 794-8349
Raceway Motel - 101 Jefferson - Monticello, NY 12701 (914) 794-6291
Pine Motel - 369 Broadway - Monticello, NY 12701 (914) 794-8660
Monticello Inn - 202 Broadway - Monticello, NY 12701 (914) 794-6500

Campgrounds

Sylvania Tree Farm - Cottages & Tent Sites - Box 18 - Lackawaxen, PA 18435 (717) 685-7001
Jack & Jill Campground - Hook-ups, laundry, rec. room, firewood. Box 34A1, Long Pond, PA 18334 off I-80
    Exit 43, Route 115 3 mile east of Long Pond road (717) 894-4388

NARROWSBURG to HANCOCK

Tackle Shops

D & K Sportshop - North Main Street - Cochecton, NY 12726 (914) 887-4857
Al Cohen's Sporting Goods- 340 Broadway - Monticello, NY 12701 (914) 794-5444
Esopus Fly Shop - 358 Vankeuren Ave. - Pine Bush, NY 12566 (914) 361-5069

Outfitters

Lander's Delaware River Canoes & Rafts - RD #2, Box 376, Dept. PM, Narrowsburg, NY 12764
    (914) 252-3925

Motels & Lodging

Long Eddy Hotel Depot - Route 97 - Long Eddy, NY 12760 (914) 887-4554
Buck Horn Lodge - East Branch, New York 13756 (607) 363-7120

Campgrounds

Narrowsburg Campgrounds - Narrowsburg, NY 12764 (914) 252-3925
Skinners Falls Campgrounds - Skinners Falls, NY (914) 252-3925